Nev   ions
in   ty

New Directions in Diversity

A New Approach to Covering
America's Multicultural Communities

George Padgett

Marion Street Press, Inc.
Oak Park, Illinois

ISBN 1-933338-04-0
Printed in U.S.A.
Printing 10 9 8 7 6 5 4 3 2 1

Marion Street Press, Inc.
PO Box 2249
Oak Park, IL 60303
866-443-7987
www.marionstreetpress.com

PART II
Covering Diverse Communities

I have a dream that my four little children will one day live in a nation where they will not be judged by the color of their skin but by the content of their character.

Martin Luther King Jr., 1929–1968

Preface

A middle-aged white male, I have no idea what it must feel like to be dropped as a five-year-old black or Asian or Hispanic kindergartener into a classroom full of white children. I have no concept of how it must feel to be a gay male or lesbian and experience the intensity of hatred that many people in our society today express openly. For that matter, I have no sense of what it must be like to be poor in this nation of astounding wealth.

I remember sitting on a Greyhound bus late one night in the sixties on the way back from an aborted trip to Mexico. A spring break excursion had ended on a highway outside Matehuala, and my three buddies and I were on the way home absent our wrecked Ford Galaxie. Seated next to an elderly black man on the crowded carrier, shameless ignorance, I suppose, led me to launch into a conversation about race. I now realize how ridiculously presumptuous I must have seemed in my attempt to appear hip. At one point I confessed that as a college student, often stereotyped and occasionally shunned (thanks to Woodstock, of course), I knew just how my seatmate must have felt many times in his life.

It took a lot of maturing for me to understand the depth of feeling in the "not 'til you've walked in these shoes," speech that wise man gave me that night on the road to Brownsville, Texas. His voice was tired and sad and angry and resentful and surprisingly forgiving as he tried to explain, as he likely had a thousand times, how it felt to live every day of your life in a society in which you are viewed as different and often something less, simply because of the color of your skin. I've never felt quite so embarrassed or humbled.

I come to this project still humbled by the strength of anyone who has endured a lifetime of difference in an unaccepting society. I was raised in a strong Christian family by a father who had contracted polio at the age of 17 and walked on crutches until he died at the age of 70. I learned much from this extraordinary man: self-reliance, determination, resilience, and the ability to forgive. A father, farmer, salesman, and elected county judge, he accomplished a great deal with what he was given. And in the 35 years I had the honor of having him a part of my life, I never heard him utter a single complaint, offer a single excuse, or ask for a single concession because of his disability. I heard ignorant people refer to him as crippled, but he never turned on them. He held his head high and went forward.

He is a part of life's journey that has brought me to this project. The other parts are my children, Joshua and Amanda Padgett, adopted as infants two years apart from Seoul, Korea. They have been raised in our blended family in a dominantly white society and have experienced the curious stares, ignorant questions, sometimes racist comments, and occasional discriminations that are common to anyone not of the currently dominant race in this country. They have been intentionally infused with a sense of positive self-image and, like my father, have learned to hold their heads high and go forward. I love and admire them both beyond imagination.

As a result of the realization several years ago that there is much work to be done before we can live peaceably together in a multicultural society, I embarked upon a purposeful study of newsroom diversity. I applied and was accepted to the Poynter Institute's excellent "Diversity Across the Curriculum" seminar and spent a wonderfully educational week at the institute's campus in St. Petersburg, Florida. Before and after the Poynter experience, I engaged in a continuing discussion of race with my colleague and good friend Byung Lee, which culminated in the presentation of a diversity paper at a Q-theory conference in Durham, England, in 2002. I also volunteered for a diversity exchange between my university and a historically black university, where I taught Media Law & Ethics for two semesters to classes almost entirely made up of black students. I learned much from the experience and can better identify with how my colleagues of color must feel walking daily into classes that are largely attended by white students.

All these experiences combined to provide the stimulus for this book. I believe that a more intellectually diverse media workforce, offering a more diverse content and creating a more realistic picture of the communities they serve, can have a significant impact on how society views difference, whether that difference is race and ethnicity, age, gender, faith, sexual orientation, socioeconomic status, physical ability, or national origin. And if that view is more understanding, more accepting of difference, and more tolerant, we can only be a better society. For my children, I surely hope so.

The approach of this book is simple. It is intended to be used as a supplemental textbook in introductory and basic media writing courses and also as a reader for professional newsroom workshops and discussion. It attempts to add to the discourse in a way that is not overly repetitious. Already numerous books in print document racism in our society. There are endless chronicles of racial stereotyping, framing, and profiling by the media. And hundreds, if not thousands, of articles point to the failure of the media to build newsrooms that meet objectives of racial parity. The premise of this work accepts that racism, prejudice, and stereotyping exist in abundance and that media are not sufficiently addressing the problem. It is my intent to create and bring together a body of knowledge that will encourage and assist in addressing these problems.

It is the goal in Part One to provide a basic framework for the discussion of diversity:

What is diversity? Why is it important? How can it be achieved? How do we begin the discussion? Part Two is devoted to concrete practical hints on covering diverse communities in general and the various diverse populations in our communities in particular. Part Three introduces practical and proven activities that can be used in either the classroom or the newsroom to teach and learn how to become better at covering the complete community. Participating in these exercises will force students and professionals to face their biases and become more sensitive to other people. Part Three also contains a list of resources that can be used to learn even more about the topics discussed.

Because of the dual nature of the book as a college- or university-level text and a guide for discussion in professional settings, various sections address both students and professionals as well as their instructors and group leaders. Occasional notes to instructors and leaders also are included.

If you have comments about this book, suggestions about things you would like to see incorporated in future editions, or additional exercises that can be used to help teach about diversity, please contact me at padgettg@elon.edu.

Acknowledgments

I offer profound thanks to the many working professionals who have made this effort possible. It is their excellent work in newspaper, radio, and television newsrooms across the nation that will help us to realize the promise of diversity.

My experience at the Poynter Institute's Diversity Across the Curriculum seminar in 2001 inspired me ultimately to pursue this project. The significant contribution to diversity by Keith Woods and others at Poynter is reflected in the numerous references to their work throughout. I also appreciate being able to use quotations from Woods and other Poynter faculty as well as their seminar handouts.

I am also grateful to the many, many members of UNITY: Journalists of Color whose wise words I have used to illustrate important points and advise strategies for better coverage of our diverse communities. My sincere thanks to everyone who advised me on the preparation of this manuscript, who read proposals or sections of the text, and who provided invaluable suggestions for making it better.

Thanks to my wife, Val, who contributed to the ongoing proofreading process, to my great kids, Josh, who currently is following his passion to become an architect, and Mandy, who is preparing to become a broadcast journalist. And finally, thanks to my parents, Ferne and Eli Padgett, who long ago taught me that we can do anything if we want it badly enough and are willing to work hard to achieve it.

Part One

The What, When and How of Diversity

In a letter to the industry dated December 5, 2004, former Unity: Journalists of Color president Ernest Sotomayor writes: "In recent years we've heard lots about how many in journalism are afflicted with 'diversity fatigue' — tired of the debate and of the opinion we've marked plenty of progress. Well, the nearly 10,000 members of Unity who make up less than a fifth of the workforce in journalism don't believe that, and they are fatigued by the constant fight to be considered for the plum assignments and the newsroom power jobs."[1]

Sotomayor goes on to note that Unity and its alliance partners, the National Association of Black Journalists, the National Association of Hispanic Journalists, the Asian American Journalists Association, and the Native American Journalists Association, will continue advocating the cause of diversity as strongly as possible. He concludes: "That's because diversity, like accuracy, fairness and honesty, is a core value of journalism. And without it, there is no excellence."[2]

Despite limited progress toward the goal of parity in the newsroom workforce, the diversity movement is far from over. Sure, every time an Armstrong Williams or a Jayson Blair fumbles the ball, diversity critics plunge front and center to pronounce the movement dead. But as Ernest Sotomayor and others maintain, diversity is a core principle of good journalism. The increasingly diverse world in which we live requires news media that can see and understand the underrepresented and underreported community. The world requires media that can report and clarify to all members of the audience the issues that are relevant in those communities. The world requires media that can contribute to a more inclusive social environment for all people regardless of their age, religion, sexual orientation, or skin color.

Organizations from Unity to Freedom Forum, the Society of Professional Journalists, the Poynter Institute, the American Society of Newspaper Editors, and the Radio-Television News Directors Association are working tirelessly to develop new programs directed at increasing diversity in the news workforce. Of course, the problem is that as the percentage of Asian American, Hispanic, black, and Native American newsroom employees crawls upward at a snail's pace, the percentage of those same racial and ethnic populations in the

U.S. community is exploding at an unprecedented rate. Current population projections estimate that the composite minority will in fact be the majority by around 2050.[3]

While the overall focus of this book is on training all journalists to do a better job of reporting on the diverse community, it is not meant to suggest in any way abandoning the movement toward parity in the newsroom. Newsrooms should better reflect the diverse communities they serve. Newsroom managers must do a better job of hiring a diverse staff of reporters, editors, and news directors. It has been an obvious need since the Hutchins Commission first broached the topic in 1947, and it continues to be an obvious need sixty years later.

However, there must be a more vigorous effort to educate journalists to be more aware of the communities they cover and to be more "diversity-smart" in cultivating sources, coming up with and selling story ideas to their editors and news directors, and creating content that tells a story about people who have never before been covered by media. That is the focus of this book.

New Directions in Diversity does not overlook the numerous efforts being made to train journalists and future journalists to better cover the complete community, but it does hope to provoke a broader and more intense emphasis on the educational aspect of the diversity movement. The movement to diversity by the impossibly slow path of recruiting and hiring journalists of color and journalists of varying ages, faiths, ethnicities, and socioeconomic backgrounds is not in itself getting the job done. No longer can the discipline or profession depend on the hiring process to right the wrong that has existed in journalism for decades.

An approach that places the burden of diversity squarely on journalism education and on newsroom training can have a tremendous impact on current and future news professionals. Imagine if every media writing and news reporting class in every journalism program in the United States gave students training and experience in reporting on the diverse community. Imagine if, in every newsroom in the country, news managers regularly took time to make diversity training a priority. Change could happen immediately. That is the objective of this book.

The focus of Part One is on the basics — the what, why, and how of diversity. Chapter One delves into the literature of journalism as it relates to diversity, provides a look at how both education and the news industry define the concept of diversity, and analyzes the current state of diversity in the newsroom. It concludes that the most inclusive of definition of diversity leads to the best journalism. Chapter Two looks at the major arguments for creating diverse journalism, suggesting that one or all of the commonly cited rationales would be sufficient for developing a program of diversity. Chapter Three discusses how to make it happen and includes a series of actions that can be taken in academic and in professional settings to teach and learn how to realize the goals of diversity. Chapter Four talks about how to begin the discussion and offers tips on creating an environment conducive to a constructive conversation.

The purpose of this book in general, and Part One in particular, like all well-meaning pro-diversity efforts, is to contribute to excellence in journalism.

Chapter One

What Is Diversity?

An administrator at a southern university, succumbing to pressure to increase diversity, told deans in charge of hiring faculty and recruiting students that he wanted to be able to see diversity walking across campus.

A 19-year-old male student in a class of 20 similarly aged white upper-middle-class men and women from the East Coast groaned about a diversity assignment. "We did diversity in high school," he said. "There are no problems any more. Why do we have to keep doing this?"

A faculty member in a communications program expressed concern about a colleague's broadly defined diversity recruitment efforts. He wanted to be assured that "homosexuals" would not be included in the department's definition of diversity.

White American university students were chided by a professor for not being more inclusive toward international students on campus. "Why should we?" they asked. "Because you are global citizens," he responded. "The world in which you're about to live is increasingly international and intercultural." A hand shot up immediately. "But we can live without ever kissing up to foreigners," a young woman in the class said. "Yeah," said another.

Although these scenarios may be anecdotal, the tendency either to define diversity as that which can be seen walking across campus or inhabiting an American newsroom, or to resist it altogether, is relatively universal.

The American Society of Newspaper Editors (ASNE), sponsors of the most comprehensive annual survey of newsroom diversity, until recently included only race and ethnicity in its yearly count of African American, Asian American, Hispanic, and Native American journalists. In existence since 1978, it included gender as a category for the first time in 1999, then only after being lobbied by JAWS (Journalism and Women Symposium) members and other interested parties.[4] A statement issued by ASNE following its decision to include women in the annual census notes that, despite the change, the primary focus of its diversity efforts would remain on hiring and promoting people of color in the newsroom.[5]

Likewise, the Radio Television News Directors Association's annual survey of employment in electronic media reflects the categories of the older ASNE study. Age, sexual orientation, and other factors easily construed as potentially affecting the news organization's ability to effectively cover the complete community are absent from the reports.

Outside those annual survey reports, contemporary journalism literature — both academic and professional — tends to be more inclusive, allowing diversity to stand for more than just race, gender, and ethnicity. Sexual orientation is the most frequent addition, followed by age, disability, faith, class and economic status, political affiliation, and geographic or national origin.

Poynter Institute dean of faculty Keith Woods writes in a 2001 Columbia University report, *Covering Race and Ethnicity*, that the single term *diversity* becomes overloaded when called on to represent so much. "Diversity," he says "is used to define everything from hiring white women and people of color to affirmative action to covering undercovered groups to uncovering racial profiling to reporting on riots to battling bias against gays and lesbians to including elderly and poor people in coverage to so called political correctness in office politics." Woods concludes that such a broad use of the word *diversity* is too much for one word to handle.[6]

However, in spite of Woods's urging that we get away from what he calls "the dysfunctional, one-noun-fits-all trap"[7] and use more words resulting in less confusion, the word *diversity*, for the time being at least, appears to be the most widely accepted term. And, perhaps proving Woods's point, there are countless definitions. Corporations, universities, and professional organizations all have gotten into the act of lexicography.

A statement by the Office of Diversity at Appalachian State University in North Carolina says: "Diversity means difference. It is inclusive, not exclusive. It embraces but is not limited to race, ethnicity, gender, sexual orientation, socio-economic class, age, geographic location, national origin, religious beliefs, and physical abilities."[8]

Iowa State University defines diversity as "that quality of its physical, social, cultural and intellectual environment which embraces the rich differences within the multiplicity of human expression and characteristics including age, culture, ethnicity, gender identification and presentation, language and linguistic ability, physical ability and quality, race, religion, sexual orientation and socioeconomic status."[9]

The University of Maryland takes a different approach, defining diversity as "otherness or those human qualities that are different from our own and outside the groups to which we belong, yet are present in other individuals and groups." Its statement of diversity then distinguishes between what the university calls primary and secondary dimensions. "Primary dimensions include age, ethnicity, gender, physical abilities/qualities, race and sexual orientation. Secondary dimensions of diversity are those that can be changed, and include, but are not limited to educational background, geographic location, income, marital status, military experience, parental status, religious beliefs, and work experience."[10]

Beverly Daniel Tatum, author of the excellent work on racial identity, *Why Are All the Black Kids Sitting Together in the Cafeteria*, writes that there are at least seven categories of "otherness" used in the United States. "People are commonly defined as other on the basis of race or ethnicity, gender, religion, sexual orientation, socioeconomic status, age, and physical or mental ability." She adds: "Each of these categories has a form of oppression associated with it: racism, sexism, religious oppression/anti-Semitism, heterosexism, classism, ageism, and ableism, respectively. In each case, there is a group considered dominant (systematically advantaged by the society because of group membership) and a group considered subordinate or targeted (systematically disadvantaged)."[11]

ASNE alludes to a similar definition in its mission statement urging comprehensive coverage of the community. "At a minimum, all newspapers should employ journalists of color and every newspaper should reflect the diversity of its community. The newsroom must be a place in which all employees contribute their full potential, regardless of race, ethnicity, color, age, gender, sexual orientation, physical ability or other defining characteristics."[12]

The Accrediting Council on Education in Journalism and Mass Communications in 2004 adopted a new diversity standard that is used in its evaluation of university journalism and communications programs. The new Standard Three requires that programs accredited by the council have a "diverse and inclusive program that serves and reflects society." Two of the indicators of inclusivity provide insight into the council's definition of diversity. Indicator (b) says, "The unit's curriculum fosters understanding of issues and perspectives that are inclusive in terms of gender, race, ethnicity and sexual orientation." Indicator (e) says, "The unit has a climate that is free of harassment and discrimination, accommodates the needs of those with disabilities, and values the contributions of all forms of diversity."[13]

Although the standard does not include all the elements of diversity present in other definitions, it is a considerable improvement over the previous standard, which said simply, "Units are encouraged to make effective efforts to recruit, advise and retain minority students and minority and women faculty members."[14]

Even diversity movement critic Peter Wood acknowledges the increasingly inclusive definition. In his 2003 book, *Diversity: The Invention of a Concept,* Wood writes, "Although the ideology of diversity was born in the discussion of differences between blacks and whites, it quickly subsumed other differences, such as ethnicity, sex (gender) and region. And it has continued to expand so that, depending on context, when Americans speak of diversity they may be referring not only to differences between whites and people of color, but also to religious differences, sexual preferences, physical or mental handicaps, or still other social differences."[15]

As it applies to the present discussion of journalism, newsrooms, and news coverage, the term *diversity* will be used in its broadest sense. Newsroom diversity refers to the mix of staff and management relative to all possible target populations. Are people of color represented? Do females have a voice in determining newsroom policy? Is the gay and lesbian community represented? Are there voices representing people of varying ages, socioeconomic backgrounds, religious and political affiliations, geographic and national origin, and physical ability? Does the diversity of the newsroom reflect the diversity of the community it serves?

Diversity as related to news content refers to coverage of the complete community. Are people of all races and ethnicities continually covered, included, and represented? Are they the subjects, as well as the sources, of news and feature coverage? Are people of all classes, ages, faiths, political beliefs, and geographic origins covered? Do people with disabilities appear as the subjects of news coverage and as news sources when appropriate?

Unlike Justice Potter Stewart's often quoted view of hardcore pornography, "I know it when I see it,"[16] diversity is more than what can be easily seen walking across campus.

Diversity Within Diversity

Just when you think you've gotten the hang of it, you realize it is not as simple as it seems. There is more to the puzzle than hiring staff who don't all look alike; are from differing political parties; and are of varying ages, faiths, and sexual orientations.

White Americans for generations have treated people of color as though they are all the same. They are not. A black television reporter who grew up in a middle-class neighborhood in Chicago took a faculty position at a selective private university in the South. After meeting with a number of the school's black students who make up about 5 percent of the enrollment, she observed, "Black students at this school don't even know they're black." With the possible exception of athletes, many of the black students attending the university had grown up in upper-middle-class and upper-class black families, but had lived in largely white neighborhoods and gone to largely white private schools.

The same is true of any racial or ethnic population. Though white people are generally incapable of distinguishing between Asians of differing ancestries, they, of course, are not all the same. Chinese Americans, Japanese Americans, Korean Americans, and other ethnic Asian populations have distinct political and cultural heritages and should not be treated as one homogeneous group. The term *Asian* itself continues to evolve. As noted in the *AAJA All-American Stylebook*, "In American usage, Asian historically has meant the countries of East Asia and Southeast Asia."[17] Increasingly, however, India, Pakistan, and other South Asian countries are included in the broader category.

Similarly, despite the tendency of many southern and midwestern whites to refer to the influx of Hispanic people all as Mexicans, they are not. Although current census reports estimate that approximately 67 percent of Hispanics living in the United States immigrated from Mexico, they also come from many Central and South American countries as well as from Cuba, Puerto Rico, and the Dominican Republic.[18]

Likewise, Native Americans are not all the same. A Lumbee is not a Lakota is not a Pueblo Indian. The Bureau of Indian Affairs in 2002 recognized 562 separate Indian tribes.[19] The *Indian Country Resource Guide* notes: "Indian tribes are as different as the Irish and Italian. Individual tribes have their own culture, language and tradition. Many groups may be strangers to one another. Some were once enemies."[20]

The Arab American is probably the least understood. Arab Americans either trace their ancestry to or immigrated from any of a number of Arabic-speaking countries in southwestern Asia and northern Africa, an area known as the Middle East. Not all Arabs are Muslims. In fact, according to the *Arab American Journalist's Guide* published by the *Detroit Free Press*, most Arab Americans are either Catholic or Orthodox Christian. Interestingly, the U.S. government does not include Arabs in minority classifications for purposes of employment and housing.[21] They are a diverse group of people in terms of ancestry, religion, cultural tradition, and skin color. They should not be grouped into one homogeneous ethnic category.

These distinctions, diversity within diversity, are important in considering newsroom employment and content. Hiring three new black reporters doesn't accomplish a lot for diversity if they all grew up in wealthy homes in white suburbia and graduated from Northwestern. Neither, of course, should they be rejected because of the circumstances of their backgrounds. The point, again, is to seek diversity. Hiring one of the Northwestern grads, but also considering the Maryland or Tennessee graduate who grew up on the streets in Baltimore or in a middle-class neighborhood in Knoxville, would begin to address the issue of diversity within diversity.

Relative to content, it also is important to recognize the diversity within targeted populations of people of color. Avoid the same old stereotypes. Don't just do stories about gays and lesbians who are interior designers. Cover the Hispanic community other than at Cinco de Mayo. Don't depict all Asians as the hardworking, intellectually superior model minority. And don't assume Arab involvement every time the government raises the terrorism alert level.

Some Troubling Terms

Terms such as race, ethnicity, and culture are used in a multitude of ways without much consistency in understanding. Similarly, racial and ethnic terms such as *black* and *African American*, *Hispanic* and *Latino*, *Native American* and *American Indian* are often used interchangeably. Terms such as *nonwhite* and *minority* also may be problematic. Hundreds of other words and phrases relating to diverse populations can be a minefield for the student or journalist attempting to get it right. Many of those terms are discussed in later chapters on covering specific targeted populations.

Although admittedly imprecise and possibly unnecessary, racial identification is historically a way of distinguishing between people. Nongeographic and noncultural, race refers essentially to skin color and physical characteristics. Don Heider writes in *White News*, "The assumption is that when people speak of race, they are talking about some way in which the world of humans has been divided. The most apparent of the markers by which these divisions has been made is physical appearance. Black, brown, red, yellow, and white skin is one system of classification. African, Latino, Native American, Asian, Caucasian may be another set of terms used to carve people up into similar categories…."[22]

Also nongeographic, ethnicity refers to a distinction based on common cultural traits. According to a "Diversity Dictionary" published by the University of Maryland, ethnicity is "a quality assigned to a specific group of people historically connected by a common national origin or language."[23] Heider notes that ethnicity is influenced by a variety of factors from skin color and geographic origin to faith, language, class, and social orientation. The Hmong people who relocated to the United States following the Vietnam war, for example, are an ethnic group, largely Laotian in national origin and Asian in race.

The word *culture* today carries a broader connotation and is widely used to link any group of people who share a set of beliefs, customs, practices, and social behavior.[24] Native Americans have cultural traditions, but then so do those who follow the music of Phish or the Grateful Dead. They are members of the culture of rock. Others may refer to the youth culture, the Internet culture, faith culture, or the culture of poverty.

Terms describing race and ethnicity are often misused. While the term *African American*, for example, is widely used and often viewed as synonymous with *black*, it is not. Not all black people are African American. In fact, 3.7 percent of the black population in the United States is Hispanic blacks.[25] A style guide published by the National Association of Black Journalists (NABJ) recommends being as specific as possible in honoring preferences, as in

Haitian American or Jamaican American. It goes on to say, however, "In a story in which race is relevant and there is no stated preference for an individual or individuals, use black because it is an accurate description of race."[26] Additionally, the guide recommends using the term *black* as an adjective only: black history, black press, or black journalists, but not blacks in television.

The choice between Native American and American Indian is less controversial. An entry in *The American Indian and the Media* says either term is acceptable. In fact, that guidebook uses the terms interchangeably. Like NABJ, the Native American Journalism Association (NAJA) recommends allowing an individual's preference to be the guide. It also suggests using the tribal association (Navajo, Zuni, Cherokee, etc.) to identify individuals when possible.[27]

The Hispanic–Latino conundrum is not so clearcut. The broader term *Hispanic* usually is used when referring to anyone with a direct ancestry from Hispanic- or Spanish-speaking countries. *Latino* refers to a person from anywhere in Latin America and to those who identify themselves as having Latin American ancestry. However, *The News Watch Diversity Style Guide* says that whereas some people of Latin American origin prefer *Latino*, others use it interchangeably with *Hispanic*.[28] Likewise, the U.S. Census Bureau uses the terms interchangeably. The National Association of Hispanic Journalists (NAHJ) uses the either/or approach, using *Hispanic* in its official name, but describing its mission as "increasing the influence of Latinos in U.S. newsrooms."[29] Like the other organizations, they recommend following the preference of story subjects.

The term *Asian American* is generally used collectively to refer to anyone from East or Southeast Asia, although increasingly the term is being applied to South Asia as well. The Asian American Journalists Association (AAJA) and the South Asian Journalists Association (SAJA) maintain separate independent websites, although the AAJA is the larger organization and includes members from South Asian countries as well. The U.S. Census Bureau groups Asian and Pacific Islander populations. Again, it is advisable to use specific country-of-origin identifications when referring to Asians or Asian Americans.

Note that some object to the very act of providing racial and ethnic qualifiers such as Asian American. They point out that while Japanese Americans and Korean Americans, whose families have lived in the United States for generations, for example, are still labeled based on their ancestral heritage, millions of ethnic whites whose origins spread across the globe are not referred to as Italian Americans, Irish Americans, and the like.[30]

The AAJA handbook explains the tendency to apply qualifiers: "Not far from the surface is the message that, unlike ethnic whites who have become American, Asians, because of their race, cannot be separated from the nations of their heritage." An unfortunate example of the media's failure to comprehend that message occurred in February 1998 on the MSNBC website when white American figure skater Tara Lipinsky defeated Michelle Kwan, also American, for the Olympic gold medal. The MSNBC headline read, "American Beats Out Kwan."[31]

All racial–ethnic stylebooks advise that terms such as *African American, Asian American, Native American,* and *Mexican American* should be hyphenated only when used as adjectives. Many consider the hyphenated use to be pejorative, due in part to Theodore Roosevelt's denunciation in 1915 of "hyphenated Americans" for not joining the American mainstream.

Two other terms deserve mention here before moving on. Both are terms that are used frequently in literature and media as a standard part of the lexicon of diversity. One is *nonwhite*. Beverly Daniel Tatum objects to the use of *nonwhite* because it classifies people or groups of people in terms of what they are not. Who wants to be nondescript, nonessential, or a nonentity? Should men be nonfemales? Adopted children nonbiological? Clean-shaven men nonbearded? People who wear clothes nonnudist? Seniors nonyoung? You get the point.

The other term is *minority*. Tatum suggests avoiding using *minority* or *minorities* because those terms "represent another kind of distortion of information which we need to correct." She accurately points out that so-called minorities represent the majority of the world's population.[32] The term also has come to have a negative connotation. The minority leader in the U.S. House is an individual who occupies a supposed leadership position in the party without power. To be in the minority on most anything in today's driven-to-succeed society is to be on the losing side.

What to Do About White People

For now at least, white people are the dominant race in the United States, being the majority tenants of every state with the exceptions of Texas, New Mexico, California, and Hawaii. Historically, they haven't come to the diversity table because as far as they are concerned, everything is just fine. Only recently have college administrators begun to see diversity as an issue and then largely as a public relations problem that can be solved by recruiting people of color who are clearly visible on campus.

Both Don Heider, in *White News*, and B. Lee Artz, in an essay published in *Cultural Diversity and the U.S. Media*,[33] blame media, at least in part, for creating the cultural hegemony that has perpetuated the dominance of whites in the United States. According to Heider, media create the frames that maintain the status quo.[34] However, as the noise of diversity chatter has become louder and louder, even threatening that status quo, members of the white majority have begun to take notice. Peter Wood's *Diversity, the Invention of a Concept* blasts the diversity movement in general, while William McGowan's *Coloring the News* has become the poster book of those opposing the campaign for newsroom diversity. McGowan, for example, writes, "Diversity has been fast becoming one of the most contentious issues in American society and in American journalism, responsible for polarizing, if not balkanizing, more than one newsroom around the country."[35]

It is easy to understand why people of color don't always welcome white people to their table, but white is a color, and all parties should be included and should show up for the discussion of diversity. When the quadrennial meeting of Unity: Journalists of Color (a coalition of NABJ, NAHJ, AAJA, and NAJA) drew over 8,000 black, Native American, Hispanic, and Asian American journalists to its 2004 convention in Washington, D.C., the Association of Education in Journalism and Communications, the nation's largest group of journalism educators, was meeting in Toronto. Journalists of color were talking about diversity issues on the East Coast, while members of the largely white AEJMC were passing a new diversity standard in Canada. That scheduling conflict was unintentional, but it was counterproductive in an era when most everyone talks about the need to bring all groups to one table to solve the diversity problem.

What about white people then? There's little likelihood of an imminent threat to the dominance of white journalists in the newsroom. Journalists of color in the newsroom are outnumbered by as many as 8 to 1, while even fewer occupy management positions. Nonetheless, this discussion assumes white journalists are a part of the diversity mix.

All About the Numbers

The six major studies referenced here contain enough graphs, tables, and figures to fill an entire textbook. The findings are summarized as succinctly as possible to provide a current and accurate picture of media diversity. Any discrepancies between surveys are most likely due to varying methodologies, survey populations, and the span of time in which the particular study was conducted and analyzed.

The Face and Mind of the American Journalist

The 2002 rendition of the "American Journalist" study (published every ten years since 1972) found that the typical American journalist today is white, male, 41 years old, college educated, and most likely to be politically Democratic or Independent. He earns a salary of approximately $46,750 and overall is happy with his career.

Only about one-third of all print and broadcast journalists are women, although that figure climbs to slightly above 50 percent when looking only at journalists with five or fewer years of experience. Over all ages and years of service, women average $37,771, more than $9,000 less than male colleagues. However, males and females with fewer than fifteen years work experience have comparable median salaries.[36]

ASNE Annual Study of Newsroom Diversity

The annual ASNE study surveys U.S. daily newspapers only, reporting employment figures for both male and female Asian Americans, African Americans, Hispanics, and Native Americans. The twenty-eighth annual 2005 census found current newsroom employment at 54,134, down from a 2001 high of 56,400.[37]

Journalists of color accounted for 13.42 percent of that total, compared to a national population in which 32.2 percent of the total are people of color in those same racial and ethnic categories, still far from the ideal of parity that ASNE established as a goal in 1978.

Broken down, the latest figures show that in the four major racial/ethnic categories, black journalists account for 5.51 percent of all daily newsroom employees; Hispanics, 4.29 percent; Asians, 3.07 percent; and Native Americans, .55 percent. Those same target groups, respectively, account for the following percentages of the national population: black Americans, 13; Hispanic, 13.3; Asian, 4.4; and Native American, 1.5.

Women occupied 37.54 percent of the jobs in daily newspapers, while making up 51 percent of the national population. Female journalists of color held 17.2 percent of the newsroom jobs held by women in 2004.

Journalists of color make up 10.8 percent of newsroom supervisors. Women account for 34.8 percent of supervisors in the nation's daily newspapers.

The 2004 census includes responses from 926 of the 1,413 daily newspapers surveyed, a response rate of 65.53 percent. Of those that responded, 37.4 percent employ no journalists of color.

Unity: Journalists of Color president Mae Cheng reacted to the new numbers by calling on editors to "personally accept the challenge of improving diversity." In response to the 2004 ASNE report, Cheng said, "It is clear that ASNE will not reach its goal of achieving parity in the newsroom by 2025 as long as this remains an institutional goal and not a personal one for its hundreds of members. . . . Editors need to make this a priority, perhaps even taking the dramatic step of making a majority of their hires over the next year qualified people of color to finally move that needle."[38] Unity is a coalition of more than 10,000 journalists representing NABJ, NAHJ, AAJA, and NAJA.

RTNDA/Ball State University Annual Survey

The 2005 study conducted annually by the Radio-Television News Directors' Association and Ball State University reports that journalists of color hold 21.2 percent of jobs in the television workforce, including Hispanic stations. When Hispanic stations are not included, the figure drops to 19.5 percent overall. People of color account for 7.9 percent of jobs in radio. [39]

Black journalists have the highest visibility in television accounting for 10.3 percent of all employees, followed by Hispanics with 8.7 percent, Asian Americans with 1.9 percent, and Native Americans with .3 percent. In radio, black employees hold .7 percent of the jobs; Hispanics, 6.0 percent; Asian Americans, .7 percent; and Native Americans, .5 percent.

People of color hold 12 percent of the news directors jobs in television and 11 percent in radio. They account for 6.8 percent of all general managers of television stations and 3.4 percent of radio general managers.

Women hold 39.3 percent of the jobs in television and 27.5 percent of the jobs in radio. Women hold news director slots at 21.3 percent of all television stations and 24.7 percent of all radio stations. They make up 17 percent of general managers in television and 20 percent of general managers in radio.

The RTNDA/Ball State survey includes the responses from 1,223 nonsatellite television stations (a 75.3 percent response rate) and 417 radio stations.

Bob Papper, who reported the study in the July/August 2005 issue of *Communicator*, sees little reason for optimism. "The minority workforce in TV has been at 20 percent — plus or minus 3 percent — for every year in the past 15," he writes. "Some years it edges up, sometimes down, but there has been no consistent change. Radio is worse, with the minority percentage in news down from 15 years ago."[40]

Diversity in the Washington Newspaper Press Corps

A census of the Washington bureaus of U.S. daily newspapers released at the 2004 Unity conference revealed that less than 10.5 percent of the reporters, correspondents, columnists, editors, and bureau chiefs in the press corps of the nation's capital are journalists of color. While only 60 of the 574 members of the press corps are people of color, only 3 of the newspaper and newsgroup bureau chiefs are journalists of color.[41]

Broken down into racial–ethnic categories, 35 or 6.1 percent were black journalists; 14 or 2.4 percent were Hispanic; and 11 or 1.9 percent were Asian. No Native American journalists were assigned to the Washington press corp.

Former Unity president Ernest Sotomayor commented: "There is no justification for any

Diversity Scorecard

Compiled from 2004–2005 surveys conducted by the American Society of Newspaper Editors, the Radio-Television News Directors Association, and Ball State University.

Journalists of color in the		U.S.population
daily newsroom	13.42%	32.2%
Black	5.51	13.0
Hispanic	4.29	13.3
Asian American	3.07	4.4
Native American	0.55	1.5

Journalists of color in supervisory roles..............10.80%

Journalists of color in the TV news workforce	21.20%
Black	10.30
Hispanic	8.70
Asian American	1.90
Native American	0.30

Journalists of color in the radio workforce	7.9%
Black	0.7
Hispanic	6.0
Asian American	0.7
Native American	0.5

Journalists of color in management

News directors in TV	12%
News directors in radio	11
General managers in TV	6.80
General managers in radio	3.40

Women in the daily newsroom	37.54%
Women in supervisory roles (daily newspapers)	34.80
Women in the TV workforce	39.30
Women in radio	27.50
Women news directors in TV	21.30
Women news directors in radio	24.70
Women general managers in TV	17.00
Women general managers in radio	20.90

Daily newspapers employing no people of color 37.47

media company to staff its bureau in Washington, D.C., without people of color. This is the seat of the most powerful government in the world, in one of the most diverse nations in the world, but the press corps doesn't come even close to reflecting what America looks like."[42]

Calling the findings dismal, Native American Journalists Association president Patty Talahongva said, "With all the talk about how much diversity matters you would think the numbers would be greater. Apparently, we are all just dreaming, but living in a journalistic nightmare."[43]

Lesbians and Gays in the Newsroom

Information about gay and lesbian employment in U.S. newsrooms is sparse. ASNE surveyed gay and lesbian newsroom professionals in 1989, reporting largely on gay and lesbian coverage and gay-bias in the newsroom. In 1993, RTNDA and the National Lesbian and Gay Journalists Association conducted a survey of broadcast journalists, again concentrating on gay coverage and newsroom conditions.

In 1999, the Annenberg School for Communications at the University of Southern California and the NLGJA surveyed print, broadcast, and new media journalists and looked at changes in coverage and attitudes over the span of the three studies. Results of the 1999 study were based on 363 responses. Both the 1989 study and the 1999 study were coordinated by Leroy

Aarons, founder of the NLGJA.

Those participating in the survey were recruited from NLGJA membership lists and from those responding to solicitations mailed to local NLGJA chapters and distributed at national meetings of media associations. The difficulty in obtaining estimates of gay numbers in the newsroom is illustrated by the response of those surveyed to the question, "What percentage of the gay men in the news operation are 'out'?" Most answered that the number of openly gay journalists ranged between 25 and 50 percent, with the average being 40.6 percent. Those responding to the same question relative to lesbians, estimated that as many as 67.2 percent of lesbians in the newsroom were "out." [44] Of those responding to the survey, 90 percent said they personally are "out."[45] The NLGJA currently has 1,200 members in 24 chapters.

Although arriving at estimates of gay numbers in the newsroom is difficult, the survey does provide some important information about gay men and lesbians working in journalism. Of those responding to the survey, 30.7 percent were employed as reporters and correspondents, 8.3 percent listed their job category as anchor, and only 1 percent said they occupied a supervisory position.[46]

Males accounted for 83.7 percent of those surveyed, females, 16.3 percent. Of those working in broadcast news, 20.2 percent worked in radio and 79.8 percent in television. Most of those working in television worked at local affiliates, 64.3 percent, compared to those who reported working at the network level.[47] Commenting on the 1999 survey, NLGJA president Robert Dodge writes:

> The findings are both gratifying and disturbing. On the one hand, results from the respondents show that there has been plenty of progress. Never before have gay and lesbian journalists felt so comfortable being out in the workplace. But the survey also points to serious deficiencies. While improved over the last decade, coverage is found lacking in quality and quantity by today's standards, our members shy away from confronting news managers and managers do not seem to be tapping into the resources available from lesbian and gay journalists.[48]

So What Is Diversity?

Industrialist William R. Wrigley, stressing the importance of diversity of opinion once said, "When two men in business always agree, one of them is unnecessary."

Just as it is important to have diversity of thought in the workplace, it also is important to have a newsroom that reflects the diversity of our increasingly complex global community: people of all races and ethnicities, ages, gender and sexual orientation, socioeconomic class, geographic and national origin, political and religious affiliations, and physical abilities.

Diversity is both that simple and that unbelievably complex.

ACTIVITY: Community Profile

1. Using the U.S. Census Bureau's latest American Community Survey (www.census.gov), profile the racial and ethnic composition of your state, county, or community.

2. Compare the composition of your community to the mix of people of color in your newsroom or in the newsroom of your local daily newspaper or television station. Although you may need to do some original investigation, information on journalists of color at most daily newspapers is available in a Knight Foundation report at www.powerreporting.com/knight/california.html. Research the diversity of local television news programs by counting the number of anchors and reporters of color.

Chapter Two

Why Is Diversity Important?

In the 1978 Bakke decision, in which the U.S. Supreme Court upheld the right of the Medical School at the University of California at Davis to consider race in admissions decisions, Justice Lewis Powell writes that "the atmosphere of speculation, experiment and creation — so essential to the quality of higher education — is widely believed to be promoted by a diverse student body."[49]

In a strong endorsement of diversity and its importance to education, he added, "It is not too much to say that the nation's future depends upon leaders trained through wide exposure to the ideas and mores of students as diverse as this Nation of many people."

Justice Sandra Day O'Connor, in her majority opinion in the University of Michigan Law School decision in 2003, echoes Powell in describing the benefits of diversity as "substantial":

> The law school's admission policy promotes cross-racial understanding, helps to break down racial stereotypes, and enables students to better understand persons of different races. These benefits are important and laudable, because classroom discussion is livelier, more spirited, and simply more enlightening and interesting when students have the greatest possible variety of backgrounds.[50]

Citing supporting documents entered in the case as *amicus curiae*, including briefs submitted by General Motors, O'Connor writes, "The skills needed in today's increasingly global marketplace can only be developed through exposure to widely diverse people, cultures, ideas, and viewpoints." She also cites U.S. military reports that assert, "A highly qualified, racially diverse officer corps . . . is essential to the military's ability to fulfill its principal mission to provide national security."

In these and other court cases, the U.S. Supreme Court has taken the lead in arguing that there is a significant societal benefit to be gained from having an educational system that is made up of a student body as diverse as the nation it serves. The same rationale applied to medical students, law students, and students in liberal arts undergraduate programs can be applied to students in journalism and communications undergraduate programs. A diverse student body will produce students who have been exposed to a greater variety of ideas, a broader understanding of other cultures and viewpoints, and an enhanced ability to communicate that better understanding to the communities they ultimately serve as reporters, news directors, and editors.

Likewise, the diverse newsroom — both in terms of numbers and in terms of attitude and ability to communicate with diverse audiences — can only contribute to a broader cultural understanding by the mass audience they serve. And a truly diverse newsroom will contribute not only to a greater understanding of racial and ethnic differences but to a recognition and understanding of differences resulting from age, class, gender and sexual orientation, faith, and national and geographic origin as well.

Although there likely are as many arguments to support the practice of diversity in the newsroom as there are organizations providing programs to increase diversity, most answers to the "why diversity" question fall into four distinct categories:

1. Ethics and social responsibility — the argument that encompasses the belief that it is the morally right thing to do.

2. Atonement — a version of the affirmative action argument or a type of reparation; the belief that there needs to be a concerted effort to make up for past inequities.

3. Good economics — the belief that a diverse work environment is more conducive to productivity and therefore more profitable, and the simple realization that as the diverse population increases, there is a greater market for diverse news. New and more readers and subscribers translate into more advertiser appeal.

4. Good journalism — the obvious argument that accurate coverage of the complete community, including uncovered and undercovered populations, is simply good journalism.

Of course, these arguments are not exclusive of one another. The real *why* of diversity likely involves a combination of two or more of these and others. It also should be noted that these are presented as rationales for practicing diverse journalism, in terms related both to creating a diverse newsroom and to providing diverse content from complete coverage of the community.

How Ethics Relates to Diversity

Ethics is viewed here as a system of principles that guide human conduct, that provide some insight into what is the right thing to do at a given place and time in history, and that are based on conscience rather than fear of retribution. While dozens of media ethics textbooks devote multiple chapters to defining ethics and ethical conduct or distinguishing between the subtleties of ethics and morals, there is value in John Merrill's simple characterization of ethics as the study of "what we ought to do."[49]

As they relate to life in general, ethical principles suggest that humans "ought" to tell the truth, share with those less fortunate, and treat others as they would like to be treated. In terms of the practice of ethical journalism, professionals "ought" to check their facts, honor the privacy of their sources and the subjects of their reporting, act independently, and minimize harm. Applied to the practice of diversity in journalism, ethics principles require that journalists use diverse sources, cover the undercovered, and avoid stereotyping and profiling.

If it is the thing that professional journalists ought to do, then ethics is central to the rationale of media diversity. Media owners and their representatives should hire and promote people regardless of their race or ethnicity or whether or not they have a physical disability. Assignments in the newsroom should be made not based on an individual's sexual orientation or socioeconomic background, but rather on his or her ability to do a good job on the story. A reporter's or editor's choice of sources should not be based on an individual's age, faith, or political affiliation. Sources should reflect the range of diversity within the community.

Ethics literature provides several systems to aid in ethical decision making or determining the "ought to" of a given ethical situation or dilemma, including The Potter Box, developed by Dr. Ralph Potter at the Harvard Divinity School, and a similar system developed by Bob Steele at the Poynter Institute.

Steele's decision-making guide provides a series of ten simple questions that help the journalist analyze the pros and cons of a particular decision and make a rational determination of the "ought to" in that situation. Using any of the decision-making systems will enable you to make better ethical decisions in general as well as to make more reasoned approaches to ethical considerations involving diversity.

Poynter's Ten Questions[52]

1. What do I know? What do I need to know?

2. What is my journalistic purpose?

3. What are my ethical concerns?

4. What organizational policies and professional guidelines should I consider?

5. How can I include other people, with different perspectives and diverse ideas, in the decision-making process?

6. Who are the stakeholders — those affected by my decision? What are their motivations? Which are legitimate?

7. What if the roles were reversed? How would I feel if I were in the shoes of one of the stakeholders?

8. What are the possible consequences of my actions? Short term? Long term?

9. What are my alternatives to maximize my truth telling responsibility and minimize harm?

10. Can I clearly and fully justify my thinking and my decision? To my colleagues? To the stakeholders? To the public?

Atonement As a Rationale for Increasing Diversity

An atonement is a reparation or compensation for a past mistake or wrong, the wrong in this case being decades of discrimination against pretty much any of the oppressed groups Beverly Daniel Tatum calls "systematically disadvantaged."

Systemic disadvantage is most obvious, of course, as relates to race. In 1947, the Henry

Luce–sponsored Hutchins Commission pointed out the need for media to provide better coverage of all groups in society.[53] The Kerner Commission in 1968 criticized media both for its discriminatory hiring practices and for its poor coverage of anything other than mainstream white communities.[54] The ASNE annual report has continued to bring attention to the disparity in hiring every year since 1978.

But the question of reparation as a rationale for supporting diversity in the newsroom does not apply just to race and gender. There continues to be an insufficient presence of gay men and lesbians as well as of people with physical disabilities. People of varying faiths, political affiliations, and national backgrounds do not have a voice in most mainstream media.

And media staff are increasingly at a socioeconomic level that puts them out of touch with their readers. "The American Journalist in the 21st Century" research shows that over 90 percent of journalists are college educated.[55] At the same time, the cost of a college education continues to rise, and journalism programs are increasingly housed at major state universities and private liberal arts colleges and universities. The increasing cost almost assures a perpetuation of the tendency for journalists to come from backgrounds limited to higher economic and social class.

Accepting that the racial, ethnic, economic, and demographic disparity has and continues to exist in the U.S. newsroom, is that alone justification for an affirmative action, or as Cornel West calls it, a redistributive[56] approach to hiring and promoting newsroom employees, making assignments, and determining content? And if so, to what extent are diversity issues to be considered or even computed in making those decisions? Should parity be used as a strict guideline? If the audience that a particular media outlet serves is 33 percent people of color, should every third new hire be a journalist of color? Should one-third of the news content relate specifically to people of color?

Although supporting the right of the University of California at Davis to consider race in admissions in the 1978 Bakke decision, Justice Lewis Powell repudiated an admissions rationale based on victimization. He argues that the goal of helping people who are perceived as being victims of discrimination does not justify imposing disadvantages on other groups.[57] He supported the right to consider race in admission decisions but not an admissions policy that reserved a certain number of positions for students of color.

Considering race, ethnicity, gender, age, class, and so on in making a decision on newsroom staff or management would be acceptable under Powell's reasoning, but setting rigid hiring standards like those proposed by management at the *Greensboro* (N.C.) *News & Record* might not. The paper's editor wrote in the newspaper's blog in November 2004 that the newspaper employed only nine journalists of color, only 7 percent of the 124 full-time journalists at the paper. The newspaper's coverage area is 35 percent people of color. His plan: "Beginning this month, at least 33 percent of our new hires will be minorities. If an editor hires two white journalists, the next hire must be a minority."[58]

The problem inherent in that plan comes about at the time of the third hire. If it is predetermined that one of every three new hires will be a journalist of color and the first two have been white, then no matter who walks through the door, that third hire has to be of a race or ethnicity other than white — regardless of the qualifications of the various applicants and regardless of any other factors relating to diversity.

According to both Powell's reasoning in Bakke, and O'Connor's opinion in the *Grutter v. Bollinger* decision, that kind of strict quota in the interest of remedying societal discrimination places "unnecessary burdens on innocent third parties who bear no responsibility for whatever harm the beneficiaries"[59] of the quota hiring system might have suffered. In other words, under the one-of-three strategy, the qualified white applicant who shows up for the third position is not even considered.

Powell preferred instead something akin to the admissions policy used at Harvard, which was cited in the Bakke decision:

> When the committee on admissions reviews the large middle group of applicants who are admissible and deemed capable of doing good work in their courses, the race of an applicant may tip the balance in his favor just as geographic origin or a life spent on a farm may tip the balance in other candidates' cases. A farm boy from Idaho can bring something to Harvard that a Bostonian cannot offer. Similarly, a black student can usually bring something that a white person cannot offer. The quality of the educational experience of all the students in Harvard College depends in part on the differences in the background and outlook that students bring with them.[60]

Justice Ruth Bader Ginsburg rejects both Powell's and O'Connor's argument in her dissent in the *Gratz v. Bollinger* decision, the companion to the Michigan law school case in which it was ruled that adding 20 points to every application from an underrepresented group was a violation of the Equal Protection Clause of the Fourteenth Amendment. "The stain of generations of racial oppression is still visible in our society, and the determination to hasten its removal remains vital," Ginsburg writes. "One can reasonably anticipate, therefore, that colleges and universities will seek to maintain their minority enrollment . . . whether or not they can do so in full candor through adoption of affirmative action plans of the kind here at issue." She said that without acceptable racially biased admission policies, higher education would resort to camouflage. "If honesty is the best policy, surely Michigan's accurately described, fully disclosed College affirmative action program is preferable to achieving similar numbers through winks, nods, and disguises."[61]

Cornell West would agree. He supports the concept of redistributive measure as a means of righting a significant wrong. He believes that equality will come only through a forced redistribution. Calling past discriminatory practices atrocious, he writes in *Race Matters*, "Given the history of this country, it is a virtual certainty that without affirmative action, racial and sexual discrimination would return with a vengeance."[62]

Of course not everyone agrees with Ginsburg and West. Peter Wood makes a point of discrediting the Bakke decision and relating the eventual suspension of Patrick Chavis's license to practice medicine based on charges of gross negligence. Chavis was the student originally admitted under the University of California at Davis's quota admissions system that resulted in the suit. Allan Bakke, plaintiff in the case, also graduated from UC–Davis and enjoyed a successful career. Wood summarizes his views on racial preference thusly: "The kind of diversity achieved by racially preferential admissions is not educationally invigorating; it is intellectually threadbare and ethically contemptible."[63]

William McGowan applies the same disdain for affirmative action to media diversity. While accepting that the media industry has in the past practiced varying degrees of racial, ethnic, and cultural exclusion, and labeling actions taken to improve newsroom diversity as worthy, he blasts the results:

> After nearly a decade of monitoring how the nation's most important news organizations cover these issues, I would say that the drive for greater diversity has failed to yield better journalism, and that this has negative implications for American society's growth as a multicultural society.... With the cultural topography of the country shifting beneath our feet, we need a press capable of framing essential questions and providing honest, candid and dependable answers.[64]

Similar to Peter Wood's enthusiasm in citing Patrick Chavis as a failure of affirmative actions, diversity critics like to point to Jayson Blair as a shining example of diversity's failure. The truth is anyone who wants to find anecdotal evidence of the failure of most any social program in the 20th century could do so with minimal effort. But the reverse is also true. The 2004 Unity: Journalists of Color conference in Washington, D.C., was attended by over 8,000 black, Hispanic, Asian, and Native American students and journalists from newspapers, magazines, and broadcast outlets from across the United States. Almost all of them are successful in what they do and are contributing to the good work of journalism. To label the entire effort a failure because of the actions of a few is misguided at best.

Taken in context, the desire to compensate for years of the media's lack of inclusiveness contributes to the broader rationale for diversity. It is reasonable to suggest that, because of the historical absence of people of color in the newsroom, the avoidance of source diversity, and the lack of significant content relating to much of anything other than the mainstream white community, media owners should treat the movement to diversity with some sense of urgency.

Cornell West comments that "Although many . . . view affirmative action as a redistributive measure whose time is over or whose life is no longer worth preserving, I question their view because of the persistence of discriminatory practices . . . ."[65]

Diversity and Profit

Like most business and social institutions, the media paid little attention as the Hispanic population began to grow in parts of the United States over a decade ago. The new neighbors were greeted with ambivalence at best. Communities had grown accustomed to an influx of new cultural groups like the Hmong or Montgnards or Somali. Though their presence had created scattered racial stirrings, there had been little impact economically.

Then the numbers exploded. Between July 1, 1990, and July 1, 1999, the nation's Hispanic population grew 38.8 percent to 31.3 million. By March 2002, the Census Bureau reported that there were 34.4 million people of Hispanic origin living in the United States.[66]

The business community began to pay attention. Signs proclaiming *en español* sprouted everywhere. ATM's offered instructions in both English and Spanish. Banks, real estate agencies, insurance offices, even car dealers hired Spanish-speaking tellers, agents, and sales staff to do business with the new Hispanic customer.

A 2005 headline in *Viva*, a Latino culture magazine, declares "Ignoring the Latino Consumer is Risky Business." The ensuing article calls the numbers "overwhelming," estimating that by 2008, 15.7 percent of the total U.S. population will be of Hispanic origin and that its purchasing power will have increased by 356 percent since 1990. The author writes: "Not too long ago, if a company made a real effort to understand and satisfy the Latino market, its executives were considered visionaries. Today, it is becoming imperative."[67]

In the premiere edition of *Viva*, a publication founded to serve the growing Latino population in the Charlotte (NC) Mecklenburg County metropolitan area, it is estimated that the buying power of Latinos in that area alone had exceeded $500 million.

While the Hispanic population has made headlines as the fastest growing ethnic group in the United States, other diverse populations have seen economic growth as well. It is estimated that black Americans have a buying power of between $575 billion and $650 billion annually, greater than all of Canada.[68] At 4.4 percent of the U.S. population, Asian Americans don't have the economic impact of the larger black and Hispanic communities, but with median household incomes at $10,000 above Caucasian households, they are getting the advertiser's attention.[69]

It also is estimated that openly lesbian, gay, bisexual, and transgender (LGBT) people compose 7 percent of the U.S. population. According to Howard Buford of Prime Access, "This consumer marketplace represents some 15 million ethnically diverse consumers with buying power of $450 billion to $500 billion annually."[70]

Yet, while taking increased notice, business is slow to react to the growing diverse population. A publication from Multicultural Marketing Resources, a consortium of marketing and advertising professionals, reports, "Of the $237 billion spent on advertising in the United States in 2002, less than 2 percent of expenditures went to programs directly targeting a consumer population which constitutes almost 30 percent of the country and commands an annual purchasing power in excess of $1.5 trillion."[71]

Media owners, also slow to realize the potential of the new multicultural market, are taking notice. The Newspaper Association of America (NAA) issued a report in 2001 called *Growth Opportunities by Leveraging Diversity.* Touted in headlines as "Finding GOLD in Diversity," the report examines from an economic perspective how appealing to diverse segments of the population can bring profits from new sources while maintaining the old.[72] Through interviews with a variety of media managers across the country and an analysis of socioeconomic trends, the GOLD project team made a number of significant observations and conclusions leading to the development of a toolkit and training materials.

Some of the conclusions from the report:

■ Newspaper revenues and profits must grow consistently from year to year.

■ Margins are at significant risk of decline from classified-ad competition and other threats.

■ Fundamental market changes are underway and recognized but are not being seriously addressed.

■ The challenge must be to find replacement revenue streams.

■ Attract Hispanic readers, taking into account specific Hispanic subgroups. The Hispanic population is not monolithic, but varies depending on country of origin and length of time in the United States.

■ Strategically attract non-newspaper readers, typically those in low-income households in ethnic neighborhoods.

■ Motivate current time-starved readers, in this case working women, to make your newspaper their first choice.

■ Establish relationships with all market segments by creating a product and derivative products for everyone.[73]

When the American Society of Newspaper Editors adopted its diversity mission statement in 1998, the role of profit as a stimulus was in clear view:

> To cover communities fully, to carry out their role in a democracy and to succeed in the marketplace, the nation's newsrooms must reflect the racial diversity of American society by 2025 or sooner. At a minimum, all newspapers should employ journalists of color and every newspaper should reflect the diversity of its community.[74]

When ASNE conducted its first Time-Out for Diversity in 2000, in which more than 150 newsrooms took "time-out" to participate in diversity discussions, a number of respondents associated diversity with economic outlooks.

Leona Allen, night city editor, *Dallas Morning News* said, "The *Dallas Morning News* readership is predominantly white, but the city of Dallas is predominantly minority and growing. Tapping into those communities is about survival for us."[75]

Peter Bhatia, executive editor, *The Oregonian* said, "It is both a moral and economic imperative . . . attracting readers from all communities is essential to our survival."[76]

There was a time in our nation's history when minority equated with poor inner city, which equated with demographics of little interest to advertisers and, therefore, of little interest to media organizations. Media did not target people of color because people of color did not have the purchasing power advertisers wanted. Wilson and Gutiérrez, in their work *Race, Multiculturalism and the Media* quote *Los Angeles Times* publisher Otis Chandler as saying it didn't make any financial sense to direct its publication toward low-income readers who have no purchasing power and are not responsive to the kind of advertising the newspaper published.[77]

With the rapid growth in the population of people of color and the increasing buying power of the Asian and Hispanic populations as well as the rising education levels and incomes of black Americans, the marketplace is becoming more diversity friendly.

Diversity makes sense from an economic perspective in terms both of staff and content. A more diverse staff will create a better product, which in turn, will appeal to a larger and broader audience, creating more advertising and marketing opportunities for the corporate office.

Diversity Is Good Journalism

This may be the simplest answer to the question: "Why Diversity?" Good journalism is the journalism of diversity. David Yarnold, former executive editor of the *San Jose Mercury News*, says: "Diversity in your content is as important as getting people's names right. It's a fundamental component of accuracy."[78]

Good journalism is all about fairness and accuracy and covering the total community without bias. If that is truly the goal, then diversity will fall into place. Accurately covering the community requires covering it completely. A standard of teaching at the Poynter Institute concerns the complete picture. A handout used in classes at the institute proclaims, for example:

> Excellent, ethical journalism honors the profession's core principles of truth, accuracy, fairness and balance. To be complete and, thus, excellent, journalists must get better at reporting and writing untold stories: at bringing the fullest possible range of people and issues before viewers, listeners and readers.[79]

Providing the complete picture requires including the undercovered in news stories of all types, not just stories about race and diversity. Include people of color as sources, as a part of informal polls and surveys, and as images in photographs and illustrations. Make the uncovered and undercovered the focus of stories about people and communities.

Poynter Dean Keith Woods writes on this topic eloquently in *The Essence of Excellence*, a report on covering race and ethnicity done for Columbia University in 2000:

> The paradox of reporting and writing well about race and ethnicity is that it is at once exactly the same as all other excellent journalism and, at the same time, unique. Those who have risen above average in this arena seem to have met the challenge of that contradiction. The two are the same in that they stand on the common foundation of journalistic excellence: factual and contextual accuracy, fairness, precision, comprehensiveness, independence, giving voice to the voiceless, holding the powerful accountable, informing, educating, taking people where they can't or won't go.[80]

The ASNE Time-Out discussion in 2001 asked newsroom managers if they agreed with the spirit of the premise: "We want to accurately reflect life in our communities. If our newspapers are not inclusive enough to regularly portray the diversity of those communities, then we are presenting a fundamentally inaccurate report. That lack of accuracy undermines our journalistic credibility."[79]

Many of the responses testified to the importance of diversity to good journalism. Otis Sanford, deputy managing editor of *The Memphis Commercial Appeal* said: "It's a no-brainer. If you continually ignore a segment of your community you are not giving a complete and accurate picture." Jeane M. DePaul, feature sections editor, at the *Lewiston* (Idaho) *Morning Tribune* said, "If we are not reporting consistently on all aspects of our community, we are not providing an accurate picture of it."

Finally, Eileen Lehnert, managing editor of the *Jackson* (Michigan) *Citizen Patriot* responded, "As a newspaper, we are creating a historical record — a reflection of life as it was at a certain time." Unfortunately, much of the news being produced does not reflect life as it is today. The underreported remain below the radars of most news organizations. Whether intentional or not, stories continue to be framed in a manner that perpetuates the same old tired stereotypes.

And that's not good journalism.

Why Do Diversity?

The ethics code of the Society of Professional Journalists tells reporters to provide a voice to those who have no voice and to "tell the story of the diversity and magnitude of the human experience boldly, even when it is unpopular to do so."[80] Serving the cause of diversity is the right thing to do.

It is the thing journalists "ought to do," whether it is done out of a sense of ethics and social responsibility, because of the need to address discriminations from the past, because it makes economic good sense, or simply because it's good journalism.

As reasoned in both the 1978 Bakke medical school admissions decision and the 2003 Grutter law school decision, diversity makes an important and positive contribution to the social dialogue. The more diverse the voices, the more mature and constructive the conversation.

In an address to the Democratic National Convention in 1984, Jesse Jackson used the analogy of a quilt to describe America:

> America is not like a blanket – one piece of unbroken cloth, the same color, the same texture, the same size. America is more like a quilt – many patches, many pieces, many colors, many sizes, all woven and held together by a common thread. The white, the Hispanic, the black, the Arab, the Jew, the woman, the Native American, the small farmer, the businessperson, the environmentalist, the peace activist, the young, the old, the lesbian, the gay and the disabled make up the American quilt.[84]

Imagine the conversation that can be had when the national media begin to pay more attention to that national quilt, to cover all the patches, all the pieces equally and without bias. Maybe then the U.S. media can truly contribute to Martin Luther King's vision of a "single garment"[85] in which all those patches are united into one.

It can happen. It's all about good journalism.

ACTIVITY: Community Survey

1. Discuss why you and others in your class or newsroom feel workforce and media content diversity is important. Make a list. Do your reasons match those discussed in the chapter?

2. Poll at least ten people outside your classroom or newsroom. Without suggesting any of the reasons in the chapter or on your personal list, ask them why having a diverse newsroom staff is important. Do their answers match those you listed in the first activity?

Chapter Three

Achieving Diversity:
A Roadmap for Success

Despite the efforts of ASNE, the Freedom Forum, the Unity partners, the Maynard Institute, Poynter, and many other media organizations, the progress of diversity is at best a slow crawl. In 1998, ASNE's annual survey reported that journalists of color made up 11.46 percent of the total workforce. Subsequent years showed minimal increases: 1999, 11.5 percent; 2000, 11.85 percent; 2001, 11.64 percent; 2002, 12.07 percent; 2003, 12.53 percent; 2004, 12.95 percent; and 2005, 13.42 percent.[86]

The industry has struggled with the numbers game since the Hutchins Commission fired the first volley in 1947, when it listed as one of the requirements of a free and responsible press the depiction of a representative picture of all groups in society. Clear in its view of the shortcomings of the press, commission authors wrote, "When the images they portray fail to present the social group truly, they tend to pervert judgment."[87]

Recommendations of the Hutchins Commission went unheeded. Race relations were largely ignored during the following decade and festered in the early 1960s, resulting in widespread civil disorder, including riots in over 150 cities during the summer of 1967.

The National Advisory Commission on Civil Disorders (the Kerner Commission), appointed by President Lyndon Johnson in 1967, echoed the Hutchins Commission's recommendations. It issued a strongly worded indictment of the media for failing to analyze and report adequately on race relations and problems in black neighborhoods, as well as for failing to bring more black journalists into the newsroom. The Commission criticized the media for ignoring its minority audience and presenting a largely white picture of society:

> The absence of Negro faces and activities from the media has an effect on white audiences as well as black. If what the white American reads in the newspapers or sees on television conditions his expectation of what is ordinary and normal in the larger society, he will neither understand nor accept the black American. By failing to portray the Negro as a matter of routine and in the context of the total society,

the news media have, we believe, contributed to the black-white schism in this country.[88]

The Commission recognized the importance not only of including people of color in news coverage, but of creating a diverse staff as well. "The journalistic profession," they wrote, "has been shockingly backward in seeking out, hiring, training and promoting Negroes." They recommended that the media "seek out young Negro men and women, inspire them to become — and then train them as — journalists"; and "publish newspapers and produce programs that recognize the existence and activities of the Negro, both as a Negro and as a part of the community."[89]

In spite of the strong words of the Kerner Commission, little progress had been made by 1978 when ASNE began its annual newsroom survey and encouraged member newspapers to commit to racial and ethnic parity by 2000. Ten years had passed since the Kerner Report, minority population was 19 percent of the total population, and minority representation in the newsroom was approximately 4 percent.

By 1998, when ASNE reaffirmed its commitment to racial diversity and revised its goal of parity to 2025, people of color had grown to represent less than 11.5 percent of the news workforce while reaching 28 percent of the total population. Little change, of course, occurred between then and 2005 when people of color were 13.42 percent of the workforce compared to approximately 32.2 percent of the population.[90]

Budget woes, changes in ownership, continued low retention of journalists of color, and downsizing in recent years have led to additional concerns about the progress of newsroom diversity. Staff reductions made strictly based on seniority led to significant layoffs of people of color both in staff ranks and in management. When the *Dallas Morning News* laid off more than 70 people in late 2004, approximately 25 percent were people of color.[91] The goal of newsroom parity, while a noble effort, faces what at times seems to be an insurmountable uphill battle. If the approximately .3 percent annual growth rate of newsroom diversity over the past five years continues,[92] employment of journalists of color will still be less than 25 percent in 2050 when it is projected that people of color will make up 50 percent or more of the national population.

The problems of retention alone are enough to stifle progress in achieving parity. Most recent research suggests that while increased efforts to hire journalists of color have produced limited success, those hired tend to leave the field at a faster rate than white journalists.

One of the most exhaustive retention studies in recent years was completed by Lawrence T. McGill, director of research at the Freedom Forum's Media Studies Center. Based on a 1999 survey of over 500 working journalists of color, McGill's analysis attempts to answer questions about retention and uses the figures to project the future of racial and ethnic parity in the newsroom. He lists the major reasons that minority journalists leave the newsroom as interest in other fields, lack of advancement opportunities, and burnout.[93]

Concerning the likelihood that newspapers will reach ASNE's goal of parity within the next twenty-five years, McGill writes, "Nearly three of every five new hires in the newspaper industry over the next 25 years (58.5 percent) would have to be journalists of color to achieve racial parity by 2025."[94] Based on participation by students of color in high school journalism programs, enrollment trends in university journalism programs, and retention, he and others conclude that the pipeline needed to reach parity in the newsroom simply is not there.

So are these discouraging trends significant reason to abandon the numerous excellent efforts directed at increasing diversity in the media workforce? Certainly not! There is every reason to continue efforts to create a national newsroom as diverse as the nation it serves. Differences disappear at a much faster pace when diverse people work together. However, the snail's pace crawl to parity may be reason to consider other strategies to accomplish good journalism with the workforce as it exists now and in the foreseeable future.

Some do argue that the ideal of numerical equality itself is limited if not flawed. Bill Kovach and Tom Rosenstiel, reflecting the work of the Committee of Concerned Journalists, write that the convention of defining diversity in terms of numbers risks confusing means with ends:

> Getting more minorities in the newsroom is a target, but not the goal, of diversity. The goal is a more accurate news organization. Ethnic, gender, and racial quotas are a means of approaching that. But they will accomplish nothing in themselves if the newsroom culture then requires that these people from different backgrounds all adhere to a single mentality. The local newspaper or TV station may "look like America," as President Bill Clinton was found of saying, but it won't think like the community and it won't understand it or be able to cover it. The goal of diversity should be to assemble not only a newsroom that might resemble the community, but one that is also as open and honest so that this diversity can function.[95]

Kovach and Rosenstiel label the goal "intellectual diversity," a group of people who are intellectually different regardless of skin color, gender, and sexual orientation.

Efforts to increase employment by people of color; people with disabilities; and people of varying age, class, gender, sexual orientation, faith, and national origin will and should continue. But there must be a commitment to hiring and training newsroom employees and managers who are intellectually diverse, who are aware of and sensitive to the issues of everyone in the diverse communities they cover, and who are eager to embrace the evolving multicultural community as their own.

Mixed Results

Most programs, most organized efforts, most professional discussions dealing with the topic of diversity focus on the parity numbers. "The numbers are bad!" "They're not getting any better!" "What can be done to make the numbers better?" There simply is not a lot of discussion about the other side. How can we, regardless of who we are, do a better job of covering the complete community?

These two concerns are not exclusive of each other. It is not necessary to focus any less on efforts to shore up the numbers, while making a concerted effort to train students and professionals to do a better job covering the community from their individual perspectives, whatever they might be.

Writing in the fall 2003 *Nieman Reports* Bryan Monroe says, "Whether it is coverage of the local Muslim community leading up to the war, or getting inside a Vietnamese-American neighborhood in everyday stories, our newsrooms too often miss nuances in coverage or miss entire stories completely because we don't have staffs diverse enough to 'get it.'"[96] Monroe talks about a few success stories, including efforts at the *Washington Post* and a joint project involving Scripps Newspapers and the NAHJ, but concludes, "While all these efforts are exciting and laudatory, it will take 10 times this activity level to even come close to hitting the parity goals for staffing and coverage that our industry has pledged."[97]

Kansas City Star reporter Mary Sanchez writes: "As journalists we are taught to keep our distance from subjects. Remain objective is the mantra. . . . And yet, there are times when a reporter needs to simply put down the pen and paper and become absorbed in the subject before him or her. . . . What journalism needs is more listening. Really listening. For a long time. Time spent building the trust that allows complex feelings to be shared."[98]

Former *San Jose Mercury News* editor David Yarnold gave his reporters time to listen. In addition to establishing the industry's first Race and Demographics department at the newspaper, Yarnold began a practice of giving all *Mercury News* reporters a week off from regular duties to identify and cultivate more diverse sources. Describing the newspaper's efforts to improve diversity of content through staff training, Carol Weber Thomas writes:

> There is no question that attention to diversity is a journalistic life-or-death situation for a newspaper like the Mercury News. The Merc covers an intensely diverse community of Anglos, blacks, Mexicans, Koreans, Vietnamese and others, in one of three states in the nation where so-called minorities are now the majority. (The other states are Hawaii and New Mexico.) With that mix, it's critical to hire a staff that reflects the community makeup, and even more critical that reporters and editors really understand the cultural dynamics of their readers.[99]

While the *San Jose Mercury News* has the advantages of size and location, others are not so lucky. The *Herald-Palladium*, serving the Benton Harbor–St. Joseph, Michigan, market, has one black female reporter on a staff of approximately thirty. Benton Harbor is 90 percent black; St. Joseph is predominately white. While acknowledging the low diversity on his staff, editor Dave Brown says, "I don't accept the notion that we can't do a good job if we don't have parity. We'll never be a perfect reflection, but the more reflective we are of our community, the better we are, and that should be our goal."[100]

The paper's single black reporter, Dana Slagle, says she supports ASNE's efforts to increase diversity, "But when we talk about diversity, it shouldn't be just about race and skin color. I'd like to see a diversity of thought."[101]

Other newspapers have similar problems but are putting forth the effort to provide diverse coverage. The *Times-News* in Burlington, N.C., serves a community of approximately 30 percent people of color, but has a history of limited or no reporters of color. Its current staff of thirty full-time employees includes a single Hispanic reporter. Both the publisher and editor have tried to hire students and journalists of color as interns and staff, but they maintain it is nearly impossible to hire journalists of color to work on a small (28,000) circulation daily and live in a small southern city the size of Burlington.

In spite of the difficulties in hiring, the newspaper tries to cover the community with the staff it has. City Editor Brent Lancaster recently did an eight-part series on local Hispanics, an attempt to educate area residents about their new Hispanic neighbors. Another reporter wrote an article about *tripas*, and the recently hired female reporter from Peru plans to do more stories about the growing Hispanic community.[102]

In addition to efforts being made by professional media, colleges and universities across the country are awakening to the needs for diversity and are integrating more content into their curricula directed at producing reporters, editors, photographers, and producers more aware of the issues of diversity and better prepared to improve coverage of the emerging community. In a study published in the spring 2002 issue of *Journalism & Mass Communication Educator*, the authors report research supporting the conclusion that journalism programs that infuse the teaching of diversity throughout their curricula have a greater success: "The importance of multicultural knowledge and sensitivity is emphasized through repetition. Students come to understand that being sensitive to and informed about various cultural groups is a standard part of a journalist's job, not an extra skill."[103]

A 2003 publication by the Accrediting Council on Education in Journalism and Mass Communications, "Diversity: Best Practices," highlights attempts by member schools to incorporate diversity into their programs and curricula. The diversity efforts range from offering a single elective course in "Media and Minorities," at the University of Alaska–Fairbanks to incorporating diversity into all syllabi for skills classes at California State University–Northridge. The dean of the Henry W. Grady College of Journalism and Mass Communication at the University of Georgia reports:

> Georgia is going through interesting changes. Students are much more aware of the need for diversity. An elective course, "Race and Media," closes within three days of registration. It's very popular; the faculty member who teaches it does it with great creativity and wit. It looks at the history of portrayals of African Americans in movies and TV.[104]

The School of Journalism at Indiana University brought in representatives of the Poynter Institute to work with them on their curriculum, resulting in a three-tier approach to teaching diversity: sensitizing students to the issues in introductory courses; immersing students in examples of good journalism of diversity; and practicing good journalism through interviewing, reporting, and writing using a diversity of sources.[105]

Michael Bugeja, director of the Greenlee School of Journalism and Communication at Iowa State University, takes the position that good journalism is diverse journalism. "I don't think a new curriculum has to be devised," he writes. "We must train the next generation of journalists to embrace diversity as a part of good journalism. . . . The community is diverse and becoming more diverse. If we think of journalism, we cover all the bases."[106]

The problem is not everyone is covering all the bases. An elective course taught once or twice a year in a program with a thousand or more students does not teach diversity. An occasional guest speaker of a color different from the majority of students does not teach students to be more knowledgeable and sensitive to issues relating to their future diverse communities. A one-time reporting assignment in a Hispanic community does not create reporters ready to cover people of all races and ethnicities, gender and sexual orientations, ages, physical capacities, class and national origins.

All these are worthwhile efforts that contribute to better informed students and future journalists. However, they need to be a part of a concentrated all-out effort to prepare students to practice good journalism reflective of the total community. Likewise, a simple declaration that students who practice good journalism will practice diverse journalism holds as much water as a bucket made from carpenter's cloth. There is truth in the statement that good journalism is diverse journalism, but seeing that it is realized in practice requires a plan.

The goals of teaching, learning, and practicing good journalism in the newsroom and on the street are obtainable if the will of those involved is strong enough and they are sufficiently determined to devote the time and resources to make it happen. It will require patience, consistency, and a resolve to not fail. But its reward will be a better workforce, a better news product, and a better community. It will, in the end, be well worth the efforts expended.

Roadmap to Diversity

The ideas presented here are not earth shattering; most are common sense. But they do require accepting that there is a problem that needs addressing, and making a determined effort to address it. As the cliché goes, you can talk the talk all day long, but somebody has to walk the walk to make it happen. All the items in the lists are intended for both students/professionals and teachers/leaders. As in all productive learning situations, success requires a partnership between teacher and learner.

A Guide to Teachers and Learners of Diversity in an Academic Setting

1. Integrate diversity into the entire journalism and communications curriculum.

Introduction to Communications — Research and discuss evolving media audiences, including changes in the U.S. population. Look at the latest census data on the race, ethnicity, gender, age, and class of the current U.S. population. Discuss what this means for media organizations. Also research the status of diversity in the newsroom. Talk about ASNE and RTNDA census results and discuss how the lack of parity might affect coverage of the community.

Basic Writing, Newswriting, Media Writing, Reporting I, etc. — This is a prime setting for diversity discussion. Diversity should be infused throughout the course beginning with the discussion of the meaning of news. Consider diversity issues in relation to story ideas, sources, and framing. Discuss racial identifications. Discuss bias. Get out of comfort zones in developing sources, story ideas, and the focus of the story. In addition to having diversity integrated into each chapter, devote at least two weeks to focus on the importance of being able to report on the entire community.

Consider Diversity Issues in Courses Across the Curriculum — Diversity can be a consideration in all writing and editing courses. Seek out diverse sources and story ideas for all of your assignments. Your writing will be more interesting and more accurate. Likewise, diversity can be incorporated in studies of media history, law, ethics, and film. Focus on the contributions of people of color; write and talk about ethical situations that involve issues of diversity; study the contributions of diverse filmmakers to the body of cinema.

2. Offer, or take, an elective course in diversity in media.

Keep it inclusive. A course that talks about all the many differences composing diversity is better than one that studies just women or a single race or ethnicity. The Newswatch website, newswatch.sfsu.edu/diversity_syllabuses, hosts dozens of syllabi taught in graduate and undergraduate courses at universities across the nation. Read what others are doing, and build a syllabus that fits your personal needs. The syllabus also constitutes an excellent source of references that can be used in research about a particular topic.

3. Bring professionals to campus.

Unity: Journalists of Color has over 10,000 members, and some of them live and work in your community. Bring them to your classes to talk about their lives and their work. But don't restrict yourself to journalists of color. Bring an older journalist from your community or someone who has a disability or someone who covers religion. Be creative.

Don't just restrict your list to journalists. Plan a panel discussion with members of the campus gay–lesbian group. Ask them questions about how they see journalists, and how they would grade the job media are doing covering people of varying sexual orientations. Or gather a group of diverse faculty members and have them discuss their opinions about media. The more exposure to the patchwork that makes up your community the better.

4. Arrange internships that offer greater exposure to diversity.

This may involve getting out of the proverbial comfort zone, but there is much value to be gained by this kind of exposure. This could involve going to a community with high diversity or simply interning at one of the excellent ethnic or specialty media organizations. Numerous Native American newspapers and magazines, for example, are spread across the country. There is no better way to learn the ins and outs of the native community than to spend some time reporting on it.

While many such internship placements involve large cities, that's not always the case. Taos, New Mexico, for example, is a small community of white, Native American, Hispanic, and black people living together in one of the most beautiful settings anywhere. Be creative and do some legwork. There are lots of good sites out there.

5. Shadow a journalist (or person) of difference.

For a week or a month or an entire semester spend time with someone who is of a race or ethnicity or sexual orientation different from your own, or someone with a disability, or someone whose socioeconomic class is different from your own. Shadow the person a few hours a week, but go beyond simply shadowing, get into the person's head. Talk to him about his life, his work, his difference. Let him know your objective is to learn and become a better journalist. Most people will go out of their way to be open with you.

6. Volunteer to do, or take, a service learning class.

Volunteer or do service at a homeless shelter, mission, food bank, or Good Shepherd kitchen. Circulate, talk to the people who pass through. Get their stories. Find out what they think about how the poor are represented in media, how they would like to be viewed. Take a class that incorporates service learning as a requirement. In some universities, such courses are identified in the registration schedule book. Take advantage of the opportunities in the course to get to know diverse people in a variety of settings whether you're working on a Habitat for Humanity house, tutoring at a Boys and Girls Club, or participating in programming at a senior citizens center.

7. Start an organization for diverse students.

Power is in numbers. Get students together to talk about issues of diversity in their disciplines. Make it inclusive: black, white, Hispanic, Asian, gay, lesbian, students with disabilities, and people of varying interests and backgrounds. Have diverse faculty from all areas of the campus come together to talk about their concerns about media and its coverage of the complete community.

Recruit speakers from the outside, both media related and not, to talk about diversity issues. Additionally, the organization might sponsor a campuswide meeting featuring speakers or a panel to stimulate discussion, a reading group, and road trips to make connections with diverse people in the community.

8. Read.

Learning is the best remedy for ignorance, and reading is still one of the basic and most important ways to learn. Read books, journals, newspapers, magazines, websites, and blogs. Scan the bookshelves in your library, at the local bookstore; use the lists included in the resources section at the end of this book. Pick up any one of those books, and its bibliography will list dozens of other books and articles.

If your library doesn't have a book related to diversity issues that you would like to read, request it through the library or a library representative in your major department. Start a book club or participate in one through your diverse student organization.

9. Get out of your bubble.

Whether it's a summer trip abroad, across country, or down the street, get out of the campus bubble and open yourself up to different people, cultures, and ideas. Shop at a Hispanic grocery or an Asian market. Have lunch at the out-of-the-way independent ethnic restaurants. Attend a black church. Volunteer at a food bank or homeless shelter. Visit a senior or independent living facility. Drive through an ethnic community. Get out and walk around. Find the hangouts. Talk to people. Attend a PFLAG meeting or social event. Visit historical sites, museums, and art displays related to diverse people. Plan trips to destinations that involve people of color. Visit an American Indian reservation. Go to a mosque. Attend a pow-wow. Eat dinner at a soul food restaurant. Take your laundry to an ethnic neighborhood.

The list, of course, is endless. Just do those things that will get you out and into the diverse community. You don't have to talk at first. Take some time to get used to being out of your bubble. Observe, and interact when it seems appropriate.

10. Study abroad.

If possible, spend a semester abroad. Very little is of more educational benefit than experiencing another culture by living for a time right in the midst of it. If your school doesn't offer a study abroad program, investigate summer programs sponsored by other universities or exchange programs where you can receive transfer credit. It doesn't really matter where you go. If you've never traveled abroad, Great Britain is a great place to start. London offers the benefit of an international setting without the hassle of language problems. Students from all over the world crowd the clubs and pubs of London year round, offering easy exposure to a wonderfully cosmopolitan setting. Wherever you go, however, get the tourist thing done as quickly as possible, then go behind the scenes to experience the real culture of the place. Enjoy, but remember your reason for being there is to learn.

A Guide to Teachers and Learners of Diversity in a Professional Setting

1. Do outreach on your local campus.

When teachers and students invite you to campus, go. If they don't invite you, invite yourself. One of the most ridiculous standoffs in the modern practice of journalism is the occasional rift between professional and academic journalists. You need each other for lots of good reasons. The goal of diversity is a good starting place.

Professionals can add much to the discussion of diversity in the classroom by talking about the importance of covering the complete community from a practitioner's point of view. In the process, the profession can benefit from a better educated class of graduates coming into the workforce. And the academic side can benefit by taking advantage of diverse voices coming from local media.

2. Practice diversity in the newsroom.

Creating an atmosphere of diversity is the first step. Make a conscious effort to hire professional and nonprofessional staff at all levels who represent the diversity of the community. Make sure your newsroom is easily accessible to people with disabilities. Develop décor or ambiance that recognizes the diversity of your newsroom and community. Eradicate stereotypes, loaded language, discrimination, and prejudice of any type from your newsroom. Practice a strict zero tolerance policy.

3. Hold diversity discussions or workshops.

Schedule regular discussions about diversity. Bring in experts from a local campus or press organizations such as the Poynter Institute to talk about providing better coverage of a multicultural community. Mix it up. Address a different topic each time, such as "Covering the Hispanic Community," "Providing Better Coverage of the Aging Community," "How to Address the Gay and Lesbian Community," and "Assessing Community Treatment of People with Disabilities."

Make it monthly, bimonthly, or quarterly. Put someone on your staff in charge of planning each event. Come up with creative ways to hold the workshops, to keep staff interested and excited. Make it a retreat. Get away from the newsroom. Serve a meal. Make the annual ASNE/APME Time Out Discussion one of your events each year.

4. Team reporters with differences.

Team a black reporter with a Hispanic reporter. Team an older reporter with a newly hired one. Put a white female reporter with an Asian male. Create assignments where they learn from each other. Send a new white reporter into the Cuban community with a veteran Hispanic reporter. Assign a black photographer to accompany a Native American writer to do a series on the impact of casinos on tourism. Pair an Ivy League graduate with a recently hired one from the South.

Put people together, have them talk, go to lunch, create stories. The white or Asian or Hispanic who accompanies a black reporter into the black community on five stories will be better prepared to go it alone on the sixth or sixteenth. It will take a proactive approach. It may not always produce the best short-term results, but in the end your staff and your coverage will benefit.

5. Send reporters out into the community.

Make a commitment to diversity. Give every reporter, photographer editor, director, producer, and anyone else who has a role in producing news one week a year to go out into the community to talk to people with differences. One newspaper sent reporters door to door in diverse communities with a set of questions to ask audiences and potential audiences about coverage: what they liked and didn't like, what could be covered better, how the coverage could be more sensitive to issues of importance to the community.

The time wouldn't need to be quite so structured. The important thing is to get people out into the community, walking the streets, going into the businesses, learning the cultures of the people they cover. A side benefit is that the people in the community get a sense that the news organization actually cares about the job they're doing and is trying to be better at covering the total community.

6. Award diversity sabbaticals on a rotating basis.

Design a sabbatical program that fits your budget, but make it as liberal as possible. At a minimum, make it a month-long program. Award at least one every six months, and more if possible. It must be educational or contribute in some way to the community. It must have at least an indirect payoff for the news organization. Other than that, keep it loose.

Let staff members design their own proposals. Here are some ideas: working in the Hispanic community to design a video on community services for new immigrants; interning on a Native American newspaper or at a Hispanic radio station; working at a community center in a newly established Hmong neighborhood; teaching ESL (English as a second language) in an after school program for Hispanic children; building a church on a Navajo reservation in Arizona; painting a building at the Penn Center (Gullah museum of slavery) on St. Helena Island; teaching a class at a senior citizen's center; working the serving line in a food kitchen. The list is endless. The benefits to the individual and to your organization are inestimable.

7. Send staff to conferences and workshops.

The Unity: Journalists of Color's quadrennial conference is not just for journalists of color. Same for the meetings of NABJ, AAJA, NAHJ, NAJA, and NLGJA. In fact, journalists outside their target audiences may benefit more from attending these conferences than members. Very few white journalists and educators attended Unity: Journalists of Color 2004 in Washington, D.C., missing out on excellent learning opportunities and numerous opportunities to interact with a wide diversity of journalists.

There also are various learning opportunities offered by the Poynter Institute on their beautiful campus in St. Petersburg, the Pew Center, the Freedom Forum, ASNE, and other press organizations. Encourage staff to take advantage of these opportunities. Some require little more than an application.

8. Establish a community advisory board.

Depending on the composition of your particular community, invite local citizens to participate on an advisory panel to meet regularly with members of your news staff to talk about coverage of the underreported community. Include a variety of racial and ethnic representatives, people of varying ages and socioeconomic backgrounds, and so forth. Don't just pick the community activists. Go out into the community and choose ordinary people, people who are not already on similar panels. Meet with them regularly. Expose them to a variety of staff at all levels up to top management. Talk in generalities, but also give them an assignment. Have them come up with a list of 50 stories that need to be covered, sources that nobody is contacting, problems that need to be addressed, and media misconceptions that need to be corrected.

9. Create a source list.

Media at all levels suffer from overused sources. The same is true in communities of difference. A community develops, activists rise to the top, and they immediately become the experts on everything in the community. The problem is their personal opinions and agendas may not accurately reflect the consensus of the entire community.

Develop other sources in the community. Find new sources at the community church, the local grocery, funeral home, barbershop, laundry, movie rental store, restaurant, newsstand, auto repair shop, real estate agency, used car dealership, and park. There are potential community experts everywhere. Seek them out. Use them. They might prove more illuminating than those tired old sources who turn up every time the six o'clock news decides to do a story on homophobia.

10. Team with leaders in the diverse community.

Establish a dialogue between community leaders and staff. Identify leaders in the diverse community. They are loan officers at the local bank. There are ministers, coaches in the little league programs, activists who speak out in the community. Invite them to your newsroom. Have them sit in on meetings where you develop story ideas. Show them how you put a paper or broadcast together. Mix it up. Let a black minister do a thirty-minute stint on an afternoon talk show while a reporter takes his or her place greeting Sunday morning parishioners. Invite a team of diverse community leaders to plan a special broadcast on the emerging community while your management team takes over weekend duties at the local homeless shelter or plans a community event to showcase the evolving culture of the diverse community.

And don't stop there. Whether you're a student or professor on a university campus, or a reporter or managing editor or news director in a news organization, the point is to experience diversity, to learn all you can learn about difference, and to produce a news product that is better and more accurate and more representative of the community you serve. It is neither complex nor difficult. But it does require someone to step up to the task and get it done.

ACTIVITY: Mapping Your Future

1. List ten activities that you can become involved with on your campus or in your community to become a better informed member of the diverse community.

2. Make a list of ten story ideas you can do on your campus or in your community that address issues of diversity.

3. Team with someone in your class or campus or in your community who is different from you. Have him or her make a list of ten story ideas, and see how they differ from your own list.

Chapter Four

The Conversation: Moving Forward

Popular radio banter these days gives much attention to the importance of "showing up," "stepping up to the plate," "sitting down at the table," and "staying in the room" as keys to success. Much like the wisdom of Dale Carnegie a generation ago, these tidbits of advice carry with them the simple truth that the most complex problems require the simplest of solutions. Want to lose weight? It's simple: eat less, eat right, and exercise. Want to stop smoking? It's a no brainer. Hide the matches. Chew gum. Get a patch. Want to raise great kids? It's simple. Engage them. Tell them how great they are. Tell them you love them several times every day. And say no once in a while.

Want to start a conversation on a difficult subject? It's quick and simple. Open your mouth and let the words come out. Unfortunately, the one thing that prevents most conversations on diversity is avoidance. Nobody wants to talk about it. It makes people uncomfortable. It makes people squirm, pace, look the other way, even sweat. People will deny there's anything to talk about. In the same room where black students huddle together in one corner, international students in another, and gay and lesbian students keep quiet for fear of being identified, students will maintain vigorously: "There's no problem. We did this in high school. Let's move on."

Others, students and your colleagues across the newsroom, will argue "Diversity is the problem. All this talk just points out how people are different. It divides people." That's the McGowan argument — diversity is the beast. But that's a ridiculous argument. Diversity is the beast only if you're a member of the dominant white class in the U.S. society. For everyone else, the beast is racism, sexism, ethnocentrism, classism, homophobia, ageism, faithism, ableism, or any other form of discrimination that has the effect of denying one group of people the same basic rights as the dominant group.

Beginning the Discussion

Step One, then, is to decide that there will be a conversation, which is not that difficult with a captive audience, say, students in a classroom or reporters in a newsroom. Put it on the syllabus, post it on a bulletin board, publish it in the newsletter: on such and such date, a discussion about diversity will begin. Bring a pencil, a notebook, and an open mind. Don't back down. Show up.

Step Two is to prepare. Whether you're the teacher or leader, a student in a classroom, or a reporter, editor, or manager in a newsroom, accept that it's going to happen. Poynter's Keith Woods says, "The challenge here is to have faith that there is gain on the other side of the pain."[107] Before the sessions begin, think about your own biases and how you can clear your way to a positive attitude and an open mind. If you are an unwilling participant in the conversation, use that as a launching point for personal self-exploration. Why are you unwilling to talk about it? What will happen if you decide to make it a positive experience?

Step Three, of course, is to show up, take a seat at the table, put yourself on the line. In a conversation among state planners published in the *Management Information Exchange*, Teresa Cosby reminds those entering into a conversation on diversity: "Remember that while diversity is an institutional issue it is also a personal issue. Success in bringing the issue to the forefront depends on the individual willingness of people within an organization to put the topic on the table and to keep it there."[108]

A conversation involves everyone in the room, not just the most vocal. Everyone should agree to some basic ground rules: Everybody at the table talks. No one has the "right" answer. All opinions are welcome and appreciated. Everyone should be honest and forthright, passionate and open minded. But don't attack, don't get personal, don't get defensive, and don't get mad.

Conversation guidelines used in a Michigan Department of Education Great Start program advise that participants:

1. Demonstrate respect by listening quietly when others are speaking.

2. Do not criticize the ideas of others; rather offer them ideas that might be different.

3. Use a round-robin approach so that each person has the opportunity to speak thoughtfully.

4. Remember that conversation is a way to think aloud together, but expect that it might be messy at times.[109]

If someone breaks a rule, call her on it, ask her to explain, help her to understand what she has done and then move on. Don't let it end the conversation. Woods advises that talking across difference requires people to:

1. Be honest.

2. Seek clarification before confusion and conflict.

3. Challenge with passion not poison.

4. Be willing to change your point of view.

5. Stay in the room.[110]

He also advises that humor helps, even when talking about the most serious topics. About the diversity conversation, Aly Colon, Poynter Diversity Program Leader, emphasizes the importance of being comfortable. He writes: "Comfort creates conversation. Conversation sparks ideas, story approaches, and management opportunities. And all of that provides the potential for engaging in a more complete coverage of the world we inhabit."[111] His suggestions for facilitating the conversation are:

1. Get comfortable. Pick a casual room where chairs can be arranged in an informal circle.

2. Have snacks and drinks available. "Breaking bread beats breaking heads."

3. Keep the group(s) to a size that facilitates discussion. There should be opportunity for everyone to speak.

4. Set the ground rules at the beginning.

5. Choose a group member to moderate. Note, that's moderate, not dominate. (Rotate the moderator with multiple sessions.)

6. Focus on journalism. You're not going to solve all the problems in the world. The point here is to create better journalism.

7. Be open to different ideas.

8. Make it possible for people to take a risk with a question or comment without feeling they'll be judged for it.

9. Listen. Listen. Listen![112]

Colon's last point is an extremely important one. A lot of people who are good talkers are not necessarily good listeners. Too often the lapse between what a person last said and what he's about to say is occupied by his own thoughts rather than what someone else is saying. And without hearing what the other person is saying, it is difficult to understand her point of view, much less see value in what she has to say.

Moderators can help group members listen with an occasional question: "Megan, what do you think about what Zack said?" or "Yolanda, how are you feeling about the direction of the conversation?" In the early stages, the round-robin approach suggested by the Michigan group is a good idea in that it assures everyone a turn. Anytime a few people seem to be dominating the conversation, the facilitator or moderator could simply say, "Let's hear from others on that point," reverting to a round-robin format.

Step Four is to get the conversation headed in a productive manner. Keep the introduction short. By this time, everyone knows the topic is diversity. The moderator might simply state the purpose of the discussion: *to learn, as journalists and future journalists, about differences in order to better cover an increasingly diverse community.* Briefly state the purpose, invite additions to it, and then seek agreement on the ground rules. Begin by inviting all the participants to introduce themselves (even if everyone knows everyone else), and ask each person to talk briefly about a way in which he or she differs from the mainstream.

Keep in mind that a person does not have to be of a different race or ethnicity to be different and to have experienced, in some way, considerable angst and discomfort as a result of that difference. Anything is accepted at this point. An alternative approach would be to have group members pair up, discuss with their partner a way in which they feel they differ, and then have members introduce each other.

Don't be surprised if it's difficult to get the conversation going. Dori Maynard, President of the Maynard Institute for Journalism Education, says: "It should not be surprising that journalists do not know how to talk across race. Little in most people's experience prepares them for these conversations. Most of us grew up (and now live) in mostly segregated communities, attended schools lacking in a diverse student body, and go to segregated houses of worship. Rarely are we in situations that give us the experience and knowledge about how to talk across race."[113]

Numerous activities might be used as an icebreaker at this stage. Have group members complete a bias survey. One is included in the activities section in Part Three, but your group could create its own by brainstorming and listing all the possible categories of people toward whom one could feel bias: a lesbian, a member of the ACLU, a campus cheerleader, a member of the KKK, a Christian fundamentalist, a pro-choice activist, a member of the campus Greek community, a black athlete who has a tuition-free scholarship, a Muslim man who believes a wife should obey her husband in all things, a gay minister, a mom on welfare, a war protester, a flag burner, and so on. Have group members anonymously rate each on a 1–5 scale with 1 being enthusiastic agreement or empathy, and 5 being a sense of anger or aversion for the person. Take up the unsigned surveys, mix them up, and pass them back out to group members. Have them talk about the results. Are there surprises? Are there trends or consensus on specific biases?[114]

Another good exercise to generate discussion in the early stages is based on Peggy McIntosh's article, "White Privilege: Unpacking the Invisible Knapsack." She maintains that there is a male and a white or dominant class privilege that males and whites are taught not to recognize:

> I have come to see white privilege as an invisible package of unearned assets that I can count on cashing in each day, but about which I was meant to remain oblivious. White privilege is like an invisible weightless knapsack of special provisions, maps, passports, codebooks, visas, clothes, tools, and blank checks. . . . I decided to try

to work on myself by identifying some of the daily effects of white privilege in my life. I have chosen those conditions which I think in my case attach somewhat more to skin color privilege than to class, religion, ethnic status, or geographic location, though of course all these other factors are intricately intertwined. As far as I can see, my African American coworkers, friends and acquaintances with whom I come into daily or frequent contact in this particular time, place, and line of work cannot count on most of these conditions.[115]

Explain the activity for group members, and have each person read aloud one of the statements, continuing until everyone has read at least one statement. A complete list of the statements from McIntosh's article is reproduced in a later section on exercises and activities. You might also have the group add statements that apply to other groups.

1. I can if I wish arrange to be in the company of people of my race most of the time.

2. I can turn on the television or open to the front page of the paper and see people of my race widely represented.

3. I can easily buy posters, postcards, picture books, greeting cards, dolls, toys, and children's magazines featuring people of my race.

4. I am never asked to speak for all the people of my racial group.

5. I can do well in a challenging situation without being called a credit to my race.

6. I can choose blemish cover or bandages in flesh color and have them more or less match my skin.

7. I can take a job with an affirmative action employer without having coworkers on the job suspect that I got it because of race.[116]

Most people who belong to the dominant race or class don't think about these things because they never come up. Going to a doctor, dentist, optometrist, or lawyer doesn't require that they sit across the table from someone with a different skin color. Visiting their representatives in the U.S. Congress or U.S. Senate or watching the evening news doesn't require being reminded once again of the extent of their exclusion from mainstream American society.

Another exercise that can get the thought processes going involves racial stereotypes, intended to point out how easily society falls into identifying particular racial and ethnic groups with stereotypes. Assign each of several groups to list stereotypical words, phrases, and behaviors that describe a particular population (good dancers, good basketball players, enjoys watermelon and rap music, and the like). Have them list ten or twelve different things, then come back together in the big group. Have a member in each group read her list, and see how long it takes to identify the population in question. This exercise often results in lots of laughter. That's good. Laughter can help set the group at ease, but be sure to remind participants of the important teaching point: stereotypes are harmful, and the media should not contribute to perpetuating their use.

Other exercises included in the later section of this book might also be used as icebreakers. The point is to get the conversation going in a fun way that suggests that everyone has a lot to learn about themselves and how they relate to difference. That understanding is the first step in the road to becoming a better journalist.

Step Five is the heart of your training effort, where you talk about the topics in this book: what is diversity, why it is important, and how it will be accomplished. Use the roadmap in Chapter Three or make up your own plan, strategy, or outline about how to accomplish the learning objectives. Combine group discussion with out-of-classroom exercises. Assign an exercise or activity, the change of perspective for example, then spend the next scheduled in-class or workshop time debriefing the exercise. A good plan would include a minimum of six sessions in an initial introduction to diversity:

Session One: Introductory information, ground rules, introduction of group members and discussion of differences, icebreaker exercise, discussion of Chapter One: What Is Diversity— Community Profile exercise assignment.

Session Two: Review briefly. Community Profile reports. Chapter Two: Why Is Diversity Important? Chapter Three: Achieving Diversity: A Roadmap for Success. Talk about objectives for your sessions. Develop a personal roadmap to improve your individual or organizational ability to practice diversity in reporting and production of news.

Session Three: Plan a listening post activity. Depending on the size of your group, divide into teams of four or five. Have one team make a connection with a gay or lesbian group on campus or in your community. Have another group go into the Hispanic or other nearby ethnic community. Have another group connect with seniors at a local independent or assisted living facility. Talk about stereotypes for these groups. Anticipate problems. Make detailed plans for accomplishing the task.

Session Four: Spend the session debriefing the listening post activities. Have each group report on its experiences, listing both successes and failures. Talk about story ideas gained from the connections, and list reporting tips for covering the targeted group. Discuss or schedule another connection activity or activities, this time investigating socioeconomic class in your community. Volunteer to work at a food bank or food kitchen. Serve a meal to the homeless. Have members circulate and record observations on the worksheets.

Session Five: Get together immediately after session four and debrief. Talk about your preconceptions and how they were or were not reinforced. How are the poor misrepresented? Does class relate to race and ethnicity or other characteristics of diversity? How? Brainstorm story ideas about how your organization might bring needed attention to this group of people.

Session Six: Report on the class exercise. Since this is the last session in the initial series, go around the room and ask each group member to talk about the experience, what they have learned, what they might do differently in the future. Discuss what needs to be done next. Make definite plans for moving forward.

Setting Long-Term Goals

Long-term change is the goal. The purpose of the training sessions is to get people fired up, get the momentum going. The challenge now is to establish ongoing goals and objectives to continue learning and improving community coverage and to keep the conversation going. Establish a diversity team or committee to head the continuing effort, but have members rotate frequently so that no one feels burdened and everyone participates.

Publish a diversity newsletter or fact sheet, which periodically summarizes information on diversity news and activities at other colleges and universities and other news organizations. Schedule times for continuing the conversation in small groups within the class or workforce. Schedule conversations with groups outside your classroom or organization. Bring in a group of pastors to talk about religious coverage in media. Bring in students who participate in school activities that are more intellectual than athletic, and hear their thoughts on being underreported. Meet with local students or area residents with disabilities. Come up with at least a dozen story ideas reflecting areas of coverage important for people affected by some type of physical or mental disability.

Plan the next series of conversations. Change it up a bit. Use different exercises. Bring in new articles on issues related to diversity. Choose different moderators. Change the location of discussions. Have the next set of discussions involve more team exercises and group projects. Vary the teams and groups. Make each as diverse as possible. Make a goal for the next series to culminate in a community conversation at a local church or community center. Bring people in your coverage area into the conversation about news content and how to make it better.

Dori Maynard writes:

> To fulfill the industry's promise to diversify its newsrooms so journalists can accurately and fairly cover our increasingly complex communities, we need to find ways to talk across our nation's racial fault lines. To do so might require retraining ourselves in how to listen and how to speak honestly and respectfully to our colleagues. If we fail to learn how to do this we stand a good chance of having these same stilted and unproductive conversations about how we once again missed the mark in the year 2025.[117]

ACTIVITY: Beginning Your Conversation

1. Complete the statements:

A. "A conversation about diversity is important to me because . . . . "

B. "I hope to learn . . . from a conversation about diversity."

C. "The thing I fear most about having a conversation on diversity is . . . ."

D. "I hope people in the diversity discussion group will . . . ."

E. "The thing that I feel is most important in having a successful conversation about diversity is . . . ."

2. Assume that you have been named moderator of the opening session on diversity. Write a brief statement of introduction, including five basic ground rules and an ice-breaker to get the conversation started. Come up with a new exercise not in this book.

3. Imagine you are moderator and the conversation gets messy. Someone in your group makes a racist, homophobic, or negative comment about a diverse group. What do you say? How do you keep the discussion from becoming an argument?

The one word more detestable than any other in the English language is "exclusive." When you're exclusive you shut out a more or less large range of humanity from your heart, from your understanding of them.

Carl Sandburg, 1954, in response to Edward R. Murrow's question, "What's the worst word in the English language?"

Part Two

Covering Diverse Communities

Walk the streets, the malls, and the campuses of most any major city in this country today and the mosaic of America is strikingly obvious. We are no longer white with a sprinkling of black. We are white and brown and tan and ebony and olive and red and mahogany and all the colors that make up a beautifully cosmopolitan-appearing society.

We are young and old and thin and thick and short and tall and gay and straight and Protestant and Catholic and Jewish and Muslim and Buddhist and Atheist and Agnostic and Republican and Democratic and Independent and Asian American and Italian American and Middle Eastern and American Indian and Hispanic and rich and poor and middle class and Dead Heads and Chicago Cubs fanatics.

Although the smaller towns dotting the landscape of rural America are not as richly diverse as the cities, they too are changing. Rapid immigration from Mexico, South and Central America, and the Caribbean Islands, as well as numerous relocations from countries such as Vietnam, Laos, and Somalia have turned once largely white Wal-mart towns into mini-melting pots (or tossed salads) where Spanish is almost as common as English. Taco trucks circulate through construction sites, and fresh homemade tamales are as popular as hamburgers and hot dogs on a weeknight out.

Long-time residents in small towns and cities alike are struggling to understand the transformation, while their new neighbors aren't sure whether to assimilate or colonize. Looking to the local media for help in most communities is an exercise in futility as the white male editor and largely white staff all are struggling to catch up with the cultural evolution unfolding before them. Most of the older reporters and editors grew up in communities where racial or ethnic diversity meant black and languages other than English were subjects, usually Latin, that only the college-prep kids took in high school.

Change comes slowly, but it comes nonetheless, to the city, the community, the campus, and the local media outlet. Help with providing better coverage of those new and changing communities is the purpose of Part Two: Covering Diverse Communities. Chapter Five presents general information, including tips from various professional journalists, for covering the diverse community as a whole. Chapters Six through Ten present specific help for covering African Americans, Hispanics, Asian Americans, Native Americans, and Arab Americans. Chapter Eleven provides help for improving coverage of gays and lesbians. Chapter Twelve offers advice for doing a better job of reporting on Americans with disabilities. Finally, Chapter Thirteen talks about other isms of diversity, including ageism, classism, and faithism, offering advice for better coverage of the complete community regardless of differences.

It would be a gross exaggeration to suggest that the content of these few chapters contains everything needed for covering these diverse populations. However, every attempt has been made to be as comprehensive as possible in providing current information. Learn and apply the lessons outlined here. Then use the resources listed later in the book to continue the process of learning how to provide better coverage of the diverse community and in turn better and more inclusive journalism.

Chapter Five

Tips for Reporting on Difference

Good journalism is hard work. It requires a creative mind and keen sense of observation to come up with interesting stories that need to be told. It requires time, determination, and a whole lot of patience. Former *New York Times* editor Turner Catledge described a journalist simply as someone who has an unbridled curiosity accompanied by an even stronger desire to tell all.[118] A journalist is that and more.

A journalist is someone who can spend hours in a cramped library cubicle digging up historical background and who is as adept at walking the streets of a new neighborhood as he is listening, observing, and experiencing. A reporter knows the feel of a good story and is willing to watch and wait for the right time, to learn, to cultivate expert sources, and to gain the respect of important community storytellers.

Good reporting on difference requires good journalists who practice good journalism. Good journalism is the journalism of diversity. Many of the ideas or tips for reporting on the diverse community suggested here are things most journalists have always been taught, simply applied to a different purpose for reporting on a different population.

What then does one need to know when approaching a new assignment that involves a diverse community? *Washington Post* writer Anne Hull, in a Poynteronline interview says, "The first thing is to admit ignorance — just get it out of the way by saying that you don't know much but are eager to learn. This opens doors. . . ." The next step is where the hard work begins, where reporter puts leather to street and goes to work. Whatever it's called, background, getting to know the community, or simply research, it is the place every good story begins.

Research: The Antidote to Ignorance

In the beginning, there is research and research and more research. Any good reporter would never think of going into an interview without having done the background research on her subject, would never think about meeting with a local school superintendent about next year's budget without having researched how state and local district budgets are put

Research Diversity

Tips from working professionals, many of them from a session at the 2004 UNITY: Journalists of Color Conference

"Before you write about a particular community, make an effort to get to know them. Break bread with them, talk to their kids, go to their places of worship — try to immerse yourself in the culture. Not only will you get a better understanding of who they are before you write about them, you will become a better journalist — and a better human being in the process."

Pankaj Paul, director of design and presentation, The News Journal *in Wilmington Del.*

"Don't overlook history. Look through clips from decades ago to learn what the big issues were. Chances are, many of the key issues are the same as decades ago."cxxi

Wanda Lloyd, executive editor, Montgomery (Ala.) Advertiser

"Get to know merchants and business owners, chamber of commerce officers and members in communities of color. Acquaint yourself with the business organizations such as the Hispanic Chamber of Commerce, the African American Chamber and the Puerto Rican Chamber."

Michele Salcedo, Asst. City Editor for Race and Demographics, Sun-Sentinel, *Fort Lauderdale*

"Take the long way home from work, shop at a grocery store in another part of town, ride the bus in an unfamiliar neighborhood. Observe the people, bulletin boards, storefronts. Stop in a local café and listen to people and talk with them.

together, and would never approach an article on a new Christian rock band without spending some time listening to the featured band as well as others of the same genre.

Covering diversity requires the same dedication to detailed research. Assigned to do a piece on the growing Hispanic community locally or over a broader geographic area? Do the research. Begin with the basic numbers, the cultural and historical facts. That's the stuff easily obtainable from books, over the Internet, or from a professor at a local university who has studied immigration patterns. Then go beyond the secondary resource materials. Take a ride through the community. Park and get out. Walk the streets. Listen. Observe. Shop at community groceries. Do laundry at a local laundromat. Eat at ethnic restaurants. Visit community agencies that serve new residents. Spend Friday night at a Latino club. Talk to a principal at a dominantly ethnic high school. Eat in the cafeteria. Sit in an ESL class. Attend a community church in which the congregation is largely Hispanic. Take a language course. Read books and novels, listen to music, and check out the movies that feature the ethnic culture of young and old Hispanics.

Then move beyond listening and observing. Talk to store clerks, wait staff in ethnic restaurants, ministers, bank tellers, realtors, people on the street. Get their stories. Ask them about media coverage. Get them to grade it: A, B, C, D, or F. Ask them how it could be improved, what they would like to see covered. Ask them how they would want to be represented in the news.

Approach every story with the same desire to learn. A story on local services for people with disabilities requires a different kind of research: admission of ignorance and scouring secondary resources, such as the library and Internet. Then what? Going into the community? Not as simple. People with disabilities don't form geographic communities. Check with social service agencies. Search out local job sites, community recreation centers, schools, and daycare facilities that cater to populations with disabilities. Research local Special Olympics programs. Rent a wheelchair and spend a week going to and from work, the grocery store, the mall, church, and the movies. Don't cheat. Try riding a bus, shopping in a crowded discount or variety store, or going to the bathroom in a fast-food restaurant. Talk with people of varying disabilities. Ask them about their experiences, significant and mundane. Ask them about media coverage of people with disabilities. What's good about coverage? What's bad?

A common theme about preparation that runs through most all the tips from working journalists involves getting out of the office or classroom and getting to know the community and the people. It really is simple and basic advice. You can begin immediately. It costs nothing other than a little time, but it is an investment that will pay off in good journalism.

Be Careful What You Say and How You Say It

A university dean of students who should have known better emailed the following note to all students on campus following an incident in a student's room:

> A female . . . student reported this morning to campus security that she awoke around 3 a.m. to find a college-age black male sitting slumped in the corner of her bedroom. . . .She yelled for him to leave and he did.[124]

The note, although unintentional, implicated every college-aged black man in the vicinity of the campus. The notice contained no identification other than an approximate

Attend community events and meetings that are not newsworthy but may lead to a better understanding of a group's issues and concerns. "
Naomi Ishisaka, Editor-In-Chief, ColorsNW

"Check out a book or film on an ethnic community you know little about. Read ethnic media. Ethnic media is full of stories by and about people of color. Read ethnic media to find the people and events the mainstream media may be missing."
Naomi Ishisaka, ColorsNW

"If you are not fluent in the language of the community you cover, at least learn how to pronounce some popular phrases or names in their native form. Circulate potential definitions of cultural terms among trusted sources so that you properly explain traditions and customs."
Elbert Garcia, Reporter, Manhattan Times

"Peel the layers and dig deeper. That's the first rule of journalism anyway. Go to the community you are covering — don't wait for them to come to you or to answer your phone calls. Let people get to know you, see you, ask you questions about what you do. Explain that you want to tell their story the right way."
Catalina Camia, Washington Editor, Gannett News Service

"Build trust with members of the community by meeting face-to-face as often as you can. Go to them as much as possible. . . . Negotiate with your editor to reserve some time — whether it's a day or a week — to broaden your source list in the community. "
Daniel Vasquez, Editorial Writer, San Jose Mercury News

"Encourage reporters on every beat (municipal, education, religion, family) to have a story-idea meeting with members of organizations from ethnic and minority groups."
Elizabeth Llorente, Reporter on Immigration and Ethnic Affairs, The Record, *Hackensak, N.J.*

"Encourage reporters to recognize (or learn about) distinctions in minority and ethnic groups. On several levels, Koreans in urban Union City, N.J., live differently than Koreans in the more suburban Palisades Park. The same goes for Cuban Americans in the urban areas of Hudson County and those in the suburbs of Bergen County and Cuban Americans in New Jersey and in Florida."[122]

Elizabeth Llorente, The Record

"Make a note of which people in the community have the ear of the power structure (municipal movers and shakers) and find out who's left outside this power sphere and why. Read up on the laws and ordinances that have divided a community."

Anne Hull, Writer, Washington Post

"Using your instincts, identify a couple people in the community whose insights you think you might trust. Make them your touchstones, not just tipsters. Talk about things you've seen or heard, and hash out what it all might mean. Don't just assign them to the duty of listening to your theories; keep learning from them. Be prepared to make culture mistakes. Be prepared to live life on their time clock, not yours."[123]

Anne Hull, Washington Post

age and the individual's race, thus served no purpose as an identifier. The description could not have formed the basis for local police to find the intruder. It is beyond insufficient for anyone to pick an individual out of a police lineup. It simply put fearful females on notice that a young black man had been an intruder in another female's bedroom, adding to any racial tensions that might have already existed.

While some would argue that racial identification is acceptable as long as it is part of an overall thorough physical description, others question whether or not it is ever appropriate. Poynter Dean Keith Woods advises: "Question the need for all racial identification. Be sure it is clear to your audience why some people are identified by race. Recognize that most racial identifiers tell you little about how the person actually looks. But they perpetuate an age-old practice of treating people who are not white as 'others.'"[125] Woods describes this alternative to using race:

> If journalists told their audience that the suspect was about 5-foot-8, about 165 pounds, with caramel-brown skin, wavy, dark brown hair about an inch long, thick eyebrows, a narrow nose, thick lips, and a light mustache, people could pick me from a lineup of men whose skin and face were different from mine. Nobody would need to know my race. It wouldn't matter if I was descended from Africans, spoke Spanish, worshipped Allah, lived on a reservation, or called a Hawaiian woman mother.[126]

Of course, Woods is totally correct that race adds nothing to description. Black is the color of carbon or coal. Few people of color who are grouped into the racial category labeled black are actually the color of coal or carbon. More likely they are brown or tan or mahogany or caramel-brown.

Similarly, as Aly Colon writes, using identifiers like white male, Hispanic female, Asian male, Native American, or American Indian female fails to make clear the color of the person's skin. Additionally, terms such as Hispanic, Asian, and American Indian all refer to ethnicity, not skin tone. Using descriptors such as these, Colon says, forces viewers, listeners, and readers to rely on their own stereotypes of what color they think the person might be.[127]

Consider the following story, which appeared in a Florida newspaper:

> A woman jogging in the darkness early Wednesday ... was sexually assaulted near a school, then forced to drive the attacker to her home nearby, where she was robbed.
>
> The woman, who is not being identified because she was raped, told deputies she was on the sidewalk, in the 5500 block of West Village Drive shortly after 5:30 a.m. when she was approached from behind by a man who put a sharp object to her throat...
>
> The suspect was described as a Hispanic male in his 20s, 5-feet-7 and 150 pounds. He was last seen wearing what looked like a basketball jersey and long pants. The car was described as an older model, white, boxy sedan. Detectives refused to say what made the victim think her attacker was Hispanic.[128]

Use of the Hispanic identifier adds nothing to the story. It doesn't describe skin color, hair, nose, eyes, mouth, or any other facial features. What it does is add to a negative ethnic stereotype, which exists in many communities

Covering Communities

"Think ordinary. Weave people of color into everyday stories, the start of fishing season, the tale of a couple buying their first home, etc. Diversity of coverage means not just reflecting people of color, different ethnicities and sexual orientations in what makes their cultures and communities special, but also how they are part of the larger community."
Maya Blackmun, Reporter, The Oregonian

"Question whether race or ethnicity is relevant in a story. Try this litmus test: Ask yourself whether you would describe a source as white under similar circumstances."
Daniel Vasquez, Editorial Writer, San Jose Mercury News

"Understand the difference between race and class, stereotypes and truths, and regional and cultural differences. What you think might be a story about racial differences might actually be about class."
Catalina Camia, Washington Editor, Gannett New Service

"Be careful about anointing sources that speak for a whole community. A city council member who happens to be Latino, for example, may not have any connection to the concerns of your Latino readers. Audit yourself (and your coverage) and keep track of how often you quote someone simply because of their race or ethnicity."
Catalina Camia, Gannett New Service

Watch your body language. Words are not the only way in which we communicate with people. We can either encourage or discourage people to come up to us by the manner in which we approach them and how we talk or listen to them. Learn the rules of eye contact and personal space — some cultures are used to having conversations in small places, while others consider such close contact to be rude."

Elbert Garcia, Reporter, Manhattan Times

"Avoid the heroes or villains dichotomy. Often the media see people of color as either heroes or evildoers. The truth is often in between. Try to avoid the temptation to either glorify or demonize people of color. Both do a disservice to a complex and balanced representation of our communities. "

Naomi Ishisaka, Editor-in-Chief, ColorsNW

"Don't pigeonhole. Incorporate diversity into all aspects of your reporting and writing. People of color should not be relegated to stories about race or used solely as sporadic person on the street sources. People of color can be found as experts in every aspect of American life and should be reflected as such."

Naomi Ishisaka, ColorsNW

"Report against stereotype. Not all immigrant children arrive in this country poorly educated. Not all Mexicans are farm workers or day laborers. Not all Asians do well in school."

Michele Salcedo, Sun-Sentinel, *Fort Lauderdale*

"Use the news as a springboard to explore the impact and opinions of people of color. For example, did Barack Obama's speech at the Democratic National Convention play differently in black neighborhoods than in other neighborhoods?"

Michele Salcedo, Sun-Sentinel

where a significant number of Hispanic people have settled in recent years.

Poynter offers the following guidelines on racial identification, suggesting that every racial reference be flagged and judged based on the following questions:

1. Is it relevant? Race is relevant when the story is about race . . . a story about interracial dating, for example.

2. Have I explained the relevance? Journalists too frequently assume that readers will know the significance of race in stories. The result is often radically different interpretations.

3. Is it free of codes? Be careful not to use welfare, inner-city, underprivileged, blue-collar, conservative, suburban, exotic, middle-class, Uptown, South Side or wealthy as euphemisms for racial groups.

4. Are racial identifiers used evenly? If the race of a person charging discrimination is important, then so is the race of the person being charged.

5. Should I consult someone of another race/ethnicity? Consider another question: Do I have expertise on other races/cultures? If not, broaden your perspective by asking someone who knows something more about your subject. Why should we treat reporting on racial issues any differently from reporting on an area of science or religion that we do not know well?[129]

What about the argument that it's okay to use racial identifiers as long as you do it for everyone? The argument goes: If it's a black man arrested, say black man, but if it's a white man arrested say white man. That makes it fair. Abe Rosenberg, a writer for KTTV Los Angeles, maintains it would not be the same story. "Right or wrong," he says "the public does not condemn all whites when a story airs about a white criminal. Tragically, the same cannot be said about black suspects, which means we have to be extra careful."[130]

Think back to the discussion of the note from a university dean of students earlier in this chapter. The note described an intruder into a coed's bedroom as a college-age black male. The inclination of many people after reading such a note might be to look at every black male they meet on campus and suspect him as the intruder. The same would probably not have been the case had the note read that the intruder was a college-age white male.

Some Final Thoughts

One of the most important things a reporter can do is to clear himself from all the personal biases that have built up over the years. Don't assume that every person over 60 appreciates being treated like an invalid. Giving a helping hand is okay, but be careful not to offend. Don't assume that lesbians, gay men, and transgender people are unhappy with their lives and would rather be straight. Don't assume that everyone living in a homeless shelter is undereducated, unemployed, shiftless, and an alcoholic. Most of these stereotypes have been perpetuated by media in the first place. You can help to correct them by breaking out of the mold and reporting accurately and objectively about all people regardless of their age, sexual orientation, skin color, and economic status.

Further, don't assume that because you've been accepted into a diverse group, that you've earned the right of familiarity. A scene in *Rush Hour* starring Jackie Chan and Chris Tucker has Chan sitting at a bar in a largely black-inhabited night club. He had heard an exchange in which black men were in good humor referring to each other as "nigger." Chan's character, in the United States for the

"To avoid using stereotypes or offensive references, contact advocacy groups (NAACP, the Arab American Institute, etc.) to point to media style guides in their cultures."

Wanda Lloyd, Montgomery (Alabama) Advertiser

"Put yourself on email lists for newsletters from targeted diverse groups; regularly attend local functions of diverse organizations; and avoid overdoing crime as a key topic on this beat."

Wanda Lloyd

"Beware of stereotypes. People in any ethnic group can have an opinion, but that does not necessarily mean that viewpoint is shared by — or is representative — of the whole group."

Pankaj Paul, *Wilmington* News Journal

"Be sensitive to cultural taboos. For example, do not go into a temple wearing shoes. Just like with any other beat, educate yourself and do your homework before you set out to report."

Pankaj Paul

"See a woman wearing a burkha? A Sikh wearing a turban? Make an effort to understand and respect why they do so. Please do not try to view other cultures and religions through the lens of your own."

Pankaj Paul

"Challenge and update existing frames. Stories of race relations are most often framed by either conflict or harmony, with clear saints and sinners. Good reporting challenges those (and other) frames and gets beyond the traditional sources used to support those frames."

Keith Woods, Poynter Institute

"Decode the language. Clarity is critical. ... Ambiguity breeds distrust and a loss of credibility. If you mean white people, don't say blue collar. If you mean it's a Latino neighborhood, don't say inner city. If you mean Hmong, don't say minority."

Keith Woods, Poynter Institute

"A good rule of thumb when handling stories about a minority or immigrant group is to ask the question: How would I feel if my gender or ethnic group were described this way?"

Elizabeth Llorente, The Hackensack Record

"Towns or states with large Hispanic populations are often described as 'heavily Hispanic,' giving the sense that there are too many Hispanics. We normally don't write or read that a town is 'heavily white' or 'heavily Irish American.' *Predominately*, without judgmental overtones, is the more common choice."

Elizabeth Llorente

"Look out for characterization of problems or qualities in minority or immigrant groups as "genetic." Stories about Hispanic dropout rates, for instance, rarely note the socioeconomic factors that contribute to the situation. They also fail to explain that in many of these homes, financial commitments are seen as family responsibilities. Kids often leave school to work and help their parents." [131]

Elizabeth Llorente

"Don't keep things to yourself. If a phrase, term or categorization just doesn't feel right, but you're not exactly sure why, read it to a colleague — or several colleagues — and ask, 'Does this bother you?'"

Abe Rosenberg, Writer, KTTV Los Angeles

first time, turned to the black bartender and with a huge grin said, "What's up, my nigger?" Of course, to Chan's surprise the bartender immediately comes at him with vengeance.

Take care in reporting on undocumented immigrants. Ask yourself if the story is worth resulting in someone's being identified by INS and deported. In most cases, it probably isn't. And if you have an attitude about the issue, you should probably leave it at home or have someone else do the story.

Know and respect the culture and traditions of all people you encounter in your job as reporter or editor or news manager. Treat them with dignity. Don't judge them; don't idolize or look down on people. Treat them as human equals. Treat them just as you want to be treated.

ACTIVITY: Examine Bias

1. Make a list of stereotypes and biases you believe many people in your community hold. Cite examples. List story ideas you might pursue to help overcome those biases.

(Example: Many people believe that senior citizens are bad drivers. Story idea: Look up statistics on traffic accidents, how many involved teenagers, adults under 65, and adults over 65. Interview seniors who have taken driver refresher courses.)

2. Make a list of your personal biases. Be honest. List everything. List things you can do to address any prejudices you have. (You're uncomfortable around gay men. Connect with a gay rights group. Attend meetings of PFLAG. Assign yourself to do a piece on civil union laws in your state. Seek out gay men and lesbians as sources.)

Chapter Six

Covering Black People in America

The headline of an Associated Press article published in numerous American newspapers on Martin Luther King Jr.'s birthday in January 2006 proclaimed, "Americans Believe We Are Closer to the Dream." Turns out the poll being reported, conducted by AP-Ipsos, had found that most white Americans completing the survey believe there has been significant progress in reaching King's dream of racial equality. Black Americans weren't as convinced.

Whether the suggestion that racism, to most white Americans at least, is a thing of the past and no longer needs addressing in any significant way is a product of intentional distortion or simple ignorance really doesn't matter. It has the same effect either way, in that it perpetuates the myth of racial harmony that stands in the way of further progress.

Several *New York Times* photographs taken at the time of Justice Samuel Alito's confirmation hearings in January 2006 illustrate the radically misinformed assumption that all is right in the struggle for racial equality. One of the photographs shows Justice Alito, a white male, seated before a Senate committee of white males, and surrounded by a support staff, which was largely white male. In fact, Alito's wife was one of the few females in the room. To complete the telling story, a throng of press photographers knelt in front of the table where Alito was seated. All were white male. Likewise, most of the reporters seated in the room also were white male. There were no articles written about the absence of gender and racial diversity in the room, no frantic media clamor to correct a societal wrong.

The problem, of course, is that there's little hope in correcting the injustice of a political system administered large by elderly men of a single race as long as the body of photographers and reporters telling the story is of the same race and gender. The result is eternal hegemony in its purest sense.

Are we closer to the dream? Of course. Black Americans no longer are subjected to the overt discrimination their parents and grandparents were forced to endure 50 years ago when everything from restaurants to public cemeteries was segregated. Are racial prejudices and discrimination merely memories of the past? Absolutely not. If you believe they are, you most likely are white.

Researchers at MIT and the University of Chicago recently sent out 5,000 résumés and job applications to 1,250 employers in response to published help-wanted ads. Every employer got four résumés: an average applicant with a white-sounding name (Greg, Megan, John, Jennifer), an average applicant with a black-sounding name (Tyrone, Shemika, Tawanda), a highly skilled applicant with a white-sounding name and a highly skilled applicant with a black-sounding name. The résumés with white-sounding names triggered 50 percent more calls than those with black-sounding names. Even those lower skilled applicants with white-sounding names got more calls than the higher skilled applicants with black-sounding names.[133]

In spite of consistent results in studies such as this, many Americans, including student and professional journalists, continue to believe that discussion of racism belongs only in history books. While the national airing following Hurricane Katrina of the unforgivable racial reality of New Orleans shocked America, bringing about an initial wave of negative reactions, any resolve to make things better soon vanished. Even though pre-Katrina New Orleans was more than 65 percent black, most of the 125,000 former residents who had returned by early 2006 were white.

The story of twenty-first-century racism in America is not being reported as it should be. And those who are responsible are not being held accountable.

Black Journalists Contribute to the Solution

The National Association of Black Journalists celebrated its thirtieth anniversary in 2005, having originated on December 12, 1975, at a gathering of forty-four black journalists in Washington, D.C. The stated purpose of that first meeting was to discuss the need for a national organization that would advocate better media coverage of black communities and black issues, and that would promote increased diversity among newsroom staffs.[134]

Founding NABJ President Chuck Stone said that in the beginning members were ridiculed, pressured, and questioned by all sorts of people. He said the organization survived because member journalists upheld the highest standards of their profession while maintaining their identity as black people.[135] And the organization continues to thrive. With over 4,000 members, NABJ is the largest organization for journalists of color in the world.

NABJ was founded eight years after the Kerner Commission had criticized national media for failing to adequately cover race relations in the United States, blaming media for contributing to the serious racial divide at the time.[136] And it was founded three years before ASNE's first pronouncement of the need to create racial parity in the nation's newsrooms.[137] Black journalists now make up approximately 5.5 percent of newspaper journalists, 10.3 percent of the television news workforce, and less than 1 percent of those working in radio news. Black people make up 13 percent of the U.S. population.[138]

Why aren't there more black journalists working in newspapers, radio, and television? Many publishers argue that they try to hire black reporters and editors but are in locations where black journalists don't want to locate. Reacting to an ASNE report showing a net increase over five years of only 34 in the number of black journalists employed by daily newspapers, NABJ President Herbert Lowe said: "Once again, this is pitiful. We have many, many black journalists ready, willing, and able to work in our nation's newspapers. So why is it that our numbers are not increasing? It's clear that not enough editors are willing to do what it takes to make the numbers grow."

Language and Stereotypes

Begin by accepting Abe Rosenberg's assertion that "It's arrogant to assume something's okay just because it doesn't grate on your personal sensitivities. Racism is in the ear of the beholder."[139] Repeat that to yourself every day until it sinks in: "Racism is in the ear of the beholder." It may not strike you as problematic to use the term *blackballed* in a story about a vote of NBA owners to exclude a particular city from ownership, but to someone who is black, it is simply a reminder that in this country for a period long enough for such terms to sneak into the lexicon, to be black meant to be excluded.

Consider these definitions of *black* from the *Encarta World English Dictionary*: "dealing with very serious things in a humorous and often macabre way; carried out in the utmost secrecy; filled with anger or hostility; so depressing as to end all hope; causing or associated with severely bad conditions or misfortune; extremely dishonorable and deserving the most serious criticism; evil or associated with evil."[140]

These definitions result, of course, in uses such as blackball, black mark, black market, black comedy, film noir, black ice, black magic, blackout, or blacklisted. They are the reason black is the color of mourning, why the bad cowboy always wore a black hat, why witch outfits are black and fortieth or fiftieth birthday parties feature black candles and black crepe streamers.

If it doesn't bother you, you're probably not black. You've never had to be subjected to the constant barrage of historical and pop culture that says your color, your race has bad, evil, or negative undertones. You or your parents or grandparents were never excluded — made to go in the back door, down into the basement to use the restroom, prevented from drinking from a public water fountain, made to enter a movie theater through a separate door and sit in the balcony, or relegated to a back seat on public transportation because of your skin color.

The teaching and learning point here, of course, is to be cognizant of the fact that using terms that cast the name of someone's race in a negative way is offensive and should be avoided. Disparaging images that remind black Americans of the subjugation of their race during a shameful period of American history are equally offensive: Black Sambo, Amos and Andy, Rochester, Aunt Jemima, and nigger Jim to name a few.

Even seemingly innocent images can cause problems. At a Fourth of July picnic, a local candidate for Congress is enjoying a slice of watermelon. A great photo opportunity? She's black. Watermelon juice running down her chin. Big smile. She's leading in the polls. Still a great photo opportunity? Consider Keith Woods' commentary about a similar situation occurring during a Poynter summer fellowship program in which participants questioned whether or not to run a photographic depiction of a stack of variegated watermelons to symbolize a rained-out celebration of Juneteenth:

> Since the earliest days of plantation slavery, the caricature of the dark-skinned child, his too-red lips stretched to grotesque extremes as they opened to chomp

down on watermelon, was a staple of racism's diet. Over time, the watermelon became a symbol of the broader denigration of black people. It became part of the image perpetuated by a white culture bent upon bolstering the myth of superiority by depicting the inferior race as lazy simple-minded pickaninnies interested only in such mindless pleasures as a slice of sweet watermelon.[141]

Woods says he would not have run it. A discussion among program participants, however, revealed that many younger students had never heard of the stereotype and didn't see a problem with using the photograph. It stayed in the story.

Images and icons that many whites look on as historical, even nostalgic, may simply remind those of another race of a time when their ancestors were routinely denigrated, often subjugated. To some people, the Confederate flag is a symbol of another era, one that they have fixated on in a kind of romantic fascination. To black men and women, it is a painful reminder of a time when their ancestors were bought and sold as chattel, whipped into submission, used as animals, then cast aside when they were no longer able to perform.

Some may view as pleasurable nostalgia the images of black men, women, and children hunched over cotton rows under the hot Mississippi Delta sun; or the obese black woman in her bandana, thick cotton dress, and apron sweeping the front porch of a stately southern mansion or tending to the plantation owner's children. To others these are, like the watermelon, images white culture has used to perpetuate the myth of racial superiority.

In many ways, the stable boy hitching posts and pitch-black coachman lantern holders, the smiling images of black Sambo, and other pastoral icons of jovial black women who would have given their lives for master's children are an attempt to soothe the conscience of the still dominant race over the reality of the atrocities their white ancestors committed. The folkloric treatment of that dark period in American history is, in modern lingo, spin at its very best, or worst. To say that these images pay tribute to black history is as uninformed as arguing that a group of teenagers in Indian costumes with tomahawks dancing around the gym floor at halftime of a high school basketball game is paying respect to the proud traditions of Native Americans.

What Can You Do?

Above all else, of course, practice good journalism. Following are suggested guidelines for better covering the black community. Most are common sense and could be applied to covering any underreported population in a diverse community. Obviously, no pretension is made or implied that this list contains everything a reporter would need to do her best. That will come only with experience.

■ Avoid the stereotypes. And that includes everything from the watermelon, cotton-pickin' stable boy images to the use of terms like blackball and blacklist.

■ Avoid the tendency to equate race with class and education. They are not the same. In fact, 19.3 percent of black adults hold a bachelor's degree or higher, which is fairly consistent with the general population, in which 21.9 percent of adults hold college degrees. Likewise, the stereotype of low-income black Americans is no longer accurate. The 2000 census reported

5.3 million black households with incomes of over $40,000 per year, making nearly half of the black population middle class and above.[142]

■ Remember that racism is in the ears and eyes of the receiver. If you are not black and are not sure about something, consult with black colleagues.

■ Don't think of, write about, or treat black people as though they are all the same. They are not. They are not all the same color, nor do they have the same facial features. They do not all talk with the same accent or live in the same neighborhood. They represent varying social and economic classes just as do other racial and ethnic groups. They are not all great basketball players or great dancers. There are good and not so good black people. They are gay and straight. They are Democratic and Republican. Think before you build a frame around people.

■ Don't overuse the same sources. The black city council member and the black associate pastor in your audience do not necessarily speak for the entire black community. The fact that they have gained a position of prominence or leadership does not render them all-knowing.

■ Understand that familiarity does not translate as knowledge. Don't assume that because you have spent three weeks or three months listening and cultivating sources in the black community that you suddenly know everything. Don't assume that you understand the culture. If in doubt, check it out with someone who would know.

■ Don't assume that all black people feel close to other racial, ethnic, or otherwise diverse groups in some kind of minority brotherhood; black people, for example, do not necessarily better understand or even sympathize with the gay perspective just because they also belong to an oppressed group.

■ Use the terms *black* and *African American* with knowledge of their specific meaning. When applying a label to a particular person, ask that person how he or she prefers to be identified. Avoid terms such as *minority* and *nonwhite*. African American is hyphenated only when used as an adjective. Black should be used as an adjective rather than as a noun. Note usage in the following clip from a 2004 AP story:

> ATLANTA — Herman Cain is a well-to-do black businessman with strong belief that the Democratic Party that blacks embraced during the civil rights struggle has swung too far to the left.
> That is why he is running for the U.S. Senate this year as a Republican.
> More black Republicans are running for office in Georgia this year than ever before, and black candidates in other southern states are also finding that declaring for the GOP is more accepted than it was just a few years ago. No blacks are running as Republican in this year's Alamance County elections.[143]

Note that in this example, *black* is used correctly as an adjective in all but two instances. In the first instance, where *blacks* is used as a noun, a simple edit to read "that black people embraced . . ." would be better. The last line, which was added by the local paper, could be rewritten, "No black Republican candidates are running in this year's Alamance County elections." Finally, note that *black* is used lowercase.

■ Editors, news directors, and other supervisory management should not assume that black reporters prefer to cover black stories. While there may be some merit to the argument that African-American sources will be more open with black reporters, many journalists of color do not want to be assigned to race stories simply because of their color.

Likewise, don't assume that a black reporter would not want to be assigned to a story on race. Some reporters of color believe that is an important role and one that they want to contribute. Talk with your reporters. Let their preferences on this question be your guide.

Where possible, team black reporters with reporters of other races and ethnicities, particularly on race stories. Not only will they pick up important reporting skills, but the joint assignment will give colleagues an opportunity to work together and get to know one another on a different level.

■ Examine your own prejudices. Don't be surprised if you're not 100 percent free of racial prejudice or at least discomfort at being around people who are in some way different from you. The point is to acknowledge it and work through it. Talk to colleagues. Talk to your managers. If you have feelings that might interfere with your ability to cover a story, let it be known. Ask to be teamed with a black reporter or ask to be reassigned until you can work through the issues confronting you.

■ Remember at all times that the end goal is to practice good journalism and that good journalism provides fair and accurate coverage of the complete community; that good journalism is inclusive in its coverage of the uncovered and the underrepresented; that good journalism is the journalism of diversity. Be open. Be honest. Be sincere. Treat people just as you want to be treated.

Getting the Right Words

Following are a few terms that may help you in reporting on African Americans, black issues, and the black community. For a more comprehensive listing, refer to the News Watch Diversity Style Guide or the NABJ style book.

African American — an individual living in the United States who has African ancestry; although often used interchangeably with black, all black people living in the United States are not of African decent. Hyphenate only when using as an adjective.

Afro-American — archaic term; avoid.

All American — can be offensive when used in a narrow sense meaning "white, blond," and the like.

AME — African Methodist Episcopal Church; independent Methodist church founded in Philadelphia in 1794.

Biracial — an individual who traces his or her heritage to two races; "mixed" is not an acceptable synonym; use only when relevant.

Black — generally the preferred term, unless subject prefers otherwise, when referring to race; use lowercase and only as an adjective: black journalist, black people; however, use only when race is relevant.

Black diaspora — referring to black people of African descent dispersed by way of slavery and colonization throughout the world.

Black Muslim — archaic reference to sect of black Muslims; members prefer to be called Muslims.

Civil Rights Act — culmination of civil rights movement in the mid-twentieth century; Congress passed the Civil Rights Act in 1964 and the Voting Rights Act in 1965 guaranteeing basic civil rights to all people regardless of race.

Colored — archaic; use only in historical quotes or referring to organizations, names, or events that still use the term as a part of an official designation.

Dark continent — offensive; avoid as a term referring to Africa.

Ghetto — avoid due to negative connotation; refers to poor inner city.

Gullah — refers to descendants of African slaves living on the barrier islands along the coast of South Carolina, Georgia, and Florida; the Gullah language can still be heard on some of the islands where Gullah culture continues to flourish.

Inner city — avoid this and other stereotypical references to poor communities of color.

Jack and Jill of America — an African-American cultural, social, and civic organization for black children; founded in 1938, currently has over 8,000 members.

Jim Crow laws — refers to laws and practices, largely in the South, that imposed racial segregation through the mid-sixties.

Juneteenth — June 19, black Emancipation Day, celebration of the end of slavery.

Kwanzaa — African-American cultural holiday, December 26 through January 1;

derived from traditional African harvest festivals.

Minority, minorities — increasingly viewed as a somewhat negative term because of the unempowered status of most things that are minor or seen in a minority perspective; people of color can be used as an alternative in most instances.

Mulatto — archaic term once used to refer to an individual with one white and one black parent; should be avoided.

NABJ — National Association of Black Journalists. Established in 1975, NABJ is the largest organization of journalists of color in the nation, with more than 4,000 members. Its mission is to provide education, career development, and support to black journalists worldwide.

Negro — while still a part of some organizational names such as the United Negro College Fund and is acceptable in such references, it should not be used in references to individuals; use black or African American.

Niggardly — tight or stingy; often viewed with a derogatory connotation due to its similarity to the word *nigger*; best to avoid.
Nigger — a highly inflammatory racial slur; should never be used.

Oreo — black on the outside, white inside; refers to a black person who acts white; similar to the use of Uncle Tom; should not be used.

People of color — increasingly popular term for describing people of diverse races and ethnicities; also use *journalists of color, students of color*, and the like.

Race — a classification of humans by skin color and physical characteristics; has little real significance and is generally inappropriate as a means of identifying people.

Uncle Tom — originates from Harriet Beecher Stowe's *Uncle Tom's Cabin*; a pejorative term referring to a black person who is unnecessarily accommodating to white people or white authority figures.

Wigger — negative term, avoid; white person who takes on the dress, language, etc. of black people; white person who wants to be black.

Chapter Seven

Covering the Hispanic Community

The wave of immigration from Spanish-speaking countries has been labeled the browning of America. According to the U.S. Census Bureau, the Hispanic population grew 58 percent between 1990 and 2000, from approximately 9 percent of the U.S. population to 13 percent. A revised census report in June 2005 showed the Hispanic population at 41.3 million, up by over 4 million between 2000 and July 1, 2004, giving the Hispanic community a 14.1 percent share of the U.S. population.[144]

The U.S. Census included in the Hispanic categorization anyone who reported their origin as Mexican, Puerto Rican, Cuban, Central and South American, or some other Latino origin. Hispanics could be of any race. Of those reported as Hispanic, 66.9 percent were from Mexico, 14.3 from Central and South America, 8.6 from Puerto Rico, and 3.7 from Cuba. The remainder, 6.5 percent, was listed as other Hispanic. Census reports use the terms *Hispanic* and *Latino* interchangeably, as do most other references.[145]

The Spanish language is the common tie that unites people who are Hispanic or Latino. Maria Arana, editor of the *Washington Post's Book World*, in an introduction to the National Association of Hispanic Journalists' guide *Latinos in the United States*, writes, "We are the only large minority group in the United States classified by our tongue, even when some of us don't speak it very well anymore." She explains the importance of language:

> We Latinos or Hispanics find ourselves here, travelers on diverse paths, with different stories trailing us. We do, however, have one important thing in common. We are overwhelmingly speakers of Spanish, and we can be as marked and molded by that language as anyone can be by the color of their skin or the history of their people. You may not be able to peg us by race. We are sometimes Asian — Peru's former president Alberto Fujimori was Japanese. We can be black. We can be Native American. We can, as the word Hispanic implies, trace our heritage to Spain. We might be Italians from Genoa, Middle Easterners from Lebanon, or Jews from Eastern European borderlands. We can be any combination of these — criollos, mestizos. But the Spanish language and its attendant culture hold us together.

A third term, *Chicano*, is also used by some Mexican Americans, mostly in California and the Southwest, but care should be taken in applying it to individuals other than at their suggestion. According to the NAHJ resource guide, the term *Chicano* was most recently made popular by Mexican Americans during the 1960s and 1970s civil rights movement. Some believe it to be outdated, even offensive, whereas others prefer it as a term that expresses their dual Mexican–U.S. heritage. As with all racial and ethnic labels, it is best to check an individual's preferences before using.

The Latin America–Central America Conundrum

Former vice-president Dan Quayle once was quoted as saying, "I was recently on a tour of Latin America, and the only regret I have was that I didn't study Latin harder in school so I could converse with those people." He obviously was confused about the language spoken there, but probably was in the ballpark on the geographic area.

Central America is the land mass between Mexico and Colombia in South America. It includes Belize, Guatemala, Honduras, El Salvador, Nicaragua, Costa Rica, and Panama. The most inclusive description of Latin America applies to the entire western hemisphere south of the United States and thus includes Portuguese-speaking as well as French-speaking countries. The NAHJ resource guide says the term is usually used to refer to the nineteen independent republics from Mexico to Chile and Argentina, including the eighteen countries in which the national language is Spanish, as well as Brazil, where Portuguese is the common language. It also notes that the term often is extended by others to include Haiti where French and Creole are spoken as well as other Caribbean and South American nations.

The *Latino* term, then, is the broad umbrella term that applies to everyone whose origins are from countries in Latin America. To be technically correct, however, use *Latino* to refer to men, boys, and mixed gender groups. Use *Latina* to refer to women and girls, unless of course they prefer to be called *Hispanic* or referred to by their country of origin.

Going Beyond the Illegal Immigrant Story

With the exception of Native Americans and those whose ancestors were brought here against their will, most of us are descended from "illegal" immigrants. Like those who were here before us, we now find ourselves not always welcoming of those who wish to cross our borders. Aside from controversial political and legal remedies, uncontested vigilantes have formed nonsanctioned border patrols in an attempt to prevent our neighbors to the South from crossing over to a potentially better life.

According to a Pew Hispanic Center Fact Sheet, as many as 40 percent of all Hispanic immigrants are undocumented.[147] The continuing story of those undocumented immigrants seems to be the most common topic of media reports about this significant and growing part of our American mosaic. Stories range from sensational tales of Hispanic men, women, and children dying of heat-related causes while trying to cross remote desert areas of the Mexican–U.S. border to dramatic data-driven reports of the cost of health and social services required to support those who do make it across the border.

And while stories related to the thousands of undocumented immigrants pouring across the borders every day are legitimate, that limited topic does not constitute the only story.

Hispanic families are more than a drain on social services. They are more than names from weekend arrest records. According to the Pew report, the Hispanic population in the United States will reach 61 million residents by 2025, accounting for 18 percent of the population. Nearly one of every five people living in the United States will be Latino. The report projects that most of that increase will come from Latino births in the United States, resulting in U.S.-born Hispanics accounting for 13 percent of the population by 2025. Immigrants will continue to account for 5 percent of the population.

The impact, particularly in the thirteen states with the highest concentrations of immigrants, is becoming more profound with each passing year. Currently, 50 percent of Hispanics in the United States live in Texas and California; the remainder are spread across New York, Florida, Illinois, Arizona, New Jersey, North Carolina, Georgia, Iowa, Arkansas, Minnesota, and Nebraska. The other thirty-seven states combined account for less than 1 percent of Hispanics currently living in the United States. In some counties of the states most heavily populated by Latino immigrants, Hispanic residents may account for as much as 25 percent of the population.

After the undocumented immigrant story is exhausted and can be put away, census data alone can be mined for numerous stories describing changes in the landscape from the city to rural areas. The average Hispanic living in the United States is from 10 to 20 years younger than the average white non-Hispanic. First-generation Hispanic households average 3.7 persons per family, compared to 2.5 for the typical non-Hispanic white family.[148]

With an extremely high percentage of the immigrants who either speak Spanish only (19 percent) or have limited English proficiency (55 percent),[149] opportunities abound for local media to provide valuable information to its new potential audience. Articles on ESL programs and other community services to help those with limited to no English skills would be beneficial. Survey articles on local businesses from banks and realtors to used car dealers who employ Spanish-speaking services, lists of Hispanic businesses, and information on immigration and naturalization processes all would make useful features. Key articles could be printed or broadcast both in English and Spanish.

For those who speak little or no Spanish, local media could provide a valuable service by publishing or broadcasting information acquainting readers with basic Latino culture, music, food, and language. One piece might deal with the new Latino club that opened in a deserted warehouse. Another would help readers understand the new foods turning up in Hispanic food sections of most every local grocery store. Still another piece, maybe a recurring article, could translate common Spanish words being repeated on signs appearing over the rapidly growing numbers of Latino restaurants, groceries, and general merchandise stores.

Perhaps even more important in incorporating Hispanic residents into regular coverage is to be inclusive throughout the content of your news package. Include Latino residents in day-to-day coverage of life in your community. Get a photo of a Hispanic family for that piece about the first spring weekend when the city park opens; on the sidelines at a youth soccer game; or enjoying a cotton candy at the county fair. Use the Hispanic banker as a source for a story on rising interest rates; the Latino student for a piece on new requirements at the local high school; or local Hispanic Catholics for a round-up of reactions to the new Pope's first sixty days.

The point is to be inclusive, to normalize the existence of this considerable new segment of your community. If one of every five or 10 or even 20 people in your coverage area is Latino, then you have an obligation to provide news content for and about that community. From an economic point of view, it makes a lot of sense; from an ethical perspective, it's the right thing to do.

Tips on Covering the Hispanic Community

It is predicted that by the middle of this century or earlier, one in every four Americans will be Latino, leaving little question about the impact the new immigrants will have on life in the United States. Communications expert Alex López Negrete believes Hispanics share much of the same hopes and dreams for their families as do other average middle-class American families. He writes, "A traditional family structure and support system, plus a strong work ethic, have helped Hispanics successfully integrate into American society and ascend into the middle class."[150] Following are some suggestions for successfully covering the Hispanic community, including suggestions from the National Association of Hispanic Journalists:

■ If no preference is indicated, use *Hispanic* and *Latino* interchangeably. Watch for trends. While there currently appears to be no preference of one over the other, that could change. When reporting on specific individuals, let their preference be your guide. Note correct use of *Latino* and country of origin in the following:

> Less than three years ago, Sindy Benavides was studying political science at Virginia State University. Today, at age 23, she's the governor's go-to person for communications with the state's growing Latino population.
> "I'm running around like a chicken without a head," the Honduran native said in Spanish on Thursday afternoon.[151]

■ Don't assume that all Hispanics are new residents of the United States. In fact, that increasingly will not be the case as the number of U.S.-born Hispanic residents continues to increase.

■ Don't assume that all Hispanics speak Spanish. Currently, as many as 9 percent of Hispanics living in the United States speak only English.

■ Don't assume that all Hispanics are Mexicans. The terms are not synonymous. While immigrants from Mexico account for nearly 67 percent of Hispanics in America, most other countries in Latin America are represented in many communities.[152] Refer to someone as Mexican only when you know he immigrated from Mexico and after you have asked his preference.

■ Don't assume that every person with a Spanish surname is Latino. Pueblo Indians, for example, often have Spanish surnames as a result of Spanish colonization . . . hundreds of years ago.[153]

■ When using Spanish words in print, be sure to get the accent marks correctly placed. The meaning of a word may change without the correct mark. Further, the meanings of words may vary depending on the country being discussed. Check with an expert or have a Spanish dictionary on hand.[154]

■ Don't make assumptions about immigration status. Language and economic level are not indicators of immigration. Never refer to someone as *illegal* or *undocumented* unless you know that to be the case. In fact, reconsider using such designations unless there is a good and justifiable reason to do so.

■ Avoid the use of *illegal, illegal alien,* or *illegal immigrant. Undocumented worker* and *undocumented immigrant* are preferred. UNITY members have taken an official stand urging that such terms not be used except in direct quotes. Such terms are considered pejorative not only by those to whom they are applied but by many people of the same ethnic and national backgrounds who are in the United States legally.[155] Consider dropping the use of *alien* altogether. In spite of UNITY's recommendation, many news organizations continue to use the term *illegal* when *undocumented* could easily be substituted. Note the following paragraph from a story on a series of fatal accidents involving Hispanic drivers:

> Moreno remained hospitalized in good condition at Carolinas Medical Center Sunday. He was charged with driving while impaired, police said.
> The wreck is the latest to affect the local Hispanic community, in the midst of a high-profile effort to educate Latinos on the dangers of drunken driving.
> The issue emerged after the August death of a Mount Holly teacher in Eastern North Carolina, in which an illegal immigrant was charged with driving drunk.[156]

The story itself is questionable in that it tends to suggest that illegal status has something to do with drunken driving. While the interchangeable use of Hispanic and Latino is acceptable, the use of *illegal immigrant* should be changed to *undocumented immigrant,* if that distinction is needed at all.

■ Avoid identifying actual subjects or sources as being *undocumented.* Journalists are not police or INS employees. Stories that have carelessly reported on the undocumented status of identified Hispanic subjects have resulted in arrests and deportation.

■ Avoid using *Hispanic* or *Latino* as identifiers in crime stories. The terms do not describe skin color or facial features. Hispanics, in fact, can be of any race. Labels serve only to stereotype individuals.

■ In Latin American countries, people generally use both the father's and mother's family names, in that order. (The father's name may be used alone in second reference unless the subject or source prefers otherwise.)

■ The singular form of *tamales* is *tamal,* not *tamale.* Spanish words do not always follow the same rules for modification as do English words. Whereas plural words in English often are made by adding an "s," that is not always the case in Spanish. [157]

■ Avoid making comparisons between Hispanic immigrants and other racial or ethnic communities. No one gets a prize for being the largest group, and phrases such as "Latinos overtake African Americans" turn population into a competition, with the obvious conclusion that someone wins over someone else.

■ As with all races and ethnicities, avoid picking out one or a few people in visible positions and having them represent the Hispanic view. Latinos are not a homogenous population and cannot be represented by a single point of view. Develop a broad source list.

■ Consider the emerging concept of America not as a melting pot in which the goal of assimilation or acculturation is primary, but rather as a kind of salad bowl or multicultural society in which immigrants maintain their own cultural characteristics while adapting to the new environment.

■ Examine your own prejudices. If you have a bias that could affect your ability to cover the growing Hispanic community, work it out, talk with colleagues and supervisors, immerse yourself in a learning process. Prejudice almost always is the product of fear and ignorance, and education is the best remedy.

It's the Right Thing to Do

Finally, it might be suggested that reporters, editors, and news directors consider taking on the social responsibility of providing increased coverage of Hispanic residents, particularly new immigrants, to assist them in adjusting to their new communities. There is a strong perception, even resentment, in many communities where Latino populations are surging that most new arrivals are undocumented, and that the new immigrants are taking scarce jobs and stressing already underfunded social services. Typically good people sometimes feel threatened and react by directing their frustrations at new Hispanic immigrants. While it is appropriate to write and talk about the negative aspects of immigration, it also is important to talk and write about the positive contributions new residents are making. Use suggestions included in this and other chapters to come up with story ideas, read as much as possible about what is going on in other communities, get out of the office and into the community, and put a face on stories you are writing and broadcasting.

Unfortunately, in many communities, the only stories involving Hispanic residents that get published or aired are those involving crime. Stories on Hispanic culture and contributions to the community are extremely important. Familiarizing communities with their new neighbors through good reporting can only help them feel more comfortable and in the end more welcomed.

Getting the Right Words

Following are a few select terms that may be useful in writing about the emerging Hispanic community. For additional terms and information, consult the News Watch Style Guide and the NAHJ Stylebook.

Alien — negative connotation; do not refer to people as aliens.

Barrio — section of a town or city dominated by Latino residents; like ghetto, it has a negative connotation and should be avoided.

Central America — the land mass between North and South America; between Mexico and Columbia.

Chicano — a popular sixties term for Mexican Americans, particularly on the west coast; not universally accepted and should not be used as an identifier without asking first.

Cinco de Mayo — May 5, a popular celebration having significance for Mexican communities in Mexico and the United States; relates to the 1862 Battle of Puebla in which Mexican forces defeated a much larger French army; sometimes mislabeled Mexican Independence Day, which actually is September 16.

Cuban American — a citizen of the United States with Cuban ancestors; one who came to the United States and became naturalized or who is of Cuban descent born in the United States.

Ethnicity — group identity based on language and social-cultural background.

Hispanic — term created and used in the 1980 census by U.S. government to describe people from or descended from a Spanish-speaking country; often used interchangeably with Latino; determine an individual's preferred identification when relevant.

Illegal alien — an individual who has entered the country without legal documentation; preferred term is undocumented immigrant.

Illegal immigrant — undocumented worker or undocumented immigrant is preferred.

Inner city — avoid this and other stereotypical references to poor communities of color.

La migra — slang for Immigration and Naturalization Service (INS).

Latin America — in its broadest sense applies to all those countries in the New World whose national language is Spanish, as well as Brazil, Haiti, and other Caribbean islands.

Latino — ethnic description; people who are from or who are descended from a Spanish-speaking country; sometimes used interchangeably with Hispanic; when appropriate to use the ethnic identification, use that preferred by the source or subject; note that while Latino refers to men, boys, and mixed gender groups, the correct term for girls and women is Latina.

Mexican — a citizen of Mexico; incorrect when used as a label for Hispanic or Latino people, all of whom are not from Mexico.

Mexican American — a citizen of the United States with Mexican ancestors.

NAHJ — National Association of Hispanic Journalists. With 2,300 members, NAHJ was founded in 1984 with the mission of improving news coverage of the Hispanic community and to increase the number of Latinos working in American newsrooms.

Nuyorican — someone who is of Puerto Rican descent but who was born and grew up in New York City.

People of color — increasingly popular term for describing people of diverse races and ethnicities; also use journalists of color, students of color, and the like.

Permanent resident — person with a green card; has legal status to live and work in the United States on a permanent basis.

Spanglish — combination of Spanish and English to create new words or sentences that combine words from both languages.

Spic — offensive term sometimes used to refer to people of Spanish or Mexican descent; do not use.

Tejano, Tejana — one of Mexican descent living in Texas.

Undocumented immigrant — preferred over illegal alien; a person living in the United States who does not have the federal documents needed to legally live and work here.

Chapter Eight

Covering Asians, the "Model Minority"

While the model minority stereotype may be one that Asian Americans would rather not perpetuate, some in the marketing and advertising world argue that it is a reality that should be exploited. "Asians not only boast the highest household income level of all groups in the U.S., but they also have the highest level of educational attainment (44 percent holding B.A. degrees or higher) and among the strongest rates of business and home ownership,"[158] says Saul Gitlin of King & Lee Advertising. "With 49 percent population growth in the last decade and a current population of 12 million, Asian Americans are the fastest growing racial group in the country."[159]

A census report issued in March 2005 lists Asian women with bachelor's degrees as earning higher salaries than white, black, or Hispanic women, earning an average of $43,700 in 2003. Asian men were the second highest male wage earners at $52,000 a year, trailing their white counterparts by more than $14,000 per year.

Comparison of Average Bachelor Degree Salaries[160]

	Female	Male
Asian	$43,700	$52,000
White	$37,800	$66,000
Black	$41,100	$45,000
Hispanic	$37,600	$49,000

According to a publication by the Asian American Journalism Association, the model minority designation was born in the 1960s and has often been used to praise Asian Americans while chastising black Americans, Hispanics, and American Indians for failing to measure up.[161]

Headlines in the 1980s and beyond praised Asian student performance and used phrases like *model minority* and *America's super minority*, creating the stereotype of an almost mythical individual. The heralded academic performance of many Asian American students even led to Asians being viewed as *honorary whites*. Academic and professional success resulted in many in society viewing Asians in a different frame from that of the so-called disadvantaged minorities: blacks, Hispanics, and Native Americans. These stereotypes, like all stereotypes, have created problems, the most significant being the fact that they fail to recognize the reality of widespread poverty and academic underachievement in many Asian groups.[162]

As C. N. Le notes on the Asian-Nation website (www.asian-nation.org), the model minority stereotype ignores a number of facts, including the reality that the Asian population is very diverse in itself and that making broad generalizations can be misleading. In spite of the overall high education level of Asians in general, for example, Southeast Asians are still struggling. Vietnamese Americans graduate from college at a rate of only 20 percent, less than half the rate of other Asian Americans. The graduation rate of other Southeast Asians, including Laotians and Cambodians, is less than 10 percent.[163]

Le also notes that references to high Asian American incomes can be misleading. He attributes the skewed income levels to characteristics of the Asian family and to the geographic distribution of a majority of Asian Americans. He notes that one of the reasons Asian American families tend to have higher median incomes than white families is they generally live in households in which more members of the family are working. He claims that as many as four, five, or even more members of an Asian family may be adding to the income of a family unit. He also notes that Asian Americans are much more likely to concentrate in metropolitan areas where both the cost of living and income levels are higher.

Who's Asian, Who's Not

The 2002 census report listed 12.5 million Asians in the United States, making up 4.4 percent of the total population. The report includes Asian and Pacific Islander populations. The Census Bureau defines those geographic terms as follows:

> Asian refers to those having origins in any of the original peoples of the Far East, Southeast Asian, or the Indian subcontinent including, for example, Cambodia, China, India, Japan, Korea, Malaysia, Pakistan, the Philippine Islands, Thailand, and Vietnam. Pacific Islander refers to those having origins in any of the original peoples of Hawaii, Guam, Samoa, or other Pacific islands. The Asian and Pacific Islander population is not a homogeneous group; rather it comprises many groups who differ in language, culture, and length of residence in the U.S. Some of the Asian groups, such as Chinese and Japanese, have been in the U.S. for several generations. Others, such as the Hmong, Vietnamese, Laotians, and Cambodians are comparatively recent immigrants.[164]

The *AAJA All-American Stylebook* cautions that "Asian is a term with cultural, historical and political overtones, and is thus a term whose use is evolving." It notes that with recent growth in the United States of immigrants from India, Pakistan, and Bangladesh, an increasing number of people put the countries of East Asia, Southeast Asia, and South Asia under the broader Asian umbrella:[165]

Traditionally, East Asia includes China, Japan, Korea, Mongolia, and occasionally, the Philippines. South Asia, traditionally comprises Bangladesh, Bhutan, India, Nepal, Pakistan and Sri Lanka. Southeast Asia includes Burma, Cambodia, Indonesia, Laos, Malaysia, Singapore, Thailand and Vietnam.166

Chinese and Chinese Americans account for the largest segment (23 percent) of Asian population in the United States, totaling nearly three million at the time of the 2000 census. Filipinos make up nearly 20 percent of the Asian population with over two million. Other Asian ethnic groups with one million or more U.S. residents include Asian Indians (16 percent of the U.S.–Asian population), Koreans (10.3 percent), Vietnamese (10.3 percent), and Japanese (9.7 percent). [167]

One of the most misunderstood Asian populations in the United States is the Hmong, an ethnic group living in southern China, Vietnam, Laos, and Thailand. Many of the agrarian Hmong living in the mountains of Laos were recruited to fight for the United States during the Vietnam War and in secret battles in Laos. Following the end of the war, Hmong were persecuted for their role in the war, and thousands attempted to escape to Thailand. Many died in the process. The first wave of Hmong refugees resettled in the United States in the mid-1970s.

Resettlement continued through the 1970s and early 1980s, slowed in the mid-1980s, and resumed in the early 1990s. As Hmong refugee camps in Thailand closed in the mid-1990s, and with talk of forced repatriation of Hmong to Laos where they feared for their lives, additional refugees were admitted into the United States, with about 3,000 relocating in 2004 and another 5,000 in 2005.

According to the 2002 census report, approximately 187,000 Hmong were living in the United States. Various Hmong websites estimate the current Hmong population in the United States at between 200,000 and 250,000. The majority of the Hmong population live in California, Minnesota, and Wisconsin with additional resettlements in several other states.[168]

Similar in background to Hmong, the Montagnards were residents of the Central Highlands in Vietnam who supported and even fought alongside American Special Forces in the Vietnam War. Following the war, they fled into Cambodia to avoid persecution by the communist regime in Vietnam. The initial resettlement to North Carolina was followed by others during the last 25 years through family reunification programs and as a result of continuing tensions between the Vietnamese government and current Montagnards living in the Highlands. Much smaller than the Hmong populations, Montagnards in the United States number between 3,000 and 5,000.[169]

The South Asian Journalist Association's website notes that there are significant South Asian populations spread across the world in a diaspora created as a result of the British colonial legacy:

> There are substantial pockets of people of South Asian origin scattered around the world (besides South Asia, of course). In some cases — Fiji, Guyana, Mauritius, Suriname and Trinidad & Tobago — South Asians make up at least 35 percent of the population. Other countries with large South Asian communities: Malaysia,

Singapore, South Africa, United Arab Emirates and the United Kingdom. The government of India puts the size of the diaspora at more than 20 million. There are more than 2 million South Asians in the United States.[170]

Additionally, some sources identify as Central Asia the former Soviet republics of Kazakhstan, Turkmenistan, Uzbekistan, Kyrgyzstan, and Tajikistan, as well as Afghanistan. West Asia may be used to refer to countries in the Middle East.[171]

Tips for Better Coverage of Asian Americans

■ It is particularly important to remember in reporting on Asian Americans that similar skin color, build, and facial features do not constitute a homogeneous group. Asian Americans are as different from one ethnic or geographic group as Irish Americans are from Italian Americans or German Americans. For that matter, all Chinese or all Koreans are not all alike. They may share race and geographic origin, but reporters should avoid making assumptions based on such similarities.

■ Avoid the model minority, super minority, and honorary white syndrome discussed earlier. It ignores the problems facing many Asian communities, creates competitive tensions among many white Americans who feel threatened, and affronts other people of color who see it as media favoritism.

■ Avoid the eternal foreigner syndrome. Don't assume that every Asian is from somewhere else. In fact, many Asians are native English speakers and are from families who have been living in the United States for generations. It is neither necessary nor appropriate to identify every American with Asian ancestry as being Asian American any more than it is necessary to identify every individual with Polish ancestry as Polish American. If in doubt, discuss the issue of identification with your subject or source.

■ Avoid the usual stereotypes. Asians are not all good at math and lousy at sports. They do not all own laundries or work as houseboys and cooks. All Asians do not necessarily like Chinese food; practice Buddhism, Hinduism, or Islam; or worship Bruce Lee, Jet Li, and Jackie Chan. Every person of Asian ancestry does not speak an Asian language, have an Asian name, or know any more about Asian history and culture than you do. U.S. State Department statistics reveal, for example, that as many as 60,000 Asian-born children were adopted into the United States by largely white families in the decade between 1989 and 2000.

■ Respect the traditions and cultures of all Asian people. Even fairly acculturated Korean Americans, for example, may follow traditional family structures where the husband is the dominant partner. As with all cultures, do not judge others through your own prism. The fact that a practice or tradition may seem unusual to you does not make it any less appropriate or important to others.

■ Do not use Chinese as a generic term to refer to all Asians. When identification is appropriate, identify Asians by their country of origin: Korean, Chinese, Cambodian, and so forth.

■ Make an effort to understand how Asian names are used. In many countries, the family name is used first, and that may still be the case among first-generation families. In Korea, for example, a name may be Yang, In Sub, but may be westernized to In Sub Yang. It is best to ask a subject or source for instructions on how to correctly use his or her name.

■ Radio and television media should make an effort to correctly pronounce Asian names. Yang, for example, may be pronounced *young,* and Li is pronounced *lee.*[172]

■ Note that Hawaiian is an ethnic group, referring to a person who is of Polynesian descent. It should not be used for everyone living in Hawaii.[173]

■ Avoid the term *Oriental.* Even though many older Americans grew up with the term, it is today regarded by many younger Asians as outdated and is often viewed as similar to the use of the term *Negro.*[174]

■ Seek out and include Asians and Asian Americans as photo subjects, sources, and features in routine news reports. Highlight Asians in nonstereotypical roles in sports, politics, and entertainment.

■ Spotlight racism, discrimination, and hate crimes committed against Asians and Asian Americans just as aggressively as you would similar crimes against other people of color.

■ In spite of preferences expressed by Asian Americans that the hyphenated identification be used only in the adjectival form (Asian-American politician), use is inconsistent. In the following samples from an article on Asian-American voting trends, *The Boston Globe* uses the hyphen whether noun or adjective:

> More than 40 percent of Asian-Americans who cast ballots last November in Massachusetts were voting for the first time, according to a survey released yesterday by a civil rights group. . . .
> The Bay State's Asian-American population soared 68 percent between 1990 and 2000, according to the U.S. Census, and individual candidates are making forays into politics most recently with a Korean-American aiming this year to become Boston's first city councilor of Asian heritage.[175]

Recognize Stereotypes

For whatever reason, Asian stereotypes and racial slurs often go unnoticed in the media, while comparable slurs toward other races and ethnicities would incite significant protest. When Senator John McCain, in his bid for the Republican presidential nomination in 1999–2000, referred to his Vietnamese torturers as *gooks,*[176] the media hardly noticed.

When student reporter Amy Leang was assigned to cover a comedy troupe performing at the 2001 ASNE convention, she was shocked to witness the Capitol Steps doing a routine in which they impersonated a Chinese official and his interpreter using stereotyped costumes and *ching ching chong chong* gibberish to get laughs. "What was disturbing," she said, "was not just the fact that this was happening, but that hundreds of editors, my future bosses, were laughing."

What Amy Leang concluded from this unfortunate experience was that while many newspapers talk the diversity talk they don't walk the diversity walk.[177]

Media need to take a position. Most editors would never have tolerated a similar mockery of black people or gays or people with disabilities. They also should not tolerate such references to Asian Americans.

In spite of efforts by the Asian American Journalists Association and other watch groups, business and credible media continue to cross the line in reference to Asian Americans and Asian culture. Style manufacturers think nothing of portraying buck-toothed, slant-eyed caricatures on clothing and then express shock when ethnic groups are offended. When Abercrombie & Fitch was criticized for its Wok-N-Bowl / Wong Brothers t-shirt series featuring Asian stereotypes a few years ago, an A&F spokesperson was quoted as saying they thought Asians would love the t-shirts.

Activist comedian Margaret Cho writes that people are surprised at the amount of resentment there is against Asian Americans:

> We are the object of hatred not only for the things we do but just for being who we are, ching-chong chinamen. Racism is one of the biggest taboos in our culture, yet most discrimination against Asian Americans goes largely unnoticed, and if it is picked up by an Asian media watch group or similar organization it's blown off by the rest of the media as a joke, as in, "Look at them. They get all up in arms over nothing." I care less about specific incidents than I do about the general disregard. The dismissal of our anger as a racial minority is worse than any slur or epithet because it undermines our ability to react to it. I would love to be a nice, happy, model minority and say that race isn't important, racism doesn't exist, but I would be lying.[178]

In her book of essays, *I Have Chosen to Stay and Fight*, Cho addresses the issue of Asian invisibility, noting that her own parents have lived in the United States since 1964, but have never voted; they feel that they don't have a right to, that they aren't supposed to. Regarding her own decision to be outspoken, Cho writes, "When you never see anyone like yourself expressing him or herself, then it makes you think that you just aren't supposed to do that, that you have no self to express."[179]

Getting the Right Words

Following are a few terms that may be helpful in writing about Asian Americans. Other more comprehensive stylebooks, such as those published by News Watch, the AAJA, and SAJA may also be helpful.

AAJA — Asian American Journalists Association. Founded in 1981, AAJA is a nonprofit professional and educational organization with 2,000 members in 18 chapters across the United States and one chapter in Asia. The mission of AAJA is to promote fair and accurate coverage of Asian Americans and Pacific Islanders and to increase the number of Asian Americans and Pacific Islanders working in journalism.

Alien — being from another planet; a citizen of another country; someone who does not belong; increasingly associated with a negative connotation, it should be avoided.

All American — can be offensive when used in a narrow sense meaning white, blond, etc.

Amerasian — a person who has both American and Asian parentage; not a synonym for Asian American, which is a term that applies to an individual whose parents are both Asian but who is an American citizen by either birth or naturalization.

America — the entire Western Hemisphere, including North, South, and Central America; not solely the United States.

Asian American — applies to someone with Asian parents who is a United States citizen either by birth or naturalization; some argue that the continued use of the Asian identifier perpetuates the sense of being outsiders regardless of how long their families have lived in the United States.

Asian Indian — avoid as a means of distinguishing from American Indians; instead, say "people from India" or "Indian Americans" when referring to U.S. citizens and permanent residents with Indian ancestry.

Banana — avoid; derogatory term referring to someone who is Asian but acts white; similar to the use of twinkie.

Biracial — an individual who traces his or her heritage to two races; "mixed" is not an acceptable synonym; use only when relevant.

Chinaman — racial slur typically used in a broad sweep to describe anyone of Asian descent; should be avoided.

Chink — negative racial term applied largely to Chinese and Chinese Americans; should be avoided.

Diaspora — refers to the dispersion of people of one race who once were concentrated in a single place; the Black Diaspora, for example, refers to black people of African descent throughout the world.

Ethnicity — group identity based on language and social-cultural background.

Eurocentric — focusing on Europe or European concerns, often in a "Europe is the center of the world" fashion.

Executive Order 9066 — 1942 order by F.D.R., which led to the internment of more than 100,000 Japanese Americans, two-thirds of whom were U.S. citizens, during WWII.

Hmong — ethnic groups inhabiting parts of China, Laos, Thailand, and Vietnam; several thousand Hmong refugees relocated to the United States following Vietnam-era fighting in Laos.

Hyphenated Americans — when referring to groups of people by their race or national origin, use the nonhyphenated form: Korean American, Asian American, African American; as an adjective, use the hyphen: Korean-American family, African-American culture. President Teddy Roosevelt, in 1915, criticized "hyphenated Americans" for not contributing to the mainstream of America. Consider if it's ever necessary to identify people by race or country of origin, particularly those who may have been in America for generations.

Illegal alien — an individual who has entered the country without legal documentation; preferred term is undocumented immigrant.

Illegal immigrant — undocumented worker or undocumented immigrant is preferred.

Inner city — avoid this and other stereotypical references to poor communities of color.

Internment — confinement of someone regarded as a security threat; often refers to the confinement of Japanese Americans, many of them American citizens, in concentration camps during WWII.

Oriental — avoid; no longer used when referring to people of Asian descent; use Asian or Asian American.

Pacific Islander — included in the Native Hawaiian and other Pacific Islander category by the U.S. Census Bureau; defined as a person having origins in any of the original peoples of Hawaii, Guam, Samoa, or other Pacific islands. Includes people who indicate their race as Native Hawaiian, Guamanian or Chamorro, Samoan and other Pacific Islander. The Pacific Islanders' Cultural Association proclaims themselves to be the children of the Pacific islands from Polynesia, Melanesia, and Micronesia.

People of color — increasingly popular term for describing people of diverse races and ethnicities; also use journalists of color, students of color, and the like.

Race — a classification of humans by skin color and physical characteristics; has little real significance and is generally inappropriate as a means of identifying people.

Refugee — a person from one country admitted to another because of a fear of persecution; Montagnards, for example, sought refuge in the United States because of their fear of persecution in Vietnam.

SAJA — South Asian Journalists Association. Founded in 1994, the South Asian Journalists Association (SAJA) is a nonprofit organization that provides a networking and resource forum for journalists of South Asian origin and journalists interested in South Asia or the South Asian Diaspora. SAJA's mission also includes acting as a resource to facilitate and promote accurate coverage of South Asia and South Asians in North America.

Twinkie — avoid; derogatory term referring to someone who is Asian but acts white; similar to the use of banana.

Tribal sovereignty means that; it's sovereign . . . it's . . . you're a . . . you're a . . .
you've been given sovereignty . . . and you're viewed as a sovereign entity . . . and therefore the rela-
tionship between the federal government and tribes is one between sovereign entities.
George W. Bush, President of the United States
Defining sovereignty, UNITY, August 2004

Chapter Nine

Covering Native Americans

While it might seem laughable, if it weren't so sad, that the president of the United States had to stammer his way through an elementary school definition of sovereignty, the reality is that most Americans, including members of the media, probably could do no better. In fact, many Americans likely do not even realize that Native American reservations are self-governing independent entities.

Many people in the United States have never been on an Indian reservation, met or talked with a Native American, picked up and read an Indian publication, or know much of anything about Native Americans other than what they've learned from popular movies and literature. General knowledge of Indian life and Indian culture is a mixture of John Wayne, Graham Greene, and public powwows. The traditional stereotypes are of brightly colored feather headdresses, war paint, teepees, restless ponies, handsome muscular men, beautiful dark-haired women, old men smoking peace pipes, and tiny dark children running naked through crowded dusty villages. Recently have those been joined by the modern stereotypes of alcoholism, gambling casinos, and Indians selling their wares on blankets spread almost anywhere tourists traveling in the Southwest are likely to pull over for a Kodak moment.

While many of the stereotypes have been updated, as in the Outkast performance at the 2004 Grammy Awards show or in the modernized versions of a less warlike Indian chief painted on gymnasium floors all over the country, the message is no less an insult to the history and culture of Native Americans. White Americans turn up in droves at school board meetings or write scathing letters to the editor demanding their Indian names and mascots not be scrapped. "The Indians should be proud," they say. "We're honoring their history."

With names like Redskins, Warriors, and Savages? With war paint, tomahawks, and wild costumed dancers accompanied by unintelligible whooping? People who have never experienced the degradation of racism argue that the repeated sensationalizing of important Native American history and culture is simply a part of their school's tradition and they mean no harm.

Barbara Munson, a member of the Oneida Nation and an activist with the Wisconsin Indian Education Association, explains:

> We experience (the use of Native mascots) as no less than a mockery of our cultures. We see objects sacred to us — such as eagle feathers, face painting and traditional dress — being used not in sacred ceremony, or in any cultural setting, but in another culture's game. ...
>
> Yes, we are proud of the warriors who fought to protect our cultures from forced removal and systematic genocide and to preserve our lands from the greed of others. We are proud, and we don't want them demeaned by being "honored" in a sports activity on a playing field.[180]

The issue of the American Indian mascot is only one of the continuing and significant misunderstandings that create tensions in media coverage of indigenous people. There is a lot of work that needs to be done, and it should begin with efforts to gain a better understanding of tribal nations and the people who inhabit them.

Native American 101

A 2004 U.S. Census Bureau report gives the population of American Indians and Alaska Natives as 4.4 million, composing 1.5 percent of the U.S. population. The Cherokee nation is the largest with a population of 234,000. The Navajo nation has 204,000 members. Other tribes with more than 50,000 members include Apache, Chippewa, Choctaw, Lumbee, Pueblo, and Sioux.[181]

Of the total Indian population, only 538,300 or about 12.2 percent of American Indians and Alaskan Natives actually live on reservations. Of the total living on reservations, approximately one-third live on Navajo nation reservation and trust lands in Arizona, New Mexico, and Utah. The Bureau of Indian Affairs reports that there are 55.7 million acres of land held in trust for American Indians and Indian tribes.[182]

There are currently 562 federally recognized tribal governments in the United States.[183] Indian tribes and Indian nations are the same. According to the "Indian Country Resource Guide," in *The American Indian and the Media*, "The federally recognized tribes are considered self governing — or sovereign nations — by Congress. . . . They have a nationhood status, enjoying the powers of government, except for those expressly taken away by Congress or overruled by the Supreme Court."[184] Tribal nations generally are organized as democracies with an elected governing body or tribal council. While subject to federal regulation, state governments do not have jurisdiction over tribal lands unless specifically given such by congressional act or court precedent.

Tribal nations have sovereignty, the freedom to govern their own territory and internal affairs, much like other individual nations. The *Indian Resource Guide* explains how sovereignty works:

> The status of tribes as self-governing nations is affirmed and upheld by treaties, case law and the Constitution. Legal scholars explain that tribes are inherently sovereign, meaning they do not trace their existence to the United States.
>
> The doctrine of tribal sovereignty was affirmed in three Supreme Court rulings in the 1800s. It recognizes the right of American Indian tribes to self-govern and run their internal affairs as so-called domestic dependent nations. It keeps states from interfering with that right, while allowing Congress to override an Indian nation's authority.[185]

Indians are both American citizens and citizens of tribal nations. They have the right to vote in local, state, and federal elections as well as in tribal elections. With some local and state exceptions, they pay the same taxes as everyone else. They serve in the U.S. military and can be elected to local, state, and federal offices just as can any other citizen.

Indians are not all becoming rich as a result of the casinos. Currently, there are some 300 casinos with annual revenues of over $13 billion. All Indian nation casinos are located on reservation land and are overseen by the National Indian Gaming Commission. Casino gambling originated with the Indian Gaming Regulatory Act in 1988, which requires states to enter into agreements with tribal governments to allow casino gambling. The most profitable casinos are those located near major population areas and major tourist attractions.[186]

In spite of these new revenues, Native Americans remain the nation's poorest population, consistently ranking at the bottom of most social and economic measures. Figures from a 2004 census report list the poverty rate for American Indians and Alaska natives as 20 percent with over 800,000 Indians living below the poverty line.[187] As many as 26.8 percent of American and Alaska Natives live without health insurance coverage, considerably higher than all other racial and ethnic groups with the exception of Hispanics.[188]

Learning the Native American Beat

Unless you live in an area with a high concentration of American Indians, the opportunity to pick up the background and skills needed to cover Native Americans and Native American issues may be a bit more complex for students and professionals than with other targeted populations of people of color. Most people do not have a reservation or native American community in their coverage area. Unlike the rapidly growing population of Hispanics, the Native American population is much smaller and much more likely to be concentrated in the West and Southwest.

The 10 states with the highest concentrations of Native Americans are, in order, California, Oklahoma, Arizona, Texas, New Mexico, New York, Washington, North Carolina, Michigan, and Alaska. And though there are significant concentrations of Native Americans in Los Angeles and New York, for example, Indians compose less than 1 percent of the total populations in those cities. Even in cities with higher overall percentages such as Tucson, Arizona, Albuquerque, New Mexico, and Tulsa, Oklahoma, Native Americans still make up less than 5 percent of the total populations. Higher percentages of Native Americans can be found in less populated areas such as the counties around the Four Corners area of Arizona, New Mexico, Utah, and Colorado; in the Great Plains of central and western South Dakota, southeastern Montana, and border areas of northern Montana and North Dakota; and in the Southern Plains of eastern Oklahoma.[189]

Thus the task of learning how to cover Native Americans may require a different kind of effort. Students or professionals on sabbatical might seek internships in locations with high concentrations of Native Americans, including major cities such as Albuquerque, New Mexico, Phoenix and Flagstaff, Arizona, or Tulsa, Oklahoma; or opt for smaller high Indian population communities like Gallup, Farmington, and Shiprock, New Mexico, or Window Rock, Tuba City, and Kayenta, Arizona. Communities such as these offer an immersion-like approach to learning.

Another possibility to help with getting an education in Native American culture might be to seek summer jobs or internships at Native American publications such as *Indian Country Today, News from Indian Country, Native Peoples Magazine, Native Voice,* and *The Circle,* or on radio programs such as National Native News and Native American Calling.

Short of work and internships, get out of the proverbial bubble and take a road trip. Pick up a map and head across country. Spend some time in the Indian country states of Arizona, Colorado, New Mexico, and Utah. Visit the Four Corners area and take any road in any direction. Visit reservations and pueblos, museums, cultural centers, and trading posts. Shop local businesses, eat at local restaurants. Give it some time. Get to know people. Show an interest. Ask questions. Many Native American people are eager to share their stories with people who are truly interested.

Tips for Reporting on Native Americans

Read the American press day after day. Watch as electronic media fill vast news holes with celebrity trials, sensational murders, kidnappings, and talking heads who can't seem to agree on much of anything. Notice that the 1.5 percent of U.S citizens who make up the American Indian population aren't there, unless of course, a story like the Red Lake shootings breaks. And even then, an initial surge of reporting dies quickly as important celebrity trials and Washington scandals reclaim the spotlight. Many Native Americans, including Mark Anthony Rolo, editor of *The American Indian and the Media,* are critical of media coverage of American Indians. In the introduction to that guidebook, Rolo writes:

> If the world allotted me only one rant it would be this: racial tension, cultural and ethnic misunderstandings rage on in America because the mainstream media fails to report fair, accurate, and timely stories about communities of color. Media research has revealed how this lack of sufficient news coverage affects racial attitudes in this county. Any honest editor would concur.
>
> When incidents of racist violence burst like geysers in all parts of America, how can one not indict the mainstream media? The media have to own up to a measure of complicity with the forces of racism and hate because they have failed miserably in covering the subject of race in the nation.[190]

As in previous chapters, the following is not an exclusive list any more than the earlier discussion of sovereignty is a full explanation of that complex topic. Reporters, editors, and news directors should view this chapter and this book as a launching point for becoming better prepared to cover people of color. Those given the responsibility of covering American Indians should immerse themselves in intensive study of Indian history, culture, and contemporary life. Visit reservations, talk with the people you are covering, and read as much of the vast library of literature as you possibly can. After all, it's all about good journalism.

■ Don't assume anything! The likelihood is that you grew up in an entirely different world, experienced an entirely different culture, and have an entirely different perspective on life than the Native American population you are covering. Don't view your subjects and sources through your cultural prism.

■ Avoid the stereotypical stories about Native American alcoholism, the impact of casino gambling on reservation economics, and desert poverty. Yes, these are important stories, but there's more to the Native American story if you're willing to take the time to go after it.

■ Most Native Americans are okay with the terms *Native*, *Native American*, and *American Indian*. However, it is always best to check since some people do react differently. Generally, the best approach is to identify people by tribal association. Besides, from a journalistic perspective, that provides the maximum information.

An informal survey of recent newspaper articles listed on LexisNexis verifies the either–or approach. An article in the *Albuquerque Journal*, for example, uses *Native American*:

> Bautista said he realized that many of his Native American students had moved to Albuquerque to take advantage of programs for the disabled that were not available in rural New Mexico and Arizona.[191]

An article distributed by Knight Ridder/Tribune Business News and appearing in *Indian Country Today* uses *American Indian*:

> American Indian organizations and individuals continue to oppose the use of an American Indian image that also involves derogatory logos and claim it is an offense to the culture and sensibilities of American Indians.[192]

There is disagreement about the use of the term *tribe*. *Indian Country Today* columnist Susan Shown Harjo told a group of reporters and editors not to refer to an Indian nation as a tribe, noting the *nation* designation is a sign of respect. Others suggest use of the term *tribe* is okay on second reference to an Indian nation. Others Indian writers use the two interchangeably.[193] That said, it's always best to err on the side of being overly careful. Check with your story sources or subjects and go with their preference.

In the following use by *The Asheville* (N.C.) *Citizen-Times*, *tribe* is used to refer to the Eastern Band of Cherokee Indians:

Principal Chief Michell Hicks wasn't up for election this year by the tribe's 6,000 registered voters. The tribe has about 13,300 members.[194]

■ Don't rush it. Ojibwe journalist Deborah Locke writes, "Relationships with Indians must be cultivated and ongoing, not one-shot hits on a single day. Indians I've known stand on ceremony and formalities, and nearly all will respond to a reporter if they are approached with respect, openness and a sincere curiosity."[195] She adds that when approaching Native sources, journalists need to think more like anthropologists.

Put a slightly different way, but worth repeating, former reporter William Claiborne is quoted as writing, "Above all, do be absolutely straight with Indian sources. . . . It's absolutely essential to gain their trust, which is the hardest part of a non-Indian covering Indian country, because for obvious reasons Native Americans are inclined not to trust non-Indian reporters. Tell them what you are going to do and do it, and after awhile they will come to trust you."[196]

■ Respect the religious, ceremonial, and spiritual beliefs that have characterized Native American culture for centuries. Religious rituals such as pipe ceremonials, sweat lodges, vision quests, and Sun Dances have been revived in recent years, and are an important and meaningful part of Native American culture.[197]

■ Recognize that all Indians are not the same. There are 562 recognized tribes ranging from the huge Cherokee Tribal Nation to the remnants of a much smaller Pueblo culture scattered largely across New Mexico and northeastern Arizona. As emphasized with other races and ethnicities, reporters should not rely on a few visible sources to represent all Indians or even all Indians of a single nation. Opinions may vary drastically depending on age, family, and education.

■ Don't act surprised when an Indian does well. One of the most clichéd story types about American Indians in recent years is the success story. People of color, like white people, should be featured when they excel because they excel, not because they are people of color.

■ Finally, this from William Claiborne: "Don't be patronizing. Don't try to curry favor by sounding overly and insincerely sympathetic to the Indian cause, or full of righteous indignation over the two centuries the white man has screwed the Indian. Obviously you should have some indignation, and presumably do since you are interested in covering Native American issues, but it shouldn't sound contrived. It should be sincere and not exaggerated."[198]

President John F. Kennedy once wrote, "For a subject worked and reworked so often in novels, motion pictures, and television, American Indians remain probably the least understood and most misunderstood Americans of us all."[199]

After all this time, perhaps it is finally time for American media to help their audiences better understand American Indians.

Getting the Right Words

Covering Native Americans requires background research and study. In addition to using the limited glossary shown here, refer to the News Watch Diversity Style Guide, the NAJA website, or to *The American Indian and the Media*.

Aboriginal — those who have inhabited an area from the earliest known times; indigenous people.

AIM — American Indian Movement; activist organization founded in 1968 to promote civil rights for Native Americans.

Alaskan Native — refers to indigenous people of Alaska.

Aleuts — refers to the indigenous people of the Aleutian Islands and the far western part of the Alaskan Peninsula.

All American — can be offensive when used in a narrow sense meaning "white, blond," and the like.

America — the entire Western Hemisphere, including North, South, and Central America; not solely the United States.

American Indian — interchangeable with Native American; use tribal affiliation (Cherokee, Navajo, and so on) depending on preference of the source in question.

Asian Indian — avoid as a means of distinguishing from American Indians; instead, say "people from India" or "Indian Americans" when referring to U.S. citizens and permanent residents with Indian ancestry.

BIA — Bureau of Indian Affairs; comprised largely of tribal members, BIA is the federal agency charged with overseeing (enhancing the quality of life, promoting economic opportunity, and the like) the affairs of tribal nations.

Brave — offensive; do not use as a term to describe American Indian males.

Buck — avoid; racial slur historically used to refer to young black and Native American males.

Eskimo — people who inhabit Arctic coastal areas of North American, parts of Greenland, and northeast Siberia; sometimes considered offensive; Inuit can be substituted in most instances, depending on the native language.

First Nations — refers to the indigenous people of North America; usage particularly popular in Canada.

Half-blood or half-breed — avoid; derogatory term, used in the past to refer to an American Indian with mixed heritage.

NAJA — Native American Journalists Association; the mission of NAJA is to help its members become better journalists and to serve as a watchdog organization to ensure Native issues are properly reported everywhere.

People of color — increasingly popular term for describing people of diverse races and ethnicities; also use journalists of color, students of color, and the like.

Powwow — a traditional Native American celebration and social gathering honoring sacred traditions through dancing, singing, drumming.

Race — a classification of humans by skin color and physical characteristics; has little real significance and is generally inappropriate as a means of identifying people.

Reservations — areas of land reserved by the U.S. government as permanent tribal homelands; only about 12 percent of Native Americans live on reservations today.

Sovereign — self-governing or independent; free from external control.

Squaw — avoid; not acceptable as a term applying to Native American women.

Tribe — historically, people united by family, language, religion, and political systems; some dislike the term, preferring instead Indian nations, legally recognized as self-governing sovereign entities; others use the two (tribes or nations) interchangeably.

Warpath — avoid this and similar terms (redskins, savages, warriors, braves), which tend to evoke stereotypical images.

Chapter Ten

Covering Arab Americans in a Post 9/11 World

In a March 2005 column about the controversy over whether it is too easy to get media access to the White House, conservative political commentator and columnist Ann Coulter wrote, "Press passes can't be that hard to come by if the White House allows that old Arab Helen Thomas to sit within yards of the president."[200]

At 84, and often referred to as dean of the White House press corps, Thomas is one of journalism's most respected Washington reporters. With the exception of a few protests, including letters from the Asian American Journalists Association, there was no outpouring of condemnation for the racist tone of Coulter's remark. The silence in itself could be viewed as symptomatic of the widespread misunderstanding of the Arab world in general and the misdirected disdain many currently have for Arab Americans.

Even prior to the September 11, 2001, attacks, most people in the United States knew very little about people of Arab descent, often confusing the terms Arab, Middle Eastern, and Muslim. Driven by misunderstanding and fear, the attacks in New York and Washington, D.C., resulted in a rash of hate crimes against Arab Americans, political references to possible internment, and continuing misinformed verbal attacks such as the tasteless Coulter remark.

Human Rights Watch reported hundreds of violent attacks immediately following 9/11:

> Monitoring groups around the country have received several hundred complaints alleging crimes apparently motivated by bias and hate. A shooting rampage in Mesa, Arizona, left one Sikh man dead, with additional shots fired at a Lebanese clerk and the home of an Afghan family. An Egyptian-American grocer was shot and killed near his store in San Gabriel, California and a storeowner from Pakistan was shot dead in Dallas, Texas. A gasoline bomb was thrown into the home of a Sikh family in California.
>
> Beatings and other violent assaults were reported across the country, as were

death and bomb threats. Mosques and Sikh temples have been shot at, vandalized, and defaced, and bricks were thrown through the window of an Islamic bookstore in Virginia. At several U.S. universities, foreign students from the Middle East and South Asia have been targeted for attacks, and some have chosen to leave the country because they feared additional attacks. Throughout the country affected community members have been afraid to leave their homes, go to work or wear traditional clothing for fear of possible hate crimes against them.[201]

While sporadic attempts were made to explain the events of 9/11 and the ensuing aftermath, the lack of understanding by many in the media left the institution as a whole largely incapable of combating the dearth of intelligible reporting on the Arab world here and abroad. Some effort was made by major media organizations to provide helpful information on covering Arab Americans. The *Detroit Free Press*, the major newspaper in a city with the nation's largest concentration of Arab Americans, responded by publishing "100 Questions and Answers About Arab Americans: A Journalist's Guide," an excellent resource of frequently asked questions. Additionally, a special *Poynter Report* on covering religion included an article on "Covering Muslims in America," and a report from the Society of Professional Journalists discussed "Guidelines for Countering Racial, Ethnic and Religious Profiling."

However, the lack of information and abundant misinformation contributed to an uneasy tension among many Arab Americans. Although most of those affected were born in the United States, still some feared for their lives. Many felt the need to abandon Arab traditions and apparel to avoid attention. Others went out of their way to express patriotism to the United States, posting American flags on their homes and in their yards or making public pronouncements opposing the attacks and professing support for the United States.

Years after September 11, 2001, many Arab Americans avoid or at least dread travel because they know they stand a good chance of being hassled at the airport and eyed with suspicion by fellow travelers, simply because of their name, their accent, the clothes they wear or the way they look. And many, like Helen Thomas, who is of Lebanese descent, know that no matter how long they live honorable and peaceful lives and no matter how much respect and credibility they may gain, there will always be the Ann Coulters of the world who will stereotype, profile, or in some way label them because of a racial, ethnic, religious, or cultural difference.

Muslim Americans, in particular, feel the tensions of exclusion. Joyce Davis, deputy foreign news editor, Knight Ridder Newspapers, writes, "Since Sept. 11, Muslims in this country say they have been living a nightmare. . . . Children have watched as the FBI searched their homes and questioned their fathers. Some say they have been harassed and ridiculed at school. Women who wear the Islamic head covering and dress say they often meet open hostility in shopping malls and other public places." They complain openly of the discrimination, and many blame the news media for spreading stereotypes and myths that reinforce the Western–Islamic divide.[202]

Who Are Arab Americans?

According to a special U.S. Census Bureau Report, "We the People of Arab Ancestry in the United States," based on 2000 census data, approximately 1.2 million people of Arab descent live in the United States. Of that number, approximately 850,000 reported Arab ancestry alone, while another 340,000 people reported both Arab and non-Arab ancestry.

Of those reporting Arab ancestry, almost 29 percent were Lebanese, followed by 15 percent Egyptian, 9 percent Syrian, and 7 percent Palestinian. Other countries represented included Jordan, Morocco, Iraq, Yemen, Kuwait, and Libya. Almost 20 percent of those included simply identified their ancestry as Arab or Arabic.

The Arab American population is more male than the general population (57 percent compared to 49 percent) and younger. Men aged between 20 and 49, for example, make up 31 percent of the Arab American population, compared to the general population in which only 22 percent fall into that age group.[203] Additionally, typical Arab Americans are better educated than non-Arab Americans, more likely to be self-employed, and have higher than average median incomes.[204]

The *Detroit Free Press* report estimates the number of Arab Americans living in the United States at about 3 million. They believe the discrepancy stems from the reality that many immigrants are reluctant to give personal and confidential information to the government, and that an increasing number of people have more than one ethnicity.[205]

The *Free Press* answer to the "Who Are Arab Americans" question is simple: "Arab Americans are U.S. citizens and permanent residents who trace their ancestry to or who emigrated from Arabic-speaking places in southwestern Asia and northern Africa, a region known as the Middle East. Not all people in this region are Arabs. Most Arab Americans were born in the United States."[206] From that point, it gets a bit more complicated. Answers to the following common question are provided by the *Detroit Free Press* in its "100 Questions and Answers About Arab Americans":

To which places do Arab Americans trace their ancestry? Arab Americans trace their roots to many places, including parts or all of Algeria, Bahrain, Djibouti, Egypt, Iraq, Jordan, Kuwait, Lebanon, Libya, Mauritania, Morocco, Oman, Palestine, Qatar, Saudi Arabia, Somalia, Sudan, Syria, Tunisia, United Arab Emirates, and Yemen. Some Arabs are Israeli citizens.

What race are Arab Americans? Arabs may have white skin and blue eyes, olive or dark skin and brown eyes. Hair textures differ. The United States has, at different times, classified Arab immigrants as African, Asian, white, European, or as belonging to a separate group. Most Arab Americans identify more closely with nationality than with ethnic group.

Are Arabs a minority group? This depends, in part, on your definition of minority. The U.S. government does not classify Arabs as a minority group for purpose of employment and housing. Arabs are not defined specifically by race, like some minority groups, but are united by culture and language. Some Arab Americans see minority classification as an impediment to full participation in American life. Others are asking for protection from the same issues affecting people in minority groups, such as profiling, stereotyping, and exclusion.

Are Arab Americans more closely tied to their country of origin or to America? Arab Americans have dual loyalties. While they may be closely tied to their countries of origin, most Arab Americans were born in the United States, and an even larger majority have U.S. citizenship. This is reflected in the expression, "Truly Arab and fully American."[207]

The Arab–Islam–Muslim Confusion

Islam is the religion. Muslims are followers of Islam, just as Christians are followers of Christianity, and Buddhists are followers of Buddhism. Not all Muslims are Arab, and conversely, not all Arabs are Muslim.

While sources may differ on even an approximate number of members belonging to or following major religions, most all agree that Islam is the second largest religion in the world with as many as 1.2 billion followers. Christianity leads all world religions with over 2 billion members.[208]

An entry in the *AP Stylebook* notes that most of the world's Muslims live in a wide belt stretching halfway around the world, across West Africa and North Africa, through the Arab countries of the Middle East and on to Turkey, Iran, Afghanistan, Pakistan, and other Asian countries, parts of the former Soviet Union and western China, to Indonesia and the southern Philippines.

Approximately 12 percent of world's Muslims are Arab. Arabs belong to many religions including Islam, Christianity, Druze, and Judaism. Most Arab Americans, in fact, are Christian (Catholic or Orthodox), though that may vary depending on the location within the United States. In some areas, a concentration of Arab Americans may be largely Muslim.[209]

The introduction to the *Detroit Free Press*'s guide to Arab Americans notes that "Culture, language and religion are distinct qualities that act in different ways to connect Arabs, and to distinguish them from one another. The differences that seem to separate Arab Americans from non-Arabs can be much smaller than the variations that at times differentiate them from one another."[210]

Keep in mind that discussions of mosques, Allah, the Quran (also Qur'an or Koran), Ramadan, Makkah (also Mecca), Sunni, Shiite, and so on are religious in nature and do not relate to all Arabs or Arab Americans. All Arabs are not Muslim or followers of Islam. And while the fact that someone worships in a mosque and reads the Quran suggests they are Muslim, that does not make them Arab.

Also note that not all people from the Middle East are Arab; Iran is not. It is descended from the Persian Empire and has a language and cultural history different from Arab countries. The Middle East also includes Hebrew, Turkish, Kurdish, and Berber language groups.[211]

One final clarification: The Nation of Islam is an African American religious group. Although closely related to Islam, it evolved in the twentieth century with some practices different from those followed by most Muslims.[212] Black American Muslims are not necessarily members of the Nation of Islam.

Covering Muslims and Arab Americans

According to Joyce Davis's report in a 2003 *Poynter Report*, many American Muslims have accused media in the United States of being biased and hostile toward Islam. She writes, "Muslims also complain that many American journalists who are writing about them have little understanding about their religion or their culture. Some even believe there is a conspiracy to defile Islam's reputation in the United States."[213]

Although the problem most likely results more from misunderstanding than from malicious intent, ignorance consistently applied over time can result in considerable harm. It is then imperative that media professionals become better educated in issues related to the Islam religion and its Muslim followers as well as those involving Americans who are of Arab ancestry.

Following are selected suggestions and guidelines for covering Muslims and Arab Americans. Many of the excellent suggestions are compiled from the *Detroit Free Press*'s "100 Questions and Answers About Arab Americans"[214] and the Society of Professional Journalists' "Guidelines for Countering Racial, Ethnic and Religious Profiling."[215] It would require a document much greater than the length of this book to explain Islam alone, so do not rely on just these few pages to provide all the information you will need to cover Muslims and Arab Americans. View it simply as a door to greater understanding.

■ The first rule or guideline, of course, is to keep them separate. If reporters, editors, and news directors can't keep the religion separated from the language and geography, then most media consumers probably won't either. This AP lead on a story about the controversial Prophet Muhammad cartoons is careful to distinguish between the two:

> Many Arab governments, Muslim religious leaders and newspapers have been calling for calm in the protests over the Prophet Muhammad cartoons, fearing the violence of the past weeks has only reinforced Islam's negative image in the West.[216]

■ Avoid depicting or implying that all followers of Islam are terrorists by using such terms as Islamic terrorist or Muslim extremist. The avoidance of stereotypes, of course, is important regardless of the race or ethnicity of the source or subject. In situations involving Arab Americans, it has become a matter of life and death.

■ When reporting on Muslims or issues related to the religion of Islam, seek objective sources who are educated on the religious issues or who have a related expertise. Reporters also should develop their own basic knowledge of world religions through reading and study. Most universities these days offer a general course on world religions. In light of the general misunderstanding of religious issues, students should consider such a course a part of their plan of study.

■ Don't assume Arab Americans or followers of Islam are involved any time there is a major catastrophe in which terrorists are suspected. Question any unsubstantiated reports making racial or ethnic links with terror attempts.

■ Remain current on spellings and follow Associated Press style where possible. Recent editions of the *AP Stylebook*, for example, have updated Koran to Quaran and Mohammed to Muhammad. While the American Muslim Council prefers Makkah, many news sources including AP and *The New York Times* continue to use Mecca:

> A stampede on Thursday at the annual pilgrimage to Mecca killed 345 people, the Saudi Arabian Interior Ministry said, the deadliest such event since 1990.[217]

■ Don't assume Arab people are foreign or alien. Most Arab Americans were born in America, their ancestors having immigrated to the United States between 1875 and 1920 during what the *Detroit Free Press* labels the first significant wave of immigration. While on the topic, consider striking the word *alien* from your lexicon entirely. It is an odd word with a negative connotation.

■ The checkered headdress worn by some Arab men, called a kafiyyeh, is a traditional garment and is not related to Islam. It is a sign of identity and pride in culture,[218] much like the plaids valued by people of Scot ancestry.

■ Be respectful of cultural traditions. The giving of gifts is considered a polite gesture in many cultures, and failure to accept may risk offense. Usual journalistic ethics aside, there shouldn't be a problem in accepting courtesy gifts even from a subject or source.

■ Approach recent immigrants somewhat differently from how you might an Arab American who was born in the United States, in that religious or cultural traditions might be practiced more rigidly by recent arrivals. For example, Muslims new to our culture might feel it inappropriate for unrelated men and women to shake hands. In such cases, take your cue from the other person and wait until he or she extends his or her hand before you offer your own. Likewise, complimenting someone's possession may be misinterpreted, with the person complimented feeling the need to offer the item as a gift.

■ Ramadan is the ninth month under the Muslim calendar and is a month of fasting between sunrise and sundown. Don't suggest a luncheon meeting during this time. The Muslim calendar is based on a lunar calendar and is about eleven days shorter than the solar calendar. Therefore, Islamic holidays move each year. In 2005, for example, Ramadan began October 5. In 2006, it began September 24.

■ Rules for entering a mosque: One generally must enter without shoes. Look for a sign from your host, or for a place to leave your shoes. Women should dress modestly and may be asked to cover their heads. Men should wear long pants and shirts. Men and women generally should pray in different areas.

■ About photographing in a mosque: Each mosque has its own rules. Ask in advance and do not assume it will be okay to photograph at will. Be prepared to make some accommodation if certain angles or parts of the mosque are off limits.

■ Generally, the use of Arab American is acceptable, but when the information is available, refer to an individual's country of origin: Lebanese, Jordanian, and so forth.

■ Don't seek out just the stereotype to depict in articles and photographs. All Arab Americans don't wear traditional clothing. In fact, most don't. So don't contribute to the perception that people of Arab descent are exotic or different. As with other racial and ethnic populations, don't allow convenient or favored sources to represent all Arab Americans. The group is far from homogeneous. Seek out lots of different voices.

Until September 11, 2001, most Arab Americans lived in peace, attended school, worked, and practiced their religions without much notice at all. Then a group of terrorists from largely Arab countries precipitated a horrendous attack on two American icons, affecting the lives of every single person of Arab descent living in the United States. Recalling a mood similar to that following the Japanese attack on Pearl Harbor, some Americans, out of confusion, fear, and even hatred of an unknown, reacted violently. As a result, many Arab Americans still fear for their safety in their own homeland.

In such times, it is the responsibility of the media to provide clear and accurate information to help people understand the events taking place and to respond in a more intelligent and responsible manner.

Getting the Right Words

Following are terms associated with Arab American life and tradition, as well as terms that relate to Muslims and the practice of Islam. For a more comprehensive listing, see the News Watch Diversity Style Guide or the *Detroit Free Press*'s "100 Questions and Answers About Arab Americans."

Abayah — long robe-like clothing worn by some Arab women; also called jilbab or chador.

Allah — God.

All American — can be offensive when used in a narrow sense meaning "white, blond," and the like.

AMC — American Muslim Council; established in 1990 to increase the effective participation of American Muslims in the U.S. political and public policy arenas. The goal of AMC is to promote ethical values that enhance the quality of life for all Americans and to encourage increased participation by American Muslims in mainstream public life.

Arab — a person from an Arabic-speaking country.

Arab American — an individual who descends from an Arabic-speaking country and who is an American citizen either by birth or naturalization. Not all Arab Americans are Muslims; not all Muslims are of Arab descent.

Black Muslim — archaic reference to sect of black Muslims; members prefer to be called Muslims.

Burka — loose garment with veiled eyeholes worn by some Muslim women, particularly in India and Pakistan.

Chador — long robe worn by some Arab women as a sign of modesty or hijab.

Eid Al-Fitr — celebration at the end of the Muslim holy month, Ramadan.

Five Pillars of Islam — refers to the sacred expectation of followers of Islam: faith in shehada (there is no god but God, and Muhammad is his prophet); salat (prayer five times daily); sharing of alms with the poor; fasting during Ramadan; and completing hajj (pilgrimage to Makkah).

Hajj — pilgrimage to Makkah; all Muslims are expected to make the pilgrimage at least once during their lifetime.

Hijab — modesty, the trait that leads some Arab women to wear robes and face scarves; also refers to a type of veil or face scarf.

Imam — one who leads prayer at a mosque; leader in an Islamic community; also called a sheik.

Islam — with over one billion followers, the Islam religion is the second largest in the world; followers of the Islam belief are Muslims.

Jihad — Arabic term referring to the Islamic concept of the struggle to do good; is not synonymous with Holy War, which is a term used by Muslim extremists.

Kafiyyeh — traditional, nonreligious, checkered head covering worn by some Arab men to exhibit pride in their culture.

Makkah (preferred) or **Mecca** — birthplace of Muhammad and Islam holy site located in western Saudi Arabia near the Red Sea; millions of Muslims make a pilgrimage there each year.

Mosque — Muslim place of worship.

Muhammad — preferred over Mohammad; the Muslim prophet and founder of Islam.

Muslim — a follower of the Islam belief, the second largest religion in the world. All Muslims are not Arabs, and not all Arabs or Arab Americans are Muslim.

People of color — increasingly popular term for describing people of diverse races and ethnicities; also use journalists of color, students of color, and the like.

Quran — the preferred spelling of the Muslim holy book; do not use Koran.

Ramadan — ninth month of the Muslim calendar, a month of fasting ending in celebration.

Chapter Eleven

Gay Men and Lesbians Take Center Stage

Twenty-five years after advertising pressure from the religious-right kept TV sitcom Love Sidney's lead gay character Sidney Shorr in the closet, the 2006 critically acclaimed *Brokeback Mountain* brought gay love to the big screen. While not the first time gay characters have been featured in a major movie, it may have been the first attempt at depicting a serious gay male relationship in a sympathetic manner. Add the traditional Marlboro-man Wyoming setting, and *Brokeback Mountain* definitely broke new ground.

The touching story of two young cowboys who fall in love, the Golden Globe Award winning movie was only one of three LGBT-themed movies lauded by the Hollywood Foreign Press Association, sponsors of the Golden Globes. *Capote*, the story of the life of gay writer Truman Capote, and *Transamerica*, featuring a transgender woman also received awards. Conservative Christian groups accused the Golden Globe Awards of promoting films with gay or leftist themes to serve a political agenda.

Of course, the big screen wasn't the only entertainment venue to catch the brunt of the Christian right's indignation over pop culture's move to inclusiveness. Even before it aired, the American Family Association urged Christians to boycott *The Book of Daniel*, an NBC television series about a self-medicating Episcopal priest whose son is gay and whose daughter deals pot. AFA Chairman Donald Wildmon called NBC's decision to run the series "Christian bashing."[219]

Much of the response to the right's heated criticism of *Brokeback Mountain* and *The Book of Daniel* came from the gay press. Mainstream media, with few exceptions, didn't simply play it neutral, they pretty much stayed away from the row entirely, missing an opportunity to provide intelligent coverage of a continuing societal issue often lacking in rational voices. Increased and improved coverage of LGBT issues, just as is the case with other target groups in the diverse community, will require students and professionals alike to become better educated and to be willing to take the risks necessary to do the job they ought to do.

Preparing to Cover LGBT Issues

In an introduction to the Journalists' Toolbox, prepared by the National Lesbian and Gay Journalists Association, Randy Dotinga writes: "No journalist would cover a professional tennis match without getting an education in backhands, foot faults, player rankings and grand slams. But some reporters step into the world of lesbian, gay, bisexual and transgender people without taking the time to know what they're reporting about."[220]

Terms like *down low, intersex,* and *pink triangle;* the acronyms FTM, MTF, and MSM; and the realities of being gay in America today likely are as foreign to many mainstream reporters as they are to the general public. Many people who are of the dominant race, ethnicity, and sexual orientation just assume everything is right because everything is right with them. They may have heard of Matthew Shepard but probably think of homophobia as a thing of the past. They may have heard of the controversies over Sponge Bob, Tinky Winky, Buster, the United Church of Christ's bouncer ad, and the same-sex marriage on *The Simpsons,* but for some people those are little more than petty fights between religious extremists and pop culture.

But it is more than an issue of censorship and pop culture. Gay, lesbian, bisexual, and transgender Americans continue to be targeted, both verbally and physically, by people who should know better. The gay marriage issue became the deciding point among many religious and morally conservative voters in the 2004 presidential election. Many states are passing laws preventing same-sex marriages, while traditional marriage proponents continue to promote a constitutional amendment to ban gay unions nationwide.

The issue of gay rights, like most all issues involving diverse groups, relates directly to misunderstanding, misinformation, and misdirected anxiety. Congressman Barney Frank, among others, has often accused the media of underreporting LGBT issues, of not providing the background and context that readers need to understand homosexuality. Speaking to a group of journalists at an Association for Education in Journalism and Communications conference in Washington, D.C., in 2001, he asserted that coverage of LGBT issues tends too often to stress the failures rather than the successes, noting that the successful civil union law passed in Vermont in 2000 was seldom mentioned.[221]

David Hawpe, editorial director of the *Louisville* (Ky.) *Courier-Journal,* believes news coverage of gay issues often leaves out important context. He cites as an example his newspaper's coverage of the Rev. Jerry Falwell's speech on a stop in Louisville during his God Save America tour. Falwell had commented on the United States Supreme Court ruling upholding the right of the Boy Scouts to ban gay scoutmasters. Falwell had expressed his shock that the decision had even been close, referring to the four dissenting justices as idiots.

Hawpe notes in an article in *NewsWatch* that the Boy Scout decision and Falwell's comments carried with it the charge that gay men are more likely than heterosexual men to commit child sexual abuse. That's the context, according to Hawpe, that the coverage was missing. He writes:

> Reading through more than 30 newspaper clippings on the court decision, which reversed a New Jersey Supreme Court ruling, I found no factual examination of the concern that lies at the bottom of the Rev. Falwell's public pronouncements on the

issue. No stories looking at the scientific evidence, which may or may not prove his point that gays shouldn't be left alone with Scouts in the woods. I don't claim to know who is right . . . . But I do know that it's part of a newspaper's obligation to help readers know what's true and what's false, with respect to such notions.[222]

It's all about truth and fairness and accuracy. It's about good journalism. Hawpe concluded the piece in *NewsWatch*: "Coverage of this important news development, and the issues surrounding it, has been full of unexamined stereotypes. We can do better."[223]

Guidelines for Covering LGBT People

Don't make assumptions. Stereotypes about lesbian, gay, bisexual, and transgender people abound. Here, U.S. Representative Barney Frank, D-Mass., responds to one of the most prevalent beliefs of many misguided people: gay people are out to promote homosexuality:

> If you gave me $1 million tomorrow and told me to promote homosexuality, I haven't the faintest idea what I would do. What do you do? Have a contest? Make up posters? Put ads on television? The notion of promoting homosexuality is preposterous. Our agenda is very simple: Please leave us alone. Please let us be what we want to be and live our lives with others.[224]

That appears to be a common sentiment among LGBT people. They want to be left alone to live their lives, with the same rights and responsibilities as everyone else. The gay marriage issue may simply be an assertion by one group of people who want to be treated to the same legal rights as other people. Granting people the right to same-sex marriage does not infringe on the basic rights of anyone else. Following are selected tips for covering LGBT people from various sources, including the NLGJA Journalist's Toolbox. The complete toolbox is available on the NLGJA website.

■ Avoid the stereotypes. Gay men are neither all effeminate nor all buff. Lesbians are not all masculine, do not all wear male clothes, and are not all coaches and gym teachers. Gay men and lesbians are no more flamboyant than anyone else. Gay men and lesbians are no more promiscuous than anyone else.

■ *Metrosexual* is not another term for gay. As opposed to a *retrosexual* (a man who spends as little time and money as possible on his appearance), a metrosexual male is one who cares about clothes, style, and his appearance in general. He may be straight, gay or bisexual.

■ LGBT people do not all wish they were straight. They are not lesbian, gay, bisexual and transgender due to rape, dysfunctional families or some other childhood trauma.

■ Being gay is not just a phase that merely requires therapy or a heterosexual relationship. Being gay is not abnormal, a mental problem, a birth defect.

■ Covering the LGBT community requires more research than a few viewings of *Will & Grace*. Consider: Transsexuals aren't the same as drag queens. Outdated phrases such as *sexual preference* make journalists look clueless at best and insensitive at worst. And outing someone without permission remains a dicey proposition, even in these days of growing sexual freedom. *Randy Dotinga, How to Cover LGBT People*

■ Reporters should be careful when identifying members of the lesbian, gay, bisexual or transgender community. Ask yourself if the person's sexuality is germane to the story. In many situations it probably isn't a matter of concern — in the same way that a person's race, ethnic background or religious beliefs are often not relevant. *Bao Ong, Is Sexuality Part of the Story?*

■ If you've decided that a person's sexuality is important to the story, consult a colleague for confirmation, particularly if you are unsure whether or not the individual is out. Unless there's a reason not to, talk to the subject or source whom you would be identifying.

■ If you're thinking about approaching a subject's family or friends and asking them about the subject's sexual orientation, do so only if the story calls for it, and with minors only if you know the subject is out to their family. *Bao Ong*

■ If you're working on a story specifically about the LGBT community, it might be appropriate to identify the straight people in your story who readers might otherwise assume are gay. The goal is providing an accurate, fair, and balanced picture of your subjects. *Bao Ong*

■ Don't assume that all gay activists and people interested in gay issues are gay.

■ Inclusion goes beyond covering gays and lesbians only when their lives are subject to political or social debate. It means inviting gay voices to participate in stories generated by commonplace life experiences. First day of school? Choose a photo of two mommies dropping off their son. Polling shoppers on what presents they're buying during the holidays? Give the man who bought a new DVD player for his boyfriend some airtime. *Jennifer Lea Reed, Why LGBT Voices Matter*

■ Don't use one gay source to speak for all LGBT people in your stories. Republicans, Democrats, school bus drivers, stock brokers, and people of different ages and races are all in the mix. *Jennifer Lea Reed*

■ Same-sex couples use a variety of terms to describe their relationship, including partners, spouses, girlfriends/boyfriends, husbands/wives, lovers, companions, etc. Don't be afraid to ask which term your subjects use. *Jennifer Lea Reed*

■ Avoid using the term *lifestyle*, as in *gay lifestyle*. Many gay people are offended by such trivialization, saying it's a life not a lifestyle, with sexuality just being one aspect of it. *Jennifer Lea Reed*

■ Be careful to use the correct pronoun when referring to a person who is a transsexual. Associated Press advises: "Use the pronoun preferred by the individuals who have acquired the physical characteristics of the opposite sex or present themselves in a way that does not correspond with their sex at birth. If that preference is not expressed, use the pronoun consistent with the way the individuals live publicly." Don't assume that all transgender people are gay. It is not necessarily the case that transgender people are automatically attracted to one gender or another. *Randy Dotinga, The T in LGBT*

■ As with reporting on other diverse groups in your community, it is important to leave your personal biases at home. If you do have a strong bias, it would be wise to discuss it with your supervisor. Ask not to be assigned to LGBT stories until you can work out your personal issues. If you do write on topics dealing with LGBT issues, ask a variety of colleagues to look over your work and check for objectivity.

■ Do not identify a person's sexuality in crime stories unless there is a significant reason to do so.

The key to successful reporting on lesbian, gay, bisexual, and transgender people is in applying Barney Frank's plea included in an earlier quote: "Please leave us alone. Please let us be what we want to be and live our lives with others." Be inclusive, but avoid stereotyping. Every story about people who are LGBT does not have to be an adversarial story, pitting one side against another. A story about the celebration of a gay union, for example, does not have to include an alternative point of view. A story about a gay couple adopting or having a child through insemination does not require that there be a quote from someone who is opposed to gay and lesbian couples having children.

In fact, those stories do not have to be gay or lesbian stories. Treat the announcement of the engagement of two men or of two women as you would any other engagement story. You don't point out the heterosexual nature of the engagement between a man and a woman; why emphasize the homosexual nature of the engagement of two people of the same sex? Same with the adoption story. When a man and a woman adopt, you don't point out that they are heterosexual. Why note that two men who are adopting are gay? They are a couple who are providing a loving family to a child without parents. Why isn't that enough?

When journalists always frame an issue in a certain manner — any mention of LGBT activity or involvement is controversial — then that is likely the way it will be viewed by the public. Certainly, media have the responsibility to report the news even when it is controversial, but they also have the obligation to go beyond the controversy.

Sorting Out the Terms

Although it is generally accepted that the commonly used letter grouping LGBT encompasses the current politically correct language, there is much more to be learned. Gay as an adjective has, according to the National Lesbian and Gay Journalists Association, replaced homosexual as the preferred term in referring to men who are sexually and affectionately attracted to other men; the term *lesbian* is most often used when referring to women who are attracted to other women; and the combined phrase gay men and lesbians is correct when including both.

Despite the preferences of the NLGJA, use remains inconsistent, as in quotes from a *Richmond* (Va.) *Times-Dispatch* article titled "Clerics Sign Ad Accepting Gays: 44 Methodist Ministers in Area Say They'll Let Homosexuals Join Church":

> A number of Richmond-area United Methodist clergy purchased advertising space in today's Times-Dispatch to say they will not use homosexual practice as a barrier to church membership. . . .
>
> Questions about church membership for practicing gays and lesbians have been raised since a South Hill United Methodist pastor refused church membership to a practicing gay man.[225]

The *NLGJA Stylebook* also notes that it is acceptable to use gay to refer to both males and females in headlines where space is limited, and that some women prefer being called gay to lesbian.[226] As is recommended when referring to members of any diverse population, it is best to ask a subject or source how he or she prefers to handle questions of identity.

Getting the Right Words

Following are a few terms that may be helpful in covering the LGBT community. Additional terms may be found in various stylebooks, including the *NLGJA Stylebook Supplement.*

AIDS — Acquired Immune Deficiency Syndrome, medical condition in which the body's immune system does not adequately combat certain diseases; caused by HIV destruction of white blood cells.

Bisexual — an individual, male or female, who may be attracted to either sex.

Civil union — refers to a legal arrangement between two people of the same sex that provides rights similar to those enjoyed by married couples.

Closeted — a person who is "in the closet" does not wish to share his or her sexual orientation.

Cross-dresser — one who wears clothing usually associated with the opposite sex; not necessarily an indication of sexual orientation. Note that the term *transvestite* is no longer considered acceptable.

Coming out — the process of coming out of the closet or making one's sexual orientation known.

Domestic partners — an unmarried couple of the same or opposite sex who live together as partners; may or may not have legal implications depending on state law.

Down low — usually refers to men of color who have sex with other men without the knowledge of their female partners; MSM or "men who have sex with men" is used to convey an equivalent meaning.

Drag — dressing in the clothes of the opposite sex.

Drag queen — usually a male performer who dresses in female clothing for entertainment.

Dyke — avoid; derogatory term for a lesbian. Note that while terms such as dyke, fag, faggot, and queer may be regaining popularity among some individuals, they are still considered extremely offensive when used as an epithet.

Fag, faggot — avoid; derogatory term for a gay male.

FTM — female to male. A transgender person who, at birth or by determination of parents or doctors, has a biological identity of a female but a gender identity of a male. Those who have undergone surgery are sometimes referred to as "post-op FTMs."

Gay — preferred umbrella term when referring to homosexual men; refer to homosexual women as lesbian; use gay men and lesbian when referring to both men and women; use only when it is appropriate to refer to individuals by their sexual orientation.

Gay lifestyle — should be avoided; being lesbian, gay, bisexual, or transgender is not just a lifestyle that one chooses; it is life.

Gender identity — an individual's emotional and psychological sense of being male or female. Not necessarily the same as an individual's biological identity.

Heterosexual — refers to people who are attracted to members of the opposite sex.

HIV — human immunodeficiency virus, the virus that causes AIDS.

Homo — pejorative term and is never acceptable.

Homophobia — irrational dislike, fear, or even hatred of people who are gay or lesbian.

Homosexual — refers to people who are attracted to members of the same sex; use lesbian and gay men instead.

Lesbian — the currently preferred term for a female homosexual when it is appropriate to identify an individual by sexual orientation.

LGBT — lesbian, gay, bisexual, and transgender.

MSM — men who have sex with men. Often used to describe men who secretly have sex with other men while maintaining relationships with women.

MTF — male to female. A transgender person who, at birth or by determination of parents or doctors, has a biological identity of male but a gender identity of female. Those who have undergone surgery are sometimes referred to as "post-op MTFs."

NLGJA — National Lesbian and Gay Journalists Association. Founded in 1990, NLGA currently has 1,300 members. Among its goals are to enhance the professionalism, skills, and career opportunities for lesbian, gay, bisexual. and transgender journalists, and to strengthen the identity, respect, and status of member journalists in the newsroom and throughout the practice of journalism.

PFLAG — Parents, Families & Friends of Lesbians & Gays; a national nonprofit organization with over 200,000 members and supporters and over 500 affiliates in the United States. PFLAG's mission is to promote the health and well-being of gay, lesbian, bisexual, and transgender persons, their families, and friends.

Pink triangle — symbol of gay pride; gay men were required to wear the label in Nazi concentration camps during WWII.

Queer — has had its ups and downs as a term for gay; once considered pejorative, it currently is being used as an umbrella term by some LGBT people; still best to avoid.

Rainbow flag — symbol of the diversity of the LGBT community.

Sexual preference — use "sexual orientation" instead; preference implies that one chooses his or her sexual orientation.

Straight — acceptable common term for heterosexual.

Transgender — applies to all stages of becoming or being transsexual (preoperative, postoperative, or nonoperative), as well as to cross-dressers and drag queens or kings.

Transsexual — a person who identifies as a member of the opposite sex; acquires the physical characteristics of the opposite sex; not an indication of sexual orientation

Transvestite — avoid; the correct term is cross-dresser.

We must scrupulously guard the civil rights and civil liberties of all citizens, whatever their background. We must remember that any oppression, any injustice, any hatred is a wedge designed to attack our civilization.

President Franklin Delano Roosevelt

Chapter Twelve

Reporting on People with Disabilities

He was a symbol of strength and perseverance during a tumultuous period of American history that included the Great Depression and World War II. After contracting polio in 1921, Franklin Delano Roosevelt served as the nation's thirty-second president from 1933 until his death in 1945.

President Roosevelt lived in an era when people with disabilities were referred to as cripples and invalids and hidden from mainstream society. He and his advisors were so convinced that public display of his disability would be a sign of weakness, he was never shown in a wheelchair. Even the media helped to keep his secret, and there are said to be only four known photographs of the president in the wheelchair that he designed for himself.

It was therefore seen as a victory for people with disabilities when President Bill Clinton unveiled the life-size bronze statue of FDR sitting in his wheelchair at the FDR National Memorial in Washington, D.C., in January 2001.

More than a half-century after President Roosevelt's death, people continue to struggle with the differences of disability. Nothing can quiet a room like a child in a wheelchair, a seeing eye dog, or an amputee. Stares and whispers are the most common signs of discomfort. Inappropriate gestures and awkward questions are the nervous outcome of many encounters.

And despite the reality that over 50 million Americans have a disability of some type and half of those have a severe disability, you wouldn't know it from reading the morning newspaper or watching the evening news. Over 2 million Americans use wheelchairs as their primary means of mobility, but months can go by without a wheelchair appearing in a newspaper photograph or on the set of a TV news program, local or national.

The most likely reason for this lack of coverage is that reporters, editors, and news directors aren't comfortable with the subject or simply don't think of disability as a factor in their efforts to be inclusive. With exceptions, of course, they likely do not have a disability, nor do they know anyone with a disability. The media they grew up with underreported people with disabilities, and they are perpetuating that same lack of inclusiveness. Ignorance, in a very real sense, begets ignorance.

The Language of Disability

Tampa Tribune reporter Vicky Beck, who is a wheelchair user, commented on the FDR memorial: "We finally have a statue of FDR in his wheelchair. It took — what? — 50 years for this country to become even close to comfortable with that image of a national leader. We may have become used to images of people with disabilities, but still trip over our tongues when we search for words to describe them. Unfortunately, words are all we have — and the choices can get strange."

While a number of euphemisms have come into common use in an era of political correctness, Beck says the clear, simple, direct words are the best. "People with disabilities are just that," she said, "people with disabilities. They are not special, differently able, handicapable, exceptional, afflicted, or victims. She adds that *challenged* or *physically challenged* and *handicapped* also are words that should not be used in describing people with disabilities.

Similarly, a style guide published by the National Center on Disability and Journalism states that phrases such as *afflicted with, stricken with, suffers from,* and *victim of* all suggest that people with disabilities are living a reduced quality of life. "Not every person with a disability suffers, is a victim, or is stricken. Simply state the facts about the nature of the person's disability. For example, 'He has muscular dystrophy,' not 'He suffers from (or is a victim of) muscular dystrophy.'"[228]

As Vickie Beck said: "Overall, most of us who are disabled are just trying to live our lives as best we can and do not feel as if we are afflicted or suffering. There are difficult days and issues, but that is true of everyone."[229]

Other words to avoid: birth defect (defect, defective), cripple (crippled, crippled with), deaf-dumb, deaf-mute (dumb, mute), invalid, lame, loon (loony, loony bin), midget, nuts, spastic, veg (vegetable, vegetative state). Though it may be the case that among friends, people with disabilities sometimes use terms like *gimp* or *cripple,* they are terms of familiarity in those limited situations and should not be used in any general sense.

While the phrase *disabled person* is sometimes used and is acceptable among some, the preferred usage is *person with a disability* in that it puts the emphasis on the person and not the disability. Do, however, avoid using *disabled* as a collective noun: "The disabled support increasing fines for parking violations." Where possible, substitute the word *disabled* even in commonly accepted phrases such as *handicapped parking.* Instead, use *parking for disabled people* or better yet *parking for people with disabilities.*[230] In an article headlined "School Board Settles Lawsuit: It Has a Plan to Address Disabled Access," the *Richmond Times-Dispatch* gets it right and wrong:

> The remediations called for in the settlement range from accessible playgrounds to elevators. Some schools lack adequate handicap parking and wheelchair ramps.

Definitions of disability status[239]

Individuals aged 15 and older were identified as having a disability if they met *any* of the following criteria:

1. Used a wheelchair, a cane, crutches, or a walker.

2. Had difficulty performing one or more functional activities (seeing, hearing, speaking, lifting or carrying, using stairs, walking, or grasping small objects).

3. Had difficulty with one or more *activities of daily living* (includes, getting in or out of bed or a chair, bathing, dressing, eating, and toileting).

4. Had difficulty with one or more *instrumental activities of daily living* (the IADLs include going outside the home, keeping track of money and bills, preparing meals, doing light housework, taking prescription medicines in the right amount at the right time, and using the telephone).

5. Had one or more specified conditions (a learning disability, mental retardation, or another developmental disability; Alzheimer's disease; or some other type of mental or emotional condition).

6. Had any other mental or emotional condition that seriously interfered with everyday activities.

7. Had a condition that limited the ability to work around the house.

8. If age 16 to 67, had a condition that made it difficult to work at a job or business.

9. Received federal benefits based on an inability to work.

Individuals were considered to have a severe disability if they met criterion 1, 6, or 9; or had Alzheimer's disease or mental retardation or another developmental disability; or were unable to perform or needed help to perform one or more of the activities in criterion 2, 3, 4, 7, or 8.

The plaintiff lost both legs during the Vietnam War and uses a wheelchair, according to court documents.[231]

Finally, as with all discussions of difference, use the distinguishing characteristic only when it is relevant to the story. If doing a story about wheelchair access to city transportation, and you are reporting the experiences of people with disabilities, then there is an obvious need to identify people with specific disabilities. However, if you are doing a story on award winners in a local chili cook-off, and one of the winners happens to be a wheelchair user, there is no reason to include that in the story. If you are unsure in a particular situation, consult with the source or subject of the story in question.

Tips for Reporting on People with Disabilities

The American Disabilities Act of 1990 defines disability as a physical or mental impairment that substantially limits one or more major life activities. According to the United States Census Bureau, in 1997, 52.6 million people (19.7 percent of the population) had some level of disability, and 33 million (12.3 percent of the population) had a severe disability. Other findings from the report issued in February 2001 are as follows:

■ Among the population 15 years old and over, 2.2 million used a wheelchair. Another 6.4 million used some other ambulatory aid such as a cane, crutches, or a walker.

■ About 7.7 million individuals 15 years old and over had difficulty seeing the words and letters in ordinary newspaper print; of them, 1.8 million were unable to see.

■ The poverty rate among the population 25 to 64 years old with no disability was 8.3 percent; it was 27.9 percent for those with a severe disability.

■ The likelihood of having a disability varies by race and origin. For all ages, the prevalence of severe disability was 8.5 percent for Asians and Pacific Islanders, 9.7 percent for Hispanics, 12.2 percent for non-Hispanic whites, and 15.7 percent for blacks.[232]

Like everyone else, people with disabilities want to be allowed to live their lives without being shunned, pitied, or spotlighted as heroic action figures who have overcome their disabilities to lead purposeful lives. Following are a few commonsense tips for covering people with disabilities. Many of the tips are from the very fine "Tips for Journalists: Interviewing People with Disabilities," published by the National Center on Disability and Journalism.

■ People use wheelchairs. Refer to them, when relevant to the story, as a person who uses a wheelchair or a person who is a wheelchair-user. Do not use phrases such as *confined to a wheelchair* or *wheelchair bound*.

■ Respect people's wheelchairs, walkers, and other mobility aids. Don't move or handle without permission. On wheelchair etiquette, Vicky Beck says, "Don't lean on my chair; don't ask how fast it can go; and don't push me without asking."

■ Avoid depicting people with disabilities as heroic, courageous, inspiring, and the like because they have a disability. It is a way of romanticizing something that is not romantic. By the same token, avoid using phrases like *overcame* or *succeeded in spite of her disability*. Such usage implies that it is surprising that a person with a disability could succeed without some sort of superhuman intervention.[233]

■ If possible, when interviewing, filming, or taking a sound bite from someone in a wheelchair, arrange to be seated at eye level with the person being interviewed. Before an interview, check with the interviewee to see if he needs any specific accommodation (wheelchair access, quiet place, interpreter, and so forth). When you are interviewing a person with a disability, you should speak directly to her and maintain eye contact rather than with an interpreter or companion.[234]

■ When talking with a person with a hearing loss, be sure to face him, and do not cover your mouth when you speak. Place yourself so that you face the light source and are not backlit. Make sure you talk when the person is looking at you.

■ When meeting an interviewee who has a visual impairment, identify yourself and others who may be with you. When talking in a group, be sure to identify the person to whom you are speaking.

■ Listen attentively when you are talking with a person who has difficulty speaking. Be patient and wait for the person to finish rather than correcting or speaking for her. Never pretend to understand if you are having difficulty doing so. Instead, repeat what you have understood and allow the person to respond.

■ When covering an event where a sign or oral interpreter is present, be aware of the communication between an interpreter or real-time captioner and the person using their services. Avoid walking between them or blocking their communication while taking a photograph. Often people who use interpreters are located near the front in a designated section. Remember, blocking this communication is like pulling the plug on the public address system.[235]

■ Focus on the person you are interviewing, not the disability. Shake hands when greeting a person with a disability just as you would anyone. If you offer assistance, wait until the offer is accepted.[236]

■ Avoid making eye contact, praising, or petting service animals and guide dogs. They are probably working when you encounter them.

■ Do be inclusive regarding people with disabilities. Include them as sources and as subjects in routine stories: children on the playground, people at the mall, parents attending school functions, speakers at events not related to disability issues, couples living normal lives.

■ Do be proactive regarding stories about disabilities. Send a reporter out to a local grocery store in a wheelchair and report on how difficult it is to shop; highlight the pharmacy that builds aisles and shelves making all products accessible to all people; do articles on new products and services that may improve the lives of a significant population of people with disabilities.

■ Be proactive in learning as much as you possibly can about disability and people with disabilities. Begin with secondary resources. Read. Talk with experts. Students can meet with their campus coordinator of disability services. Professionals can talk with local social service organizations that provide services to people with disabilities. Attend conferences featuring sessions on media and disability. Meet and talk with people who have disabilities. Ask them about media coverage, how it could be better. Participate in activities that expose you to the difficulties and frustrations of people who have disabilities.

Writing for the *Spinal Network*, Kathryn Coffin, a program coordinator on disability issues, says, "The way we use language affects the way people think and believe about other people, ideas and things. If we use language that values people, affirms people, language that is positive about them, we can shape attitudes and thinking about those people."[237]

Reminding media managers of the importance of incorporating people with disabilities into the newsroom, Vickie Beck says: "Journalists with disabilities can help create more balanced coverage. Readers benefit because they get a clearer picture of a large segment of the population, what their needs are and why certain laws exist to assist them. As the news industry continues to discuss diversity and reaching undercovered communities, journalists with disabilities may be the only voice reminding the newsrooms that diversity means more than just race and ethnicity."[238]

All reporters, editors, news directors, and producers, not just those with disabilities, have an obligation to help bring disability out of the closet as a difference that affects how people live their daily lives, not who they are.

Following are a few of the more common terms used and misused in reference to people with disabilities. Additional terms may be found in various stylebooks, including an excel-

Getting the Right Words

lent guide published by the National Center on Disability and Journalism.

Afflicted with, suffers from, victim of — avoid the assumption that every person with a disability "suffers" or is a "victim."

Birth defect — avoid; when appropriate, use "born with a disability" or "person who has had a disability since birth."

Blind — adjective; describes a person with complete vision loss; a person may be legally blind but still have some vision. When appropriate to refer to the disability of those who are not totally blind, use "visually impaired" or "partially sighted."

Confined to a wheelchair — avoid; people with disabilities who "use wheelchairs" don't think of themselves as being confined; in fact, a wheelchair provides mobility.

Cripple, crippled — avoid; if necessary to describe a person's disability, use an accurate description: "walks with assistance" or "uses a wheelchair."

Deaf — adjective; refers to a person with total or near complete hearing loss. Those whose hearing loss is not as advanced may, when appropriate, be referred to as "hearing impaired," "hard of hearing," or having a "hearing loss."

Deaf-dumb, deaf-mute — avoid; these terms have a negative connotation.

Deformed — avoid; has negative connotation; if necessary, describe the specific disability.

Differently abled, handi-capable — avoid

trendy terms such as these and others like "physically challenged" and "inconvenienced". "Person with a disability" is preferred.

Disabled, disability — preferred terms; when possible use "person with a disability" rather than "disabled person."

Fit — seizure is preferred.

Guide dogs — also called assistance animals, service animals, and Seeing Eye (registered trademark) dogs.

Handicap, handicapped — avoid due to the negative connotation ; "disability" or "person with a disability" is preferred; replace even terms like "handicap parking" or "handicap seating" with "parking" or "seating for people with disabilities."

Infantile paralysis — polio.

Invalid — avoid; pejorative term that refers to someone with a disability.

Lame — avoid when referring to a person.

Little person — refers to a person of short stature; avoid dwarf or midget; avoid the trendy "vertically challenged"; if necessary to refer to the height of a person of short stature, ask for his preference.

NCDJ — National Center on Disability and Journalism; its stated mission is to work with journalists and educators about disability reporting issues in order to produce more accurate, fair, and diverse news reporting.

Nondisabled — reference, if necessary, to a person who does not have a disability; avoid the trendy "temporarily abled."

Special, special needs — avoid when referring to people with disabilities.

Wheelchair — when necessary to the story, refer to a person as one who "uses a wheelchair" rather than as being "wheelchair bound" or "confined to a wheelchair."

Chapter Thirteen

Covering Other "Isms" of Diversity

The best advice is to never make assumptions about anything. People don't quit having sex when they turn 60 or 70 or even 80. Not all Christians swear off an occasional glass of beer or wine. Not all Christians are "born again." Not all born again Christians are fundamentalist or evangelical. Not all people of faith are Christian. People of all socioeconomic backgrounds do not aspire to be Bill Gates or Donald Trump. Everyone who is poor does not live in a trailer. Everyone living in a trailer is not poor. People under 18 and over 65 are not the cause of all traffic accidents. Not all adoptees spend years of their lives searching for their biological parents.

The homeless are not all dirty alcoholics with tattered clothing, greasy hair, and bad teeth. In fact, many of the people encountered at the local homeless shelter may look just like a typical reporter sitting in a newsroom. On the street or in a mall, you probably wouldn't know the difference. It's the assumption that creates the stereotype that most people hold. Imagine this scenario. It's Thanksgiving or Christmas. The assignment editor sends a reporter and photographer to the local Good Shepherd kitchen to get a cover photo or footage for a holiday news show.

On arrival the reporter finds an assortment of people. There are several older people, seniors. They wear decent clothes, tennis shoes, and have lots of good stories to tell. There are a couple of younger men in jeans and sweatshirts from a local university. They look as if they could be almost anyone on a weekend off.

Over at a table in a corner sit two small children eating as if they haven't had a meal in two days. They both are dressed in old sweatpants and nonmatching t-shirts with faded lettering and tears at the collar and sleeves. A very young, skinny mom is dressed in a cheap department store outfit and a worn man's sweater. Her hair is tangled. The three are anything but clean. They look and smell as if they may have slept on the streets for the past several nights.

Odds are the news team will go back to the office with photos or footage of the dirty kids and skinny mom. They look the part. They're what the editor has in mind. They're what the audience expects. Job well done. Another stereotype reinforced by a media organization taking the easy way out.

Wouldn't it be better to do a piece about homelessness that surprises, even educates a few people? Wouldn't it be better to write or talk about all the people who are at the shelter, including those who aren't alcoholics or drug users? How about people who lost factory jobs because of a bad economy or outsourcing, or those who were just barely getting by before bad luck pushed them over the line? Wouldn't it be better to break the stereotype and feature one of the men who looks as if he's on a weekend camping trip? How'd he get here? What's his story? The audience might get a different view of homelessness.

Although there are doubtless endless possibilities when considering societal isms, this final chapter on covering difference in the evolving community will focus on faithism, ageism, and classism. The grouping of these particular issues into one chapter does not imply that they are any less important than other issues. To those people affected by discrimination based on age or class or faith, they are every bit as important. Neither is the exclusion of other possible isms intended to be a statement on the difficulties or challenges of being short, tall, obese, bald, a low talker, a fast walker, or any other way an individual might differ from the established norm.

Covering Religion

Google "world religions," and the popular Internet browser spits out 26 million possibilities. Type in "God," and an immediate resource of over 172 million sites is displayed, just in case you have the next several years to run through them all. Interestingly, the major religions of the world yield the following results when Googled: Christianity, 36.1 million sites; Islam, 55 million; Buddhism, 15.2 million; Hinduism, 6.6 million; and Judaism, 16.5 million.

Although those figures tend to change, sometimes drastically, from month to month and vary widely depending on the browser used, they do provide an indication of the level of interest in the major religions. Obviously these figures do not reflect the actual memberships of the major religions, but perhaps they do support the general belief that while Christianity is still by far the most popular religion in the world with over 2.1 billion members, it is declining; and Islam, with over 1.3 billion members, is growing. Similarly, while there appears to be more Internet interest in Buddhism than in Hinduism, there are some 828 million Hindus in the world compared to only 364 million Buddhists.[240]

Note, too, the level of interest in Judaism, third on Google after Christianity and Islam, though it ranks twelfth in numbers with an estimated 14 million adherents worldwide. It is the second largest organized religion in the United States with nearly 3.9 million members (1.3 percent of the population) behind Christianity with 224.4 million members (76.5 percent of the population). The abundance of Internet sites related to Judaism reflects its popular interest and obviously its importance from a media perspective.

Finally, in terms of raw numbers, 16 percent of the world population, about 1.1 billion people, are categorized as secular, nonreligious, atheist, or agnostic. In the United States alone, that figure is about 14.1 percent or 41.3 million people.

Wars in the Middle East have brought religion, particularly Islam, back onto the front page. *ReligionLink* editor Diane Connolly writes, "While religion was once the domain of a lone newsroom reporter whose stories were destined for the church page, it is now a potent force in stories about terrorism, schools, sexual abuse, civil rights, entertainment, social services and more." She warns about missing the religious angle in any story:

> All reporters should take notice. Why? Because if they ignore the way faith shapes people's actions, they're missing a critical part of the story. Religion is one of the most powerful and unpredictable forces in the world. It brings out the very best and the very worst in people. And it binds and divides people in the deepest ways imaginable. That makes for compelling stories.[241]

Terry Mattingly, author of a weekly "On Religion" column for the Scripps Howard News Service, writes, "I am convinced that issues related to religion, faith, and morality remain at the heart of many clashes between journalists and their readers, a source of misunderstanding and lost opportunities for understanding."[242]

Covering religion requires the same level of training and dedication as covering issues related to race or ethnicity or sexual orientation or any of the other differences discussed here. Mattingly says the road to improving coverage of religion is for news professionals to do the same things they would do to improve coverage of other areas: "They should hire qualified specialty reporters who have demonstrated a commitment to the beat and then give these reporters the time and space necessary to do their jobs."[243]

Following are some tips for covering religion better based on an article by David Crumm, religion writer for the *Detroit Free Press*:

■ Do your homework. Explore alternative religious media, including *Christianity Today*, the *Christian Century*, *Parabola*, *Tikkun*, and *Hinduism Today*. Explore religion on the Internet, including the Religion Newswriters Association website www.rna.org and its companion sites www.religionwriters.com and www.religionlink.org.

■ Double check every detail. Words like baptism, sanctuary, mass, and prayer can vary drastically in meaning from one church to another.

■ Use caution in quoting an expert in one faith about other faiths. Crumm writes: "It's stunning to realize how little scholars in one faith tradition know about other faiths. Just because they're bishops, or academics, or authors doesn't mean they know much outside their own disciplines."

■ Don't assume that a particular religious leader speaks for all of his or her members or that all members of a particular religious belief follow all of the established traditions of faith.[244]

Following are additional suggestions included in a 2003 *Poynter Report* article by Diane Connolly:

■ Be timely, but don't worry too much about time pegs. With religion, some of the best stories result from following up later to find out what effect a vote, a change in leadership, or a new policy had on real people's lives.

■ When possible, be local and national. Localize national stories and connect local events with national trends. When parents in a local school district complain that an elementary school is allowing a religious group to meet in its facilities after school, see what's happening nationally. Have there been court cases about the issue? If a student is being prevented from reading a prayer at graduation in a high school three states away, find out what the policy is in your school district.

■ There is no such thing as a sacred cow. Question everything. While it is important to treat faith groups with respect, reporters should never skip questions or background checks just because they're dealing with religious issues or people.

■ Treat everyone's beliefs with fairness and respect, even if you disagree with them.[245]

■ While every news organization can't afford to have a position designated as a religion beat, every reporter, editor, and news director can ensure better reporting on religious issues by becoming better educated and more aware. Whether it's sexual scandals among Catholic priests, the integration of gay and lesbian ministers into more progressive churches, campaigns against gay marriage by more fundamental churches, or the death of a pope, religion is an increasingly important fixture in the daily news. It is imperative that media practitioners be prepared to cover it.

Ageism and Media Today

Ageism is a chronic and consistent problem in today's society. People much past 55 generally are portrayed as Viagra users, denture wearers, bingo players, targets for term life insurance, and wrinkled castaways who while away their days in a trailer park in Florida wondering just when the dreaded Alzheimer's will strike. Every good sitcom has to have a cranky old couple to make jokes about sex and memory loss. The stereotype of silver-haired couples playing tennis and golf, dining in fancy restaurants, or walking barefoot on the beach, sweaters tied around the waists, staring wistfully out to sea plays over and over in all kinds of magazine ads.

The baby boomer story appears and reappears. It's coming. It will have a significant impact on the workforce, housing selection, healthcare, leisure time opportunities, government programs, and on and on. Yes, it is an interesting story and should be reported regularly. At the time of the 2000 census, for example, 35 million or 12 percent of the U.S. population were age 65 and over. The median age had increased from 32.9 to 35.3 in only ten years. Baby boomers (people born between 1946 and 1964) represented a whopping 28 percent of the total population.[246] Senior living, independent living, and assisted living complexes as well as nursing homes are being built and filling at an increasingly rapid pace. Public relations, marketing, and advertising are awakening to the profit possibilities.

But there's more to the story than numbers, economic impact, and marketing strategy. Like stories on the browning of America or the coming of a minority majority, the graying America story lacks the personal element. It leaves out people. Who are the people behind the statistics? What do they do? What do they hope for in the future? They are story subjects, sources, and resources. They are news stories and features and human interest stories. They are stories of success and triumph and celebration. And they are stories of sadness and sorrow.

Following are tips for reporting on seniors:

■ Don't make the mistake of treating all senior citizens as though they are the same. They are not. Seniors are of every race and ethnicity, of varying class and economic backgrounds, and of differing sexual orientations. They come from the farm and the city. They are Arab American and Amerasian. They are gay, lesbian, bisexual, and transgender. They are poor, middle class, and wealthy. Stories should reflect that diversity when it is appropriate.

■ As with other targeted populations, don't assume that because a particular senior is vocal or visual that he speaks for all seniors. Seniors are not all of one mind. Even the AARP, though it represents itself as the voice of seniors, does not represent the views of everyone who is past 55 years old.

■ Surf the senior websites, especially AARP.com, for information on current events and issues of relevance to seniors. Become acquainted with senior, retirement, and health magazines to learn more about issues and the language of seniors.

■ Avoid the stereotypes. Every senior story is not a health crisis or Medicare story. Neither should every story about seniors feature a 90-year-old marathon runner or a birthday story on a centenarian. Not that those aren't good stories. They are. But reporting should go beyond the extremes.

■ When interviewing an older person, accommodate obvious special needs, but don't assume every senior has a hearing difficulty. And do not speak to a senior as though she were a child or cute or sweet. While some may like the tease, others will be offended.

■ While most working-age Americans identify who they are as what they do for a living, many if not most seniors don't identify themselves that way. And while that in itself is an interesting story, it also is a cue to not dwell on the fact that one is a retired pharmacist or school teacher or assembly-line worker. Ask what a person does now, what he enjoys, what he wants the world to know about him.

■ Become familiar with local social services for seniors. Spend a day at an activity center. Get to know the directors of local senior apartments and assisted living centers. Arrange for interviews or visits with a variety of seniors just to talk about how seniors are portrayed in news media.

■ Seniors are a tremendous resource for historical perspectives on most any topic from the economy to military affairs, and a source of reactions on any current issues. A little research and an effort to make connections should yield good results.

Covering Class and Poverty

According to U.S. Department of Health & Human Services Poverty Guidelines, a family of four earning less than $19,350 per year lives in poverty.[247] The U.S. Census Bureau's 2003 report on poverty listed the poverty rate in the United States at 12.5 percent or nearly 36 million people living below the poverty threshold at that time. At the same time, over 45 million people lived without health insurance.

Poverty rates broken down by race and ethnicity looked like this:

Non-Hispanic whites	8.2%
Blacks	24.4
Asians	11.8
Hispanics	22.5
American Indians	23.2

The states of Arkansas, New Mexico, Mississippi, Louisiana, West Virginia, and the District of Columbia had the highest three-year poverty rates, all averaging 18.5 percent.[248]

In 2000, the average CEO made as much as the combined incomes of 1,223 minimum-wage workers. A member of Congress earned nearly fourteen times that of a minimum-wage worker.[249]

According to a Ford Foundation Project, *For an Economy that Works for All*, policy changes that could help low-wage families include a higher minimum wage, job training, affordable early childcare and education, and access to health insurance. The ability to achieve such policy changes is affected by attitudes that, according to the report, are based on a fairly complex and ingrained set of values, perceptions, and experiences that the media in many instances tend to perpetuate. Some of those perceptions are as follows:

■ Anyone can achieve great wealth with hard work and good luck.

■ Many people on welfare don't want to work.

■ Poverty is, at least partially, the fault of the poor person.

■ Poverty is a given — there always will be poor people.

The Ford Foundation report states: "Most coverage [of the poor] is framed in terms of sympathy for the poor and entails telling compelling personal stories. The sympathy frame provokes a charity response, not systemic change. Compelling personal stories focus readers on what is wrong with and how to 'fix' the person in the story, not on fixing the broken system."[251]

Reporters are encouraged to frame stories on poverty in a way that will contribute to solving the problem rather than simply generating pity. For example, the report says, "Stories about individuals who 'make it' reinforce the problematic notion that anyone can make it if they try hard enough." Other examples of how frames affect stories on low-wage workers:

■ Stories about individuals who fail to get a decent paying job or support their families financially lead people to focus on individual reasons for that failure, such as drug use, bad marriages, dropping out of school, or teen childbirth.

■ Stories about government incompetence and how various government policies have made matters worse can lead many readers to conclude that government should not play a role in solving the problems of poverty and low-wage work.

■ Stories about poverty also run headlong into the obstacle of the strongly held view that poverty is part of the natural order.[252]

Focus on the economy and jobs rather than the poor or working poor, on inadequate wages as opposed to not wanting to work or not working hard enough, and on system failures rather than individual failures.

And avoid the stereotypes. Dirty children, old men in torn blankets on park benches, and hobos gathered around a fire under a busy cloverleaf may make good copy, but they are not necessarily representative of the nation's poor. Poverty is a social and systematic problem that cripples the present and future of millions of people in a land of affluence. Good journalism should contribute to the solution rather than the problem.

Still More "isms"

Anytime an individual's difference is used, intentionally or not, to distinguish him from others, a possibility of framing or profiling or stereotyping is created. It is obvious when it is race or ethnicity: "The woman was attacked by an unidentified college-aged black man." College-aged black men in the community beware. You've been profiled. It may be less obvious when it is something else: "He was identified as a Southern Baptist." Images of a fundamentalist or evangelical. "He was described as a loner. He is a Vietnam veteran." Brings to mind crazed veterans suffering postwar stress syndrome. "The 19-year-old runaway, adopted when she was an infant, was arrested for shoplifting." Right, those adoptees. They're all maladjusted. Wait long enough and they'll get into trouble. "Deadheads." Drugged-up groupies of the Grateful Dead.

Here's some final advice on covering people with difference. Don't make assumptions. (Yes, you've heard that before.) Don't perpetuate pointless stereotypes. There is absolutely no reason to ever identify someone as adopted, unless it is a story about adoption: "Wendy's founder Dave Thomas, himself adopted, created a foundation that raised millions of dollars for causes related to adoption." Avoid regional labels, which suggest a negative connotation: Yankee, for example.

Avoid any and all language that implies a difference unless the difference is important to the story.

Getting the Right Words

Following are terms related to those topics, including the coverage of faith, class, poverty, and senior citizens.

Ageism — discrimination or prejudice against people based on age.

Agnostic — a person who believes that, at our present level of knowledge, we cannot know whether or not a God exists.

Anti-Semitism — hatred toward Jews; discrimination or prejudice against people because of their belief in Judaism.

Atheist — someone who does not believe in the existence of God or other deities.

Blue collar — refers to a manual laborer, usually one who works for wages as opposed to a set salary or commission.

Born Again Christian — a person who has repented of his sins and accepted Jesus as Lord and Savior. Conservative Protestants believe that this is the only way one can get to heaven. Some of these denominations do not require that a person repent first.

Classism — discrimination or prejudice against people based on economic or social class.

Disadvantaged — social class of people who are historically oppressed because of a lack of economic, social, and political power.

Evangelical — strong believer; one who is zealous in her support of the Christian religion and extremely eager to have other people share her beliefs.

Faithism — discrimination or prejudice against someone based on faith or religious belief or nonbelief.

Fundamentalist — one who believes in strict adherence to the basic beliefs of a faith; often associated with the Evangelical Christian movement.

Inner city — avoid this and other stereotypical references to poor communities of color.

Minimum wage — the minimum amount required by the federal Fair Labor Standards Act for qualifying employees; currently $5.15 per hour. A person earning minimum wage and working forty hours per week with no time off would make $10,712 in a year.

Mosque — Muslim place of worship.

Muslim — a follower of the Islam belief, the second largest religion in the world; all Muslims are not Arabs, and not all Arabs or Arab Americans are Muslim.

Poverty — according to the U.S. Department of Health and Human Services, a person who earns less than $9,310 or a family of four earning less than $18,850 would fall below the poverty threshold.

Religion — an organized system of beliefs by which someone lives; usually associated with a belief in the existence of a divine power.

Synagogue — Jewish house of prayer; place of worship and communal center for followers of Judaism.

Part Three

Activities, Assignments, and Resources to Improve Diversity Reporting

The days of a talking head lecturing students for 50 minutes and expecting them to retain much of anything are long gone. *Active learning, collaborative, engaged, experiential.* Those are the new buzzwords. Pedagogical evidence is fairly clear that when learners take an active role in the process, when they work together, when they experience what is being taught, when they become stakeholders, they learn more quickly and retain what they learn for a longer time.

A teacher could lecture for hours about how it feels to have a severe physical disability in a society dominated by people with healthy bodies, but those who have never experienced the stares, whispers, and hardships won't get it. Put the same students in a wheelchair and drop them at a local department store with a shopping list and orders not to get out of the chair for anything, and the learning curve surges upward.

Try to explain how a black student feels walking into a dominantly white classroom on a largely white campus or into a largely white newsroom, and blank stares indicate zero comprehension. Arrange with a professor at a historically black college or university to have white students attend classes for a week. They may resist, but they will learn.

Students and professionals alike will learn how to be better journalists by learning how to deal with their biases; by experiencing what diverse people in their media audiences experience every day; and by connecting with people of color, people of varying economic and social backgrounds, and people of varying sexual orientations. By building partnerships and collaborating with members of the community, by engaging in community issues, and by experiencing the daily lives and routines of the people they cover, they will become better reporters, editors, and news managers.

The activities and exercises included in Part Three are designed to serve a number of functions from ice-breaking in mixed groups to exposing and overcoming personal biases. Some are simple and may be completed in a single class period or workshop session. Others are more involved and may require several sessions. Some exercises require equipment or special supplies. Some may be more or less relevant depending on the location and composition of a particular community.

The activities need not be completed in any particular order. It is important, however, to discuss the exercises in full before completing them and to debrief fully following completion. Some of the exercises will create discomfort among some participants. That is expected and not necessarily a bad thing. However, it is important to always leave the possibility of an "out" or "pass" should a participant resist for personal reasons. The last thing a learning exercise should do is create a bad experience.

Any of the exercises may be changed, shortened, or adapted to fit a particular situation. New exercises may be added to the mix. If you come up with a variation or other new exercises not included here but that work, please let me know so that it can be included in future editions or made available on a website for other learners to use in their training programs.

Finally, learn, enjoy, and become better journalists.

Chapter Fourteen

Exercises to Break the Ice

Anyone who has ever taught school or led a workshop or seminar group knows the toughest part sometimes can be to get people talking, regardless of the topic. The most brilliant and creative schemes can result in stone silence and dead stares. Throw in the diversity angle, and the audience reaction from a convention of mimes might produce more noise.

There are lots of ways, none guaranteed, to get students active and involved from the beginning, and none of them include a 50-lecture. Save the facts and figures for later, after creating some interest. Here are some exercises that can be used to break the ice and get participants talking.

Ten Questions

Members of the group should take some time to write the answers to the following questions. Sitting in a circle, take turns reading the questions and talking about each person's answers.

1. What is the thing you like most about being who you are?

2. What is the thing you like least about being who you are?

3. If you could experience being a person of another race or ethnicity, who would it be and why?

4. In what ways can people be different? List as many as you can.

5. Name something that is different about you.

6. List ways in which that difference has had an effect on you.

7. Has that difference resulted in any negative implications for you?

8. Have you ever been prevented from doing something you wanted to do because of your difference?

9. What do you consider to be the silliest, most stupid, or most unfair assumption about you because of the difference you listed?

10. What one thing do you wish people would notice about you?

Take One Step Forward or Backward

This one has been around for a long time in a number of different formats. It's an easy illustration of the impact of discrimination. Instructors or group members should prepare tags on string or labels for everyone in the group. Write racial, gender, sexual orientation, age, and ethnic designations on each tag or label: Black, Asian, Latino, non-Hispanic White, Male, Female, Gay/Lesbian, over 55, under 55, and so forth. The instructor or group leader should be creative in assigning the labels, making sure no one gets a label that reflects his or her actual race or ethnicity.

If you are on or near a college or high school campus with a football field, take the participants there and have them line up across the 50-yard line facing the home goal. Otherwise, use a cleared room or hallway. Instruct participants, for the sake of the exercise, that they are who the tag says they are. Begin by asking everyone with white male labels to move forward by 10 yards (or two steps in a smaller room setting). Next ask white females to move forward 5 yards (or one step), and white males to move forward another 5 yards. Next ask all Asians to move forward 5 yards, white females another five yards, and white males another 5 yards as well. Next ask all Latinos to move ahead 5 yards, and everyone in front of them to move forward another 5 yards as well. Instruct all blacks to remain on the 50-yard line.

Next, instruct all those who are over 55 years old to move backwards by 5 yards regardless of their race or ethnicity. Then ask everyone who is gay or lesbian to move backwards by 10 yards regardless of age, race, or ethnicity. At this point, participants are spread over 50 yards or so of the field.

Announce that there's a prize or prizes (use gift certificates to a favorite restaurant, for example) under the home goal, and the first person there on the count of "1, 2, 3, go" wins the prize.

Later, back in the classroom, the group should have a discussion about how difference creates an unlevel playing field dictated by race, ethnicity, age, gender, and sexual orientation.

Name That Group

This exercise illustrates the degree to which everyone is continually exposed to stereotypes. Lead students in defining terms such as *stereotyping, prejudice, bigotry, discrimination, racism, oppression, exclusion, right,* and *privilege.*[253]

The instructor should list the following groupings of terms and ask participants to identify and discuss the stereotype being portrayed:

1. athletic, good dancers, lazy (don't work), gold-chain wearing, good singers, like rap music, have lots of kids, criminals, good basketball players, aggressive, cliquish, on welfare, drink malt liquor, love soul fool

2. dumb, lazy in school, sexually active, stupid, healthy, dedicated, greedy, rich, sleep around, strong, body odor, mean and vain, on steroids, get special treatment

3. have fun, weight conscious, sex objects, easy, dumb, sleep around, cheerleaders, conceited, airheads, materialistic, big breasts, fake, shallow, naive

4. affectionate, have fun, laid back, smoke weed, talk fast, steal, work cheap, religious, family oriented, dirty, mechanics, migrant workers, smell bad, carry guns, drive gaudy cars, low riders

5. can't drive, penny pinchers, stubborn, child-like, slow, go to bed early, don't have sex, can't see, poor memory, paranoid, wise, senile, overly conservative, always cold, can't hear, can't take care of themselves

6. racist, drive pick-ups, drink beer, live in trailers, heavy accents, wear boots, dumb, hunt deer, line dance, like country music, work in factories, wear cowboy hats, love confederate flag, chew tobacco, get into fights

7. short, computer skilled, studious, smart, eat weird foods (raw fish), intelligent, gymnasts, good at math, good at karate, smell bad, bad drivers, good at business, hard working, good financial planners

8. love to party, heavy drinkers, dreamers, risk takers, self-centered, insecure, know-it-all, drive too fast, studious, grade conscious, sexually active, defy authority, expect life to be easy, always broke, want to be rich, late sleepers

Answers: 1. African-American males 2. Athletes 3. Blondes 4. Hispanics 5. Elderly 6. Southern rednecks 7. Asians 8. College students

Racial Passing and Privilege

The racial passing exercise was created by Peggy McIntosh and appeared in her classic article "White Privilege: Unpacking the Invisible Knapsack." It is an excellent exercise in helping members of the currently dominant racial group realize the privilege they are granted on the basis of being white. Following is a quote from McIntosh's article that describes the thinking behind the exercise:

Through work to bring materials from Women's Studies into the rest of the curriculum, I have often noticed man's unwillingness to grant that they are over-privileged, even though they may grant that women are disadvantaged . . .

Thinking through unacknowledged male privilege as a phenomenon, I realized that since hierarchies in our society are interlocking, there was most likely a phenomenon of white privilege which was similarly denied and protected. As a white person, I realized that I had been taught about racism as something which puts others at a disadvantage, but had been taught not to see one of its corollary aspects, white privilege, which puts me at an advantage.

I think whites are carefully taught not to recognize white privilege, as males are taught not to recognize male privilege . . . I have come to see white privilege as an invisible package of unearned assets which I can count on cashing in each day, but about which I was meant to remain oblivious. White privilege is like an invisible weightless knapsack of special provisions, maps, passports, codebooks, visas, clothes, tools and blank checks.[254]

As a class exercise, take turns reading from the list of white privileges, add your own and discuss changes in society that may or may not have outdated some of the statements.

The following is a list of conditions a white person can for the most part count on in daily living in the United States (at least in terms of race, if not in terms of sex, class, sexual orientation, age, physical ability, religion, and the like):

1. I can — if I wish to — arrange to be in the company of people of my race most of the time.

2. If I should need to move, I can be pretty sure of renting or purchasing housing in an area that I can afford and I want to live in.

3. I can be pretty sure that my neighbors in such a location will be neutral or pleasant to me.

4. I can go shopping alone most of the time, assured that I will not be followed or harassed.

5. I can turn on the television or open to the front page of the paper and see people of my race widely represented.

6. When I am told about our national heritage or about "civilization," I am shown that people of my color have made it what it is.

7. I can be sure that my children will be given curricular materials that testify to the existence of their race.

8. If I want to, I can be pretty sure of finding a publisher for this piece on white privilege.

9. I can go into a music shop and count on finding the music of my race represented, into the supermarket and find staple foods that fit with my cultural traditions, into a hairdresser's and find someone who can cut my hair.

10. Whether I use checks, credit cards, or cash, I can count on my skin color not to work against the appearance of financial reliability.

11. I can arrange to protect my children most of the time from people who might not like them.

12. I can swear, or dress in secondhand clothes, or not answer letters, without having people attribute these choices to the bad morals, the poverty, or the illiteracy of my race.

13. I can speak in public to a powerful male group without putting my race on trial.

14. I can do well in a challenging situation without being called a credit to my race.

15. I am never asked to speak for all the people of my race.

16. I can remain oblivious of the language and customs of persons of color who constitute the world's majority without feeling in my culture any penalty for such oblivion.

17. I can criticize our government and talk about how much I fear its policies and behavior without being seen as a cultural outsider.

18. I can be pretty sure that if I ask to talk to the person in charge, I will be facing a person of my race.

19. If a traffic cop pulls me over or if the IRS audits my tax return, I can be pretty sure I haven't been singled out because of my race.

20. I can easily buy posters, postcards, picture books, greeting cards, dolls, toys, and children's magazines featuring people of my own race.

21. I can go home from most meetings of organizations I belong to feeling somewhat tied in, rather than isolated, out-of-place, outnumbered, unheard, held at a distance, or feared.

22. I can take a job with an affirmative action employer without having co-workers on the job suspect that I got it because of race.

23. I can choose public accommodation without fearing that people of my race cannot get in or will be mistreated in the places I have chosen.

24. I can be sure that if I need legal or medical help, my race will not work against me.

25. If my day, week, or year is going badly, I need not ask of each negative episode or situation whether it has racial overtones.

26. I can choose blemish cover or bandages in "flesh" colors and have them more or less match my skin.

Conclude by discussing the following statements from the McIntosh article:

To redesign social systems we need first to acknowledge their colossal unseen dimensions. The silences and denials surrounding privilege are the key political tool here. They keep the thinking about equality or equity incomplete, protecting unearned advantage and conferred dominance by making these taboo subjects. Most talk by whites about equal opportunity seems to be about equal opportunity to try to get into a position of dominance while denying that systems of dominance exist.

It seems to me that obliviousness about white advantage, like obliviousness about male advantage, is kept strongly inculturated in the United States so as to maintain the myth of meritocracy, the myth that democratic choice is equally available to all. Keeping most people unaware that freedom of confident action is there for just a small number of people props up those in power, and serves to keep power in the hands of the same groups that have most of it already.

Chapter Fifteen

Listening Posts and Connections

Experience, of course, is a great teacher. And listening is an overpowering resource. Put them together in a listening post experience, and learning is the significant byproduct. Actually, there's really nothing new about the concept of listening posts. Reporters have been doing it forever. Police reporters hang around the station, ride or walk the cop's beat, learn the right coffee shops and diners. Courthouse reporters do the same thing. They learn the people, the filing cabinets, and the court records. Sports reporters hang out in locker rooms, business reporters in the board rooms, and education reporters on the school grounds. The better the reporter knows how to listen, the better the reporter.

But the police beat, the courthouse, and the donut shop are good only for developing the traditional sources, the routine of journalism as Poynter's Keith Woods calls it. To go outside the unusual, to report the uncovered or undercovered, reporters have to find new listening posts.

And that means leaving the classroom and the office, getting into the neighborhoods of the undercovered, going outside the comfort zone, or breaking out of the campus bubble. Spend a few weeks hanging out at the senior citizen center. Participate in daily activities or help plan a special event. Spend time listening to what the residents are saying. Don't play journalist at this point. Don't ask questions. Just listen.

The emerging Hispanic community is on everyone's mind. In communities across the country, as their numbers grow, Hispanic people are becoming an important economic reality to businesses and advertisers. They are undercovered and need to be brought into the media audience. As in any beat coverage, the first step is research. The reporter must get out into the community. Drive. Locate Hispanic businesses, concentrations of Hispanic residents, where they shop. Draw a map. Get out and walk around. Eat at a local Mexican or Honduran restaurant. Mark potential listening posts on your map, including community centers, day-care centers, churches, even street corners.

Following is a listening post assignment as described by Keith Woods at the Poynter Institute. Woods designed a project called "Making Connections," in which reporters were sent out into the community with the primary goal of uncovering new story ideas. They visited an Asian Community Center, a Muslim cultural complex, a leather factory that employed a large number of Bosnian, Mexican, and Cambodian immigrants, a seafood processing plant, and a neighborhood funeral home. They observed, listened, and finally asked questions.

Listening Post Learning Experience[255]

Send reporters or students out to establish contact with one or more listening posts. Here's one set of criteria for their choices:

1. It must be a place where you are not likely to go otherwise.

2. It should include a group of people who are poorly understood or poorly covered by the media.

3. It should offer a window onto a community of people who might provide information on the group beyond people who come there.

Give the participants a set of questions to answer while at the listening post:

1. Who comes here?

2. What can I learn about the community from this place?

3. What stories might I do about this place, the people who come here, or the things I've learned from looking around?

4. How might the people I encounter here fit into my (and my organization's) everyday coverage of other beats?

A number of things may come from the day(s) out. Spend some time debriefing the exercise in class, discussing not just what you learned, but how you felt. Put the information into an essay, or write it in a journal kept during the class.

Students also could be required to produce stories from the listening post. They could be asked to use sources found at the listening posts in stories unrelated to that place. They might be asked to write a few descriptive paragraphs for a feature-writing class or project, produce a source list for a beginning newswriting class, or analyze the way the group is portrayed as an advanced assignment.

This exercise strikes at many levels of diversity. It raises awareness, often in introducing students for the first time to a group of people, a faith, a condition — whatever the source of difference being explored. It informs, providing primary (though very limited) information to the students, information that will have immediate applications in their assignments. Talking to Muslims at a mosque demystifies the faith, expands the student's vocabulary, and makes it all the harder to stereotype or demonize a whole group of people. It energizes often abstract discussions about story ideas or ethics or diversity.

A conversation with students should probe for any or all of these results, reinforcing and expanding the learning by the degree to which students shared similar experiences or added new perspectives for the class's consumption.

This exercise offers a good opportunity to reconcile one of the abiding dichotomies of diversity; undercovered people want to be treated no differently from anyone else, but they want their differences recognized by the media. This exercise emphasizes the ordinary nature of beat reporting while demonstrating the need for — and advantage of — going to places no one else goes. It contributes to sensitizing journalism students to the world around them, helps reporters and photojournalists improve the range of their coverage, helps copy editors know more about the names and places that will be mentioned in stories or the language usually associated with a particular group.

Pushing the Edges

Ruth Seymour at Wayne State University conducted a similar long-term project called "Pushing the Edges." The project paired community and journalism fellows who promised to spend time getting to know the other side. Journalists spent time in the community where they dug city gardens, did routine office work at Arab community agencies, and served as greeters at a gay and lesbian community center. Community fellows spent an equal amount of time working in newspaper and broadcast newsrooms. In the process, they learned more about each other. Describing the ups and downs of the project, Seymour writes:

> In the 12 months of the fellowship, we delved into many local communities. Because the group was so mixed, this meant that Chicana and Pakistani community activists studied Detroit Jewry, and African American and lesbian journalists learned the basics of Islam. Everyone spent time in wheelchairs. Once, with a panel of Latino community representatives, we brainstormed 105 stories in 90 minutes.
>
> We spent a day in intercultural skills training, and a morning debating media coverage of hate crimes. The hard way, we learned to be wary with the word objectivity. Several days, Journalism Fellows and Community Fellows didn't even come close to seeing eye to eye. But throughout it probably helped that we sat in one unbroken circle upon the advice of Native Americans among us. Most of the year, we were pushing the edges of what would be possible to learn and share with strangers.[256]

Although these particular exercises may sound a lot like something that might fit under the umbrella of civic journalism, the distinction is in the overall objective of these and similar projects. They share the goal of civic journalism to mutually engage the community in journalism and journalists in the community. However, the primary goal of the projects conducted by Woods and Seymour was to improve the quality of reporting on diverse communities. The broader goal of civic journalism is to engage the community in the civic process of self-governing.

Listening Post Tips from the Pros

Following are a few tips on conducting a listening post as presented by the Poynter Institute:

Get out of the office. Take a tour of your own city to learn about the diversity. Use public transportation and walk around the neighborhoods.

Expand and nurture your source network. Eat at different restaurants, go to meetings, invite community groups or experts to your paper for brownbag talks.

Be aware of what you put in your newspaper and on the air. Daily stories about a community can show demographic shifts in a city as much as a single, major project.

Resist easy answers in framing and presenting stories. There can be multiple layers to stories, and context is needed for readers and viewers to better understand a community or issue.[257]
Victor Merina

Find organizations and institutions that devote themselves to the ethnic community you are covering. Examples are churches, political groups, social service or business organizations, and college ethnic associations.

Go to local ethnic diners or community centers or a school to meet parents as they pick up their children. You often get more candid comments because people won't feel compelled to promote an organizational opinion about an issue.

To avoid the common problem of representing an ethnic group as a monolith, make sure the organizations you contact represent a variety of interests and viewpoints. If you are doing a story about how Cuban Americans feel about the U.S. trade embargo, you would be wise to reach out to organizations representing Cuban Democrats as well as Cuban Republicans, young U.S.-born Cubans as well as senior citizens.

You need a lot of patience and understanding. Keep in mind that it may take several visits to get some immigrants to truly open up. Many come from countries where the press was a quasi-governmental organ. Immigrants may be leery of speaking to you and puzzled about why you would want their opinions.

The most provocative and evocative quotes are the ones that come from "real people" rather than community leaders. Words from the heart are the ones readers and viewers will remember.

Once you find cooperative "real people," ask them to introduce you to others. Also ask them for story ideas.

If you know a community's language, read the ethnic newspapers and listen to foreign lan-

guage TV and radio programs. They often cover ethnic issues and debates before these issues make mainstream media.[258] *Elizabeth Llorente*

Combining Research and Connection

The first part of this assignment involves secondary research only. In this part of the assignment, the class is divided into groups of from three to five, and each group is assigned to research any of several targeted populations (Asian Americans, people with disabilities, the homeless, African Americans, gays and lesbians, Arab Americans, and others).

The teacher or group leader should select the groups and assign the topics. It is also best to have all the group members operate across differences. So don't assign blacks to groups researching African Americans, or identified gay and lesbian students to a group researching that topic. Assign each group to research the following questions:

1. What is the current status (raw data) of the designated population within the national community?

2. What is the status of the designated population within the newsroom (again, comparative data)?

3. If the goal of having a diverse newsroom is to provide better coverage of the diverse community, what is being done to increase representation of the designated population in newsrooms? List efforts by professional organizations, educational institutions, and individual media companies.

4. Consider the question of numbers versus training. Is the solution to achieve representative diversity within the newsroom, simply to train all reporters to be able to report on diverse communities, or some combination of the two? What are experts saying? Find a variety of voices.

5. What can media do better than they are doing to cover the designated population? What are they doing wrong? What are they doing right? What do reporters, editors, and news managers need to know? Again, survey the literature and find a variety of opinions on the issue.

The second part of the assignment is to make a connection in the community. Students and workshop participants should go into the community to talk to diverse groups of people about news media, to get their views about how good or bad a job media are doing in covering the total community, and to get suggestions about how to make it better.

Ground rule, particularly in the college classroom setting: Students are required to talk to people they don't know. Students assigned to research seniors, for example, can't simply talk to their grandparents. Following are suggested questions:

1. Where do you get most of your news? Daily newspaper, news magazine, television, radio, Internet?

2. Overall, how good of a job do media do in reporting the news? A, B, C, D? Explain your grade. What's good? What's not so good?

3. What kinds of stories in general would you like to see reported that currently are not covered?

4. How good a job do media do in covering issues related specifically to (the targeted population)? A, B, C, D? Explain. What's good? What's not so good?

5. Let's say I'm a reporter in need of story ideas. I want to do more stories about (targeted population). Give me some ideas.

6. I want to write a story about you. What's my angle? What do you want the world to know about you?

7. Do you think it's necessary for stories about a particular community, Hispanics, for example, to be written by a member of the same racial or ethnic group? Why?

8. Could the same thing be accomplished by training reporters to be able to report on all groups within a diverse community? Why or why not?

Incorporating Service into Listening Post Exercises

Another buzz phrase on colleges campuses today is "service learning," which means simply to combine learning with some type of service to the community. In many basic classes, it turns out to be volunteer service, followed by classroom discussion of the value of giving back to the community. In other classes, it might be a direct learning experience: making a brochure or information video for a Boys and Girls Club, designing a newsletter for a local church, or planning and promoting an event to raise money for the Make a Wish Foundation.

Service also can create new listening post opportunities. Serving a meal at a local homeless shelter, for example, gets students or participants involved with the people they need to hear. Serving a Thanksgiving Day dinner or conducting a Christmas Cheer or Santa Claus project for the needy during the Christmas season exposes students to people and lives they would never encounter inside their everyday bubble. Working with Hispanic kids at a community center or helping their parents learn English can offer a view not easily available by just observing.

It's also an easy way to make a connection to assess media performance and generate story ideas. Service connections should be easy to obtain on a campus where there is a volunteer office or a person in charge of service learning. Likewise, it should be relatively easy from the newsroom. Contact any local social service agency for ideas.

It Works

An article from a Knight Ridder company magazine is reprinted on the following pages. The article describes listening post and connections type activities that have worked extremely well at the *San Jose Mercury News* in California. Read the article and discuss how some of the techniques mentioned could be applied in your community.

It works
Strong connection to changing communities produces richer, smarter stories[259]

By Carol Weber Thomas

Reprinted with permission from Knight Ridder News

In a nation so diverse and so fluid that each census paints a new community portrait, newspapers are grappling with how to reach readers from strikingly different backgrounds. "All papers want a strong sense of place," said San Jose Mercury News Editor David Yarnold. "That's just good journalism."

Nowhere is that quest more demanding, or more focused, than at the Mercury News, which covers one of the most diverse markets in the country.

A San Jose high school dropped its football program, a fact reported in one sentence in a prep sports column. End of story? No. Sportswriter Elliot Almond developed a strong piece on the changing face of sports in an Asian-majority school.

El Tri, Mexico's longest running rock act, might have been ignored in the daily paper because it performs only Spanish-language songs. But pop music reporter Brad Kava immersed himself in Spanish to do a better job on his beat. He actually played with the musicians as he got to know them.

A planned one-year-later update on the first babies born in 2002 — one Asian, the other Hispanic — hit a snag when the Asian family couldn't be found. So Viet Mercury, the newspaper's Vietnamese-language publication, asked its readers for help. One put the paper in touch with the family.

"We're a majority-minority community," Yarnold said. "One in every six babies born in Santa Clara County are of mixed race. The name most often given to boy babies in our area is Juan. Fifty-two percent of our population is non-white. This is what America will look like in the future."

Building on a team set up seven years ago, Yarnold has created the newspaper industry's first Race and Demographics department, with a department head, team leader and six reporters. In addition, a dozen satellite reporters from every part of the newsroom volunteer to brainstorm weekly. Their mission: to help look at the community with fresh eyes. Their stories and their suggestions play out in every section of the newspaper.

As part of the effort, all Mercury News reporters were given a week away from regular duties to identify and cultivate more diverse sources in areas they cover.

"Readers want a lot of what we already give them: hard news, investigations, information about schools and health," Yarnold said. "But they want news to be told through people . . . to the extent that people see their communities represented in our pages, they view us as credible. Credibility and coverage are inextricably linked — and therefore vital to our future."

"It's everybody's job to cover these stories," said team leader Anne Vazquez. "We're looking for more sophisticated ways to tell our stories, throughout the paper."

There is no question that attention to diversity is a journalistic life-or-death situation for a newspaper like the Mercury News. The Merc covers an intensely diverse community of Anglos, blacks, Mexicans, Koreans, Vietnamese and others, in one of three states in the nation where so-called minorities are now the majority. (The two other states are Hawaii and New Mexico.)

With that mix, it's critical to hire a staff that reflects the community makeup, and even more critical that reporters and editors really understand the cultural dynamics of their readers.

Newspapers in communities where the change is less dramatic may feel they have less to worry about. But none can disagree that the newspaper is enriched when the news staff really gets to know the community it serves.

"Every community has its subgroups," said Executive Editor Susan Goldberg. "I'm Jewish. I react to some things differently than someone who is Catholic. Women react to and read different things than men. Having a race and demographics focus helps us see the broader picture in all stories."

It also helps find the stories in the first place.

"I talked about the football team at Mission High in one of our satellite diversity meetings and came away with the idea of addressing the issue head on with Asian American students," said Elliot Almond. "The kids were thoughtful and combative in their debate. They didn't have a united front, and offered a variety of insights. I knew I had a story: Mission lost its football program because the school had become predominantly Asian. Asians didn't turn out for football because they were raised competing in things like badminton and ping pong. Asian men also tend to be smaller than American-bred men, and it makes it harder to compete — another issue."

But even that is changing, Almond reported. The school hopes to reactivate its senior football squad some day. Coaches are focusing on students eligible for the junior varsity — younger boys more acclimated to American sports — to start building a team.

"This wasn't simply a sports story," Almond said. "It was a story of social changes and how American institutions are not always relevant to new faces in our country, and how this is not only all right, but something enriching for all of us."

"We are making inroads to readers who weren't on the radar years back," said pop writer Kava. "I started listening to Rock en Español as an intellectual exercise. I thought it would help the newspaper if I had a grasp of it. My first response was that it sounded OK but was alien. Then I hit on El Tri. The music bowled me over. It was as good as U2, the Stones, the Beatles, and I realized that if those groups had recorded in Spanish or Portuguese, most English speakers wouldn't have heard of them either."

His first interview with the group turned into an all-night jam session, with Kava on harmonica. He ended up playing with the group in six cities across the country for a week.

Is all this good for business? Kava received dozens of notes from readers thanking him for covering something so important to them. And a promoter said the fresh approach to Latin music coverage had convinced him to use his Spanish-language advertising budget to buy ads in the Mercury News promoting another act, Shakira.

While the ethnic makeup of the community commands much of the newsroom focus, the staff also is becoming more sensitive to race and gender issues.

A piece on triple-digit homicides in nearby Oakland, which is largely African-American, looked beyond a wide spread perception that the crimes are an issue of race.

"The real story is not about race," said R&D team leader Vasquez. "It's about people killing people. It's much more a socioeconomic issue than race. If you wanted to stereotype, you could say because they are all renters instead of homeowners, it's a renters issue."

Gender is also a focus in San Jose, where 49.3 percent of the population consists of women.

"With the 30th anniversary of Roe v. Wade coming up, we didn't want to rehash all the political arguments for and against abortion," said Vasquez. "We found women who've gone through the experience and have different opinions. One, who had an abortion before Roe v. Wade made it legal, has a hair-raising story. Another had an abortion four or five years ago and now feels abortions shouldn't be allowed."

Vazquez, a Cuban-American from Miami, brings her own life experiences to her job. She helped plan coverage of Elian Gonzalez, the Cuban child who was returned to his father in Havana after his mother drowned while trying to bring him to the United States. To capture the emotion of the story, someone suggested interviewing people in the Latino community.

"But our Latino community is mostly Mexican," Vasquez reminded her colleagues. "Latinos are as differentiated as anyone else. They have different points of view. The Mexicans weren't running from a communist dictator when they came to the United States. They didn't relate to Elian's story. The staff found more empathy in the Vietnamese community, where fleeing for life and freedom was a much bigger issue.

Understanding a community is much more than just acknowledging that groups with different backgrounds exist, Yarnold insists. It's a matter of getting into their minds and hearts to find out just what matters.

Chapter Sixteen

Change in Perspective

Administrators on college and university campuses talk a lot about bursting the bubble. Most students on most campuses fit snugly into a healthy, white, middle to upper-middle class, increasingly female, mold. Most of them have lived in that bubble their entire lives and have little experience with or knowledge of the diverse groups around them. Based on annual figures from ASNE and RTNDA, a similar conclusion could be made about most newsrooms.

Unfortunately, the same sort of bubble can be attributed to many students of color on increasingly exclusive university campuses. Fewer and fewer middle to lower income students can afford to attend either smaller private colleges or major public universities. Therefore, the students of color in the ivy elite often grew up in upper income families and attended private elementary and secondary schools. They arrive on campus with the same limited experiences as everyone else.

Still the natural tendency for everyone is to avoid difference, to seek the shelter of that which is comfortable. Therefore, as described in Beverly Daniel Tatum's *Why Are All the Black Kids Sitting Together in the Cafeteria*, people typically seek out those people who are most like themselves and those situations with which they are most accustomed. Most people tend to maintain distance from those things that are different. With few exceptions, black or Asian students group together in classes, in cafeterias, and in other public gathering places. White students seldom venture into a group of students of color.

For that same reason, students with disabilities seem to be a lonely population on campuses. A student who uses a wheelchair or walking aid or who has some other disability is avoided. They're not avoided because they are bad people but because they are different, because people who have not experienced disability are uncomfortable with those who have.

This exercise calls for a shift in perspective, for students and participants to put themselves into a situation outside their comfort zone, for a day, a week, or even a few hours. This and other perspective exercises allow students to feel the challenges and frustrations of being outside their personal comfort zone.

Although this particular exercise involves the use of wheelchairs as a perspective shift, the same type of exercise could be designed using blindfolds, crutches, or other walking aids; or a totally different type of perspective shift could be assigned. Straight students could be assigned to participate in a gay or lesbian day of silence, or students could be required to take on the life of a homeless person for an assigned period. Be creative. The objective, after all, is to have students experience life outside the bubble.

The perspective shift here is based on an assignment taught by Ruth Seymour at a Poynter Institute diversity seminar.

Perspective Shift — Disability[260]

As assigned by your instructor, choose a partner and plan to meet at a department or grocery store that has wheelchairs available for customers. Make sure the store has a sufficient number of wheelchairs available so that shoppers who need the chairs aren't inconvenienced. You should notify the store manager that you are there and the purpose of the assignment. *(Instructors may want to pre-arrange this assignment, or provide the students with a letter to the store manager, which explains the assignment.)*

Your assignment is to spend a minimum of one hour shopping from the wheelchair. Don't explain the assignment to anyone other than the store manager. A part of the experience is to observe how others react to you, a person with a disability.

Have your partner meet you at your vehicle with the wheelchair and push you during the first half hour. During the second half hour, your partner should leave you alone while you navigate through the aisles without assistance. You should do some actual shopping, try all the aisles, determine if all items are accessible to you or if store workers are available to secure items not reachable, and attempt to use a public restroom.

If possible to do so discreetly, you may shift roles in the store. It would be preferable, however, to go to a different store when you change roles. For example, you could complete half the assignment at K-Mart and the other half up the street at Wal-Mart.

Obviously this limited exercise does not pretend to provide the able-bodied with an experience equivalent to that which persons with disabilities experience on a daily basis. It does, however, provide an opportunity for participants to gauge their own reactions to negotiating from a different perspective. It also provides a chance to generate story ideas. Is the store as accessible as it should be? Are there sufficient chairs? Are store employees available to assist when needed?

Your instructor may ask you to write a reaction paper (about 500 words) about the experience to be shared with the class. Be thorough in describing observations. Include any anxieties you might have had and how you felt at the end of the experience.

Consider the following questions as you write:

1. How did you feel while you were in the wheelchair?

2. How did you feel while pushing or walking beside your partner in the chair?

3. Did you notice behaviors on the part of other people that differ from how they would normally react to you?

4. What did you learn from the experience?

5. What's all this have to do with journalism?

Additional assignment: Your instructor may ask you to keep a log of articles and media images of people with disabilities, to include in class discussion. Record whatever media you happen to read, listen to, or watch, and whatever images of disability appear in that media. Remember that disability includes a broad range of things from deafness and blindness to chronic illnesses like diabetes or asthma. The definition of a physical condition is anything that affects one's ability to perform normal life functions: eating, walking, getting out of bed, driving, writing, standing.

Notes to Instructors:

1. An on-campus variation of this assignment might be to rent wheelchairs and have student pairs or groups spend an entire day or significant part of a day navigating the obstacles on campus to learn about the challenges that wheelchair students face every day. Again, you could use blindfolds or crutches to provide a perspective on other disabilities.

2. Be sensitive! If there are students with disabilities in your class, you might want to discuss the assignment with them before introducing it to the entire class. Be sure they know the intent of the assignment is to make future journalists more aware and more sensitive to issues facing people with disabilities. You should also stress the importance of taking the assignment seriously to your class. No one should get the impression that you or your students are making light of living with a disability.

Chapter Seventeen

Getting at Personal Bias

Bias: an unfair preference for or dislike of something, one that inhibits impartial judgment; **biased**: one who possesses a highly personal or unreasoned distortion of judgment.

Prejudice: opinions based on insufficient knowledge; an unfounded hatred, fear, or mistrust of a person or group, especially one of a particular religion, ethnicity, nationality, or social status.

Much if not all prejudice is the direct result of fear or ignorance. People who experienced Pearl Harbor and were a part of the ensuing wave of hatred for anyone and anything Japanese responded initially based on fear, but allowed the fear to lead them in irrational directions, including the internment of Japanese Americans. Similarly, fear and ignorance led to an anti-Arab American sentiment following the terrorist attack on New York City and Washington in 2001. Hate crimes and civil rights violations against Muslims in the United States continue at an unprecedented rate, resulting directly from rhetoric born of ignorance and fear.

The bias survey and subsequent assignment presented here are designed to expose students to individual biases and help them see how those biases can interfere with their ability to report objectively.

The "Bias" Assignment[261]

Discuss prejudice and realize that everyone, intentional or not, has some sort of bias, and that the best way to deal with bias is to confront it. Students and workshop participants should complete the bias survey anonymously. The survey contains blanks so that students can add target groups that have not been included. Produce a range of numbers indicating different levels of bias from none to extreme. It shouldn't take more than ten minutes or so of class time to complete the survey.

1 . . . . . 2 . . . . . 3 . . . . . 4 . . . . . 5 . . . . . 6 . . . . . 7 . . . . 8 . . . 9 10

Makes me feel nauseated	I have no real feeling	I support
I strongly disagree	I don't care	I feel friendly towards
Makes me angry	I'm neutral	I agree or endorse

We are human and we react to people. It's important to be self-aware of our voluntary and involuntary reactions in order to do our best reporting. Using the scale above, assign a number to the various individuals, according to how easy it would be for you to interview them.

_____ a pro-choice activist, or person who supports (or who has had an) abortion

_____ a member of the KKK, Aryan Brotherhood, or other white extremist group

_____ a member of the Christian right, fundamentalist, evangelical

_____ a gay professor

_____ a gay student

_____ a Muslim woman who believes a woman should obey her husband in all things

_____ a Muslim man who believes a wife should obey her husband in all things

_____ a Muslim who supported Taliban

_____ a hawkish pro-war student or professor

_____ a war protesting student or professor

_____ a member of the ACLU

_____ an adult book store owner

_____ a homeless man who begs at the side of the road

_____ a homeless woman

_____ a mom on welfare

_____ a single man on welfare

_____ a pro-life proponent

_____ an Asian businessman

_____ a lesbian student

_____ a lesbian professor

_____ a formerly gay person who has been "cured" thanks to Christianity

_____ an atheist

_____ a Hispanic man or woman

_____ a Japanese student or group of Japanese students

_____ anyone of a different race from your own

_____ a senior citizen living in a nursing home

_____ someone with a severe mental disability

_____ someone with a disability (uses a wheel chair or seeing-eye dog)

_____ someone who has served time in prison for a crime against another person

_____ anyone who has served time in prison

_____ a registered child molester

_____ other: _____

_____ other: _____

_____ other: _____

After everyone completes the survey, circle or put a star by the three or four highest and lowest numbers. Discuss the results, keeping in mind that this is a learning exercise, that some aspects of the discussion may be uncomfortable, that no one should get personal, and that everyone should respect the feelings of their classmates and colleagues. Don't take off on gays or lesbians or anti-war protestors or evangelical Christians. Talk about feelings, not people.

Following a few minutes of general discussion, everyone is asked to identify the group that received the lowest score. If more than one group was rated at the 1 level, identify which of those causes the most anger, resentment, or distaste. Students may be assigned to make a contact with someone in that group and produce a profile of that person or group of people.

The assignment includes researching (including observation) the targeted group, making contact with a subject, and scheduling meetings with the subject person or group. Students should remember that in all cases a reporter is trying to be an unbiased observer whose goal is to present an objective picture to the reader, listener, or viewer.

More time should be given for this story than the typical piece. Schedule class or workshop time to discuss progress, problems, and the like. When the project is completed, students are asked to read or present their articles in class, talking about the experience, and whether or not it changed their thinking in any way.

Chapter Eighteen

The Power of a Word

Author's note: This assignment originally was written by Keith Woods, dean of the Poynter Institute. I heard him present this as a teaching module at a seminar in 2001. It was excellently presented and extremely powerful. As a teacher, I would only hope that it could work as well in all classes. Because his words are so effective, I am presenting the exercise, with permission, largely as it appears on the handout distributed at the seminar.[262]

The strength — and weakness — of communication lies in individual words. Journalism emphasizes precision as one of the essential building blocks of excellence. It's in the choice of strong, active verbs or vivid, descriptive adjectives that a journalist takes ordinary sentences and transforms them into compelling stories. The choice of words can also betray a bias or cause harm, even when the bias is unseen and the malevolence unintended.

This issue can be highlighted at any point during the school term in any reporting, writing, or editing course and in any medium. The lesson need not take an entire class and, once taught, could form the foundation of many discussions to follow.

Methodology

In talking about diversity, it's best to move from a universal point (excellent journalism is concise journalism) to the specific point (inner city is not a racial description). There are several reasons:

1. The point is grounded in immutable journalistic principle. If we are not talking about journalistic principle, then we are simply suppressing or mandating language choices.

2. It is easier to begin a difficult conversation — and these conversations are almost invariably difficult — with a point upon which all are likely to agree. It is easier to learn when assured that the goal is to improve journalism, not fix people.

Actual published stories, rather than hypotheticals, should be used whenever possible. While hypothetical stories may help get a point across, they typically seem less believable than the real thing. Additionally, brief stories work better for in-class reading.

The Lesson

Use the stories reprinted on the following pages. Students should have a quick conversation with a neighbor (or small group) about the meanings of the words in the stories. Take five minutes or so for the conversation. Everyone in the group should participate. Debrief the small-group conversations and create a list of the ways the stories might reveal bias or cause harm.

Opening Discussion

There are ostensibly neutral facts in the two stories. The essential five-W facts are there. The ages and genders of the victims and/or perpetrators are there. Both stories involve fire and death. Things change, though, when a common fact — military service — is included in the two stories. In the case of the Fort Walton Beach story, is the phrase "Persian Gulf War veteran" a neutral fact or one that heightens the tragedy of the man's death? In the Lakeland story, could "Vietnam veteran" be viewed as a synonym for "mentally unbalanced"?

The point here is that "facts" are seldom neutral, and journalists need to be accountable for the direction in which they guide readers. Underscore the words "be accountable," because that phrase demands not that journalists leave out essential facts, but that they make clear the relevance of the facts they put in. In the Lakeland story, it is reasonable for the reader to conclude that the man's stint in Vietnam somehow contributed to his death, though that point is never engaged directly.

A great many of the complaints about bias in the media gain strength from loaded language that implies and insinuates. Problems with diversity and language grow from the same seed.

The Transition

Read a second set of stories where language can cause trouble, this time dealing with the issues of race, class, gender, sexual orientation, or faith. Talk in small groups again, then debrief as a class. In this case, use the "cross-dressing story" out of New Port Richey, Fla. With awareness raised from the first discussion, the power of verbs and adjectives should be more clearly obvious. Talk about the effect of words like "shuffled," "daintily," and the phrase "particularly harsh." Talk about the subtext of the story, the tone of the story as established by those words.

Does the story make fun of cross-dressers (though this man is likely transgendered)? Does it make light of the probability that the man will be mistreated (the subtext suggests raped) in prison? The bias of the reporter and the newspaper comes through.

Summary

Groups are almost always hurt when stories lean upon stereotypes, racial shorthand, and euphemisms. Many of our biases are so ingrained, so institutionalized, so normalized, that they often glide unchecked through the reporting, writing, and editing processes. Spend time learning about the abiding, destructive stereotypes in play for different groups. Bring particular care to reporting, writing, and editing stories about these groups, turning a careful eye to powerful verbs and descriptive language in use.

Dead man had gasoline stashed throughout his home[263]

LAKELAND — A 51-year-old recluse was found dead Wednesday inside his fire-charred home, where 22 gasoline-filled containers forced the temporary evacuation of houses within a one-block radius.

Alfons Draht's unburned body was found with a gunshot wound in the head, police said.

His death initially was ruled a suicide, said Michael Holder, a spokeswoman for the Polk County Sheriff's Office. An autopsy is planned for today.

Firefighters found the gasoline containers throughout the home where an arson fire was reported at 3:57 a.m., said Capt. Mike Douglas of the state fire marshal's office. Two erupted in the fireplace, he said.

A bedroom and a car in the back yard also were set on fire, Douglas said.

Neighbors said the house did not have electricity and that Draht, described as a Vietnam veteran, rarely left home during the day.

"Nobody's really seen him, knows much about him," said neighbor David Little.

3 teens charged with man's murder[264]

FORT WALTON BEACH — Two teenage girls and a boy were charged Thursday with tying a man to a tree, setting him on fire and then killing him — after he survived being burned — by slitting his throat.

The apparent motive was anger over the 31-year-old man's alleged sexual advances toward one of the girls, who were renting a room in the victim's apartment, according to Okaloosa County sheriff's deputies.

Ronald Lee Bell Jr., 17, Renee Ko Lincks, 15, and Kristel Rose Maestas, 17, each were charged with murdering restaurant worker Cordell Richards, a Persian Gulf War veteran.

A sheriff's department statement gave this account:

The two girls lured Richards into a sexual encounter at his Fort Walton beach apartment in early February so Bell could sneak up from behind and hit the victim on the head.

The teens bound Richards, put him in the trunk of a car and drove to a secluded area west of the city near Santa Rosa Sound, where the victim was tied to the tree and set on fire.

When the fire went out, his throat was cut. The teens returned about two weeks later to set a second fire in an attempt to destroy the body, investigators said. A boy discovered the remains in a vacant lot about a month later on March 4.

Woman loses 3 of 8 fetuses[265]

LONDON — Her doctors say she needs a miracle.

Mandy Allwood, who conceived eight fetuses with the help of fertility drugs then peddled her story to a British tabloid, was hospitalized in stable condition Tuesday after losing three of the fetuses.

She runs a serious risk of losing more, doctors say.

Allwood, 32, is receiving drugs to stop her uterus from contracting and delivering the remaining five fetuses prematurely.

Now in their 20th week, the fetuses need five more weeks in the uterus to have a chance of surviving, doctors say.

"I think that is unlikely, but we do not give up hope," said Donald Gib, a consulting obstetrician at King's College Hospital in London. He said the drugs are effective for days, at most.

"I don't normally use the word miracle, but it was something I nearly said to Ms. Allwood," when she gave birth to three male fetuses Monday, Gibb said. Each weighed less than 7 ounces "and would fit in the palm of my hand," he said.

Gibb said he had seen the remaining fetuses on an ultrasound Tuesday, and all had heartbeats and were moving. There are no fears for Allwood's health, he said.

The babies' father, Paul Hudson, 37, was with her. Their relationship was strained when newspapers disclosed that he has another lover and two children. Both Allwood and Hudson are on welfare. Allwood, who is divorced and has a 5-year-old son, received fertility drugs from the free National Health Service.

Max Clifford, the publicist Allwood hired, insisted the loss would not affect her lucrative deal with the News of the World tabloid, which he has estimated could be worth up to $1.5 million.

Cross-dressing man sentenced for battering woman at bar[266]

NEW PORT RICHEY — Patrick Hagan shuffled off to serve his 2 1/2-year state prison sentence wearing a black-and-pink print dress and a matching pink blouse.

But before he held out his wrists to accept a bailiff's handcuffs, the 6-foot-3, 280-pound Hagan asked for a moment to remove his jewelry.

Off came the earrings and the rings. Hagan struggled with his gold necklace, and a bailiff daintily helped him undo the clasp.

And then the bailiff tightened the cuffs around Hagan's wrists and escorted him toward the beginning of what is likely to be a particularly harsh prison term.

Appraising Hagan's appearance before imposing the sentence Friday morning, Circuit Judge Stanley Mills acknowledged that.

"It's not a pretty picture in the state prison system," Mills told Hagan, a cross-dresser who is awaiting sex-change surgery.

Hagan was convicted in July of punching a fellow bar patron in the mouth. The victim, 40-year-old Cheryl Partsch, lost five teeth and could end up paying as much as $60,000 in medical bills.

A jury found Hagan guilty of misdemeanor battery, punishable by up to a year in jail. But Hagan was on probation from a felony illegal dumping conviction at the time, and the recent conviction also meant he had violated his probation, which can be punished with state prison time.

The battery occurred in November at BT's, a Port Richey bar frequented by cross-dressers. Hagan was accused of battering Partsch because she questioned his presence in the women's restroom.

Mills heard testimony in Hagan's sentencing one day late last month and on Friday.

Defense lawyer Robert Attridge argued a prison sentence would be especially difficult for Hagan, given the level of violence in Department of Corrections facilities and the hostility to which cross-dressers often are subjected.

Hagan took the stand to say he punched Partsch in self-defense after she kicked open his stall door.

Gay man barred from adopting[267]

LANTANA — In five years as a foster parent, Kenneth Suber took more than 20 troubled children into his Lantana home, coaching their Little League teams and attending their school PTA meetings.

But when he tried to adopt, state officials declared him unfit.

Their only problem: Suber is gay.

"I can be a foster parent and take care of children from the time they are born up until 18 years of age, but I can't adopt," said Suber, 40, a mortgage banker. "Why? That's the law."

Florida is one of only two states that bans gays from adopting.

State officials stepped in to overturn Suber's adoption of a 4-year-old boy this month. Only a month before, they had chosen Suber as the best potential parent among several people seeking to adopt the boy named Brandon.

Beth Owen, spokeswoman for the state Department of Children and Families, said her agency didn't know Suber was gay when it endorsed the adoption on Sept. 3.

Suber acknowledged that, on a form required by the agency, he did not check off that he was gay or bisexual.

When officials confronted him later he admitted he was gay. State officials removed Brandon from Suber's home on Oct. 16 and put him back in foster care.

Owens said the agency had no choice. It's not up to her agency to offer opinions on the law, only to uphold it.

"When he admitted to the department what his sexual preference was, we had no choice but to remove the child," she said.

Suber, who does not have a partner, said he lied on the adoption forms because "I just thought it was none of their business."

Florida's law prohibiting gays from adopting was passed in 1977; it applies to private adoptions as well as those sought by the state. New Hampshire is the only other state with such a law.

Suber's only hope of getting Brandon back is to have the Legislature change the law or for the courts to declare it unconstitutional. In hopes of doing so, he said he has filed a petition for adoption in Palm Beach County Circuit Court.

Similar efforts have failed.

Several times, members of the state Legislature — including state Rep. Suzanne Jacobs, D-Delray Beach — have proposed deleting the part of the law prohibiting gays from adopting, but it has always failed.

One gay couple took the issue to the state Supreme Court but dropped the appeal before it was resolved, said Boca Raton attorney Charlotte Danciu, who handled the adoption cases of Suber's children.

Tim Fisher, executive director of Gay and Lesbian Parents Coalition International in Washington, D.C., said it is a tragedy to prevent gays from adopting when so many children need good homes.

"Just look at the kids who have been adopted into loving, caring homosexual households, who are thriving. We should talk to them about what our real family values are," Fisher said.

But David Canton, president of the American Family Association of Florida, argued that it is wrong to subject children to a "dysfunctional lifestyle."

"And a child who's going to be placed in a home is already coming from a dysfunctional atmosphere. It's not fair to the child."

Chapter Nineteen

Diversity and Ethics

Diversity is an ethical issue. It is all about the question of the right and wrong thing to do. Coverage of the uncovered and undercovered is a contemporary continuing ethical issue, just as are the perpetuation of racial and ethnic stereotypes and the problem of inclusion in entertainment as well as in news.

Most professional journalism organizations address the issue of diversity in their ethics codes. The RTNDA Code of Ethics says that electronic media should "Seek to understand the diversity of their community and inform the public without bias or stereotype."[268] The SPJ Code says journalists should "Avoid stereotyping by race, gender, age, religion, ethnicity, geography, sexual orientation, disability, physical appearance or social status."[269]

Yet, examples of racial stereotyping abound in news reporting, both in print and electronic media, advertising, public relations, and entertainment media. Native Americans are lazy drunks, gay men are effeminate, lesbians are "butch," African Americans are best known for athletic prowess and rap, the aged are senile and in nursing homes, the homeless are under-motivated drunks and drug abusers, Hispanics are stealing American jobs, and Asians are either buck-toothed cooks and launderers or the high-achieving chosen minority.

For the most part, the only mention of Hispanic or Latino residents in local media are in Monday morning arrest reports or the local sheriff's not-yet-proven theories on drug trafficking. The image then that our audiences have of our Latino neighbors is of largely young men who drink too much on Saturday nights and cut each other up over young women. Little do they know of the lives left behind, the struggles to become citizens, to earn decent wages and send money home to needy families. Seldom are their triumphs in school, business, or church reported.

The same could be said of any undercovered population. The homeless are poor and uneducated and must surely have untreated alcohol or drug problems. Why else would they be homeless? It's just not that simple. And if more reporters and editors would bother to get into the streets, and listen — really listen — they might begin to better understand the communities they serve.

The best way to explore ethics and diversity is to look at specific situations that require some kind of solution (print or not print), or broader policies on covering the community. Guide the decision making using either the Poynter *Ten Questions for Making Ethical Decisions* presented in Chapter Two, "Why Is Diversity Important?" or follow the steps of the Potter box shown here.

Potter Box Decision-Making System[270]

1. Define the situation or explain the basic facts of the ethical dilemma.

2. Consider the values that you would apply to a particular situation — humanistic and journalistic values: truth, objectivity, accuracy, responsibility, human compassion, and so on.

3. Consider the following principles on which a decision might be made:

A. Aristotle's Golden Mean — That the moral virtue is a mean between two extremes.
B. Kant's Categorical Imperative — "Act on that maxim which you will to become a universal law." Make decisions in a manner you wish similar situations to be decided; or simply be consistent.
C. Mill's Principle of Utility — The right decision is the one that does the greatest amount of good for the largest number of people.
D. Rawl's Veil of Ignorance — Justice emerges when negotiating without social distinctions. All prejudices should be blocked when making ethical decisions.
E. Judeo-Christian Concept of Agape — Unselfish love, "love your neighbor as yourself," accepting a person's existence as it is; to love a person as he is.

4. Consider those to whom you owe loyalties: self, employer, audience, society.

5. Decision should emerge from your analysis.

Ethical Situations Involving Issues of Diversity

Some of the following scenarios involve diversity issues and questions that require a decision. Others may be used simply to provoke discussion of diversity issues.

1. You are a reporter for a media organization. Like most newsrooms, staff diversity is far from meeting parity standards. When your employer hires an inexperienced but well-educated Asian American woman, you suspect it's all about diversity. Coffee room rumor says she was hired instead of more qualified Anglo candidates. How do you respond?

2. You are a reporter for a midwestern television station. A representative of one of the two candidates for governor leaves a message on your phone suggesting that the opposition and front-running candidate is a lesbian. You check around and find that the rumor is probably true. You report what you've found to your news director who wants to go with it. She

says, "voters have a right to know." You're not so sure. Do you agree? Will you do a story? Why or why not?

3. You are a sports reporter for a local media organization. You are contacted by a Native American in your community asking that you discontinue referring to local teams by their Indian-related mascot names. The largest high school in the area, for example, labels all its sports teams the "Warriors." The caller complains that the name as well as the half-time "powwow" imitations are an insult to Native American cultural and spiritual traditions. He notes that media in other areas have agreed to go along with the pleas of Native Americans to not use Indian names and imagery in sports reporting. What is your reaction? Is it your responsibility, or is it up to the schools to change their sports names?

4. You are reporting a story on the arrest of a murder suspect. The victim and the suspect were friends and in their 50s. They got into an argument over a woman both of the men had at times dated. One of the two ended up dead. The murder occurred in the victim's trailer. The suspect is unemployed and a veteran of Vietnam. The woman over whom the two argued was a younger Hispanic woman. Which of these facts do you include in your report? Why or why not?

5. You are doing a feature profile — a day-in-the-life-of story — on a young single Hispanic immigrant living in your community. His name was given to you by a social worker. You write about his job, his religion, his life in his new community. He is excited and eager to cooperate with your visits to his home and work in order to get the story. On the third or fourth visit, you discover he is an undocumented immigrant. In fact, he talks very candidly about the night he left his home in Mexico, crossing the border and dodging border patrols. You tell him that this information, if published, would very likely lead to his deportation. He gives you the okay to continue with the story. Do you write the story, including immigration status? Do you write everything but his lack of papers, knowing that even that would be a risk? Do you tell the story, but disguise his identity? Do you drop the story rather than put him at risk? Are there other possibilities?

6. Some reporters and editors argue that the one time race should be used is when a crime has been committed and police are searching for someone. Yet there are countless examples of erroneous accusations, which have led to the harassment of minorities. A Boston murder offers a classic example. A man took out a huge insurance policy on his pregnant wife. He then murdered her, shot himself in the stomach, and called the police. His story was that a black man had jumped into the backseat of their car at a stop light, had forced them onto a back street, stolen their money, and left them both for dead. The media ran with the story. Black men were routinely stopped and frisked. One particular black man was arrested and identified by the victim. Ten weeks later, the police discovered the truth.

A similar result could have occurred in South Carolina when a young mother buckled her children into the back seat of a car and drove them into a lake, where they drowned. She claimed that a black man had kidnapped them. Again, the media ran with the story, creating suspicion of every black man driving on the interstates out of South Carolina. A local law enforcement officer eventually found inconsistencies in the woman's story, leading her to a confession.

In a series of rapes on a campus in Pennsylvania, the victims repeatedly identified the perpetrator as "a large black man" with little other description. The media repeated the description. Large black men all over town became suspect. Parents of female students put pressure on the college to stop the rapes, make an arrest. They arrested a black maintenance worker at the school. Even though he was later released, the damage was done.

You are the news decision maker in all these instances; how do you report the story?

7. Your editor is planning a special Thanksgiving Day story on homelessness and asks you to go to the local shelter for pictures and a story. "Get me a real tear-jerker," he says. "Skinny kids with sad faces. Dirty teenage girls with big tummies." Though disgusted by your editor's attitude, you need the job and do as ordered. At the shelter, you take a couple rolls of film: dirty sad-faced kids, pregnant moms, bearded older men with the shakes. But you also discover a number of "normal" looking residents — clean shaven, decent and clean clothes (mostly white). You take their photos, too. Is this an appropriate story in the first place? Do you play it the editor's way? Do you include the "normal" photos in the story?

8. You are a reporter in a southern newsroom, fully aware of lingering racial biases in your community. But when an editor tells you not to run photos with an accident story in which one black youth was killed and another seriously injured, you disagree. Here's the editor's reasoning: The young driver and his sister were on their way to school on an early and snowy January morning. Most every school system in surrounding counties had canceled school for the day because of icy road conditions. Your county had not. Your editor says to you: "It was a mistake not to cancel school. If I were a parent, I would be outraged. Someone's head needs to roll over this, but if we put these kids' pictures with this story, there will be considerably less outrage than if we let them think these kids are white." How do you react?

9. On three consecutive days, you notice that there are separate nonfatal traffic accidents in your city involving drivers who are 75 and older. You want to do a story tying the three together with age as the common angle. Your editor, herself over 60 years old, says she wouldn't run the story and even argues that you should not use age as an identifier in these stories, that doing so will contribute to an inaccurate stereotype that seniors are bad drivers. She points out that in two of the three accidents, the fault had been placed on the other drivers (in both cases younger than 50). How do you respond?

10. You are working on a series of stories on poverty in your community. You go to a homeless shelter, an unemployment office, and finally to local projects. You talk to a few people and get lots of photographs. You put the first piece together and it runs. Calls from the African American community begin immediately. With the exception of a couple photographs of recently arrived Hmong refugees, all the photographs are of African Americans. The callers claim this is just another example of the media's history of perpetuating the stereotype of a dominantly black lower class. How do you respond? Could you have done the story any differently?

Chapter Twenty

Story Stances

Ruth Seymour, a professor at Wayne State University, maintains that too much diversity coverage is created from a dominant group's perspective. As an alternative to mainstream America's point of view, she offers the following four points of view from which diversity coverage can be accomplished: neo-traditional stories, inner-sanctum stories, service stories for the smaller group, and "We're watching you, too" stories.

Seymour says all four are sometimes published and broadcast by U.S. media though the first is the most common. The last three have the greatest potential of producing stories with surprisingly fresh points of view.[271]

1. Neo-traditional: Seymour claims most newsrooms adopt this stance most days of the week without thinking. "I call it neo-traditional," she says, "to acknowledge that it is a clear and important improvement over the content of American media, say, in the 1950s, when mainstream media paid attention almost exclusively to white, straight, Christian America. Today's neo-traditional stance intentionally covers other religions, social and racial groups."

The neo-traditional stance works something like this: Scanning the community, a newsroom notices someone or a group of people who are different. They then attempt to fairly, fully, accurately, and authentically explain the difference. Following are examples of this kind of coverage:

Debbie Wilbourne is deaf, but she also is a successful psychotherapist. (How does she do it?)

Instead of relaxing after Christmas, many African American families celebrate Kwanzaa. (How Kwanzaa is celebrated and what families say they get out of it.)

Muslim women are showing up in greater numbers on college campuses these days. (Are they required to wear those veils and scarves?)

2. Inner-sanctum: Seymour says she used to call these voyeur stories. Inner-sanctum stories are about issues and events and people typically visible only within an undercovered community. The only way to get these stories is through connecting with friends or trusted acquaintances of these people and through them gaining access to their private inner sanctums. These are areas of American society that are basically invisible from the point of view of most Americans. Examples:

Debbie Wilbourne is deaf and a psychotherapist, but some of her deaf acquaintances consider her a sell-out because she prefers lip-reading to signing. (Young deaf professionals: straddling two worlds.)

Mark Egglesworth III refuses to teach his kids the Swahili words that are principles for Kwanzaa. He cites recent genetic evidence suggesting that the ancestors of many African American families were more likely kidnapped from West Africa than from the southeastern parts of the continent where Swahili is more commonly spoken. (Why some black families dislike Kwanzaa.)

One suggests Turkey, another Iran. One suggests devoutness, another a possible willingness to test the limits. (The subtle but communicative language of Muslim chadors, or headscarves.)

3. Service stories for the smaller group: These are stories that address your nonmainstream communities as people you want to serve. Examples:

When John Essed arrived at Macomb Mall, he easily found a handicapped parking spot big enough for his van. Then he found out why: The automatic door for wheelchairs — the only one in the entire shopping complex — was on the backside of the mall, near a different parking lot. (An investigative accessibility survey: Which department stores, or which malls, are the best and most useful to wheelchair-using customers? Which have the highest percentage of broad, open aisles? The best bathrooms? How about trained and instructed sales staff — say for when a customer walks in the door with white cane or dog? And how about movie theaters, restaurants, supermarkets?)

The hottest Kwanzaa Kinara around the country this year is . . . (What new styles of kinaras — Kwanzaa candleholders — are sure-to-please holiday gifts? Where are they sold or manufactured locally?)

When Aisha Rahman was asked in an employment interview whether she would be willing to take her scarf off during sales presentations, she knew what to do. But it worries her that many American Muslim women don't. (What legal remedies — list organizations and phone numbers — exist for Muslim women in your community who are either fired from jobs, or not hired, because they want to cover their head? How can women best document the experience to help their case?)

4. "We're watching you, too!" stories: This stance attempts to flip the coin and view the majority or mainstream community from the other side. How do Hispanics view their new American neighbors? How do gay men view straight men? Seymour tells a story about an interview in which a radio talk show host asked this question of an openly gay male guest: "The talk show host said: 'We all know the names you get called: fag, homo, queer . . . What I want to know is: What do you call us?' Caught by surprise, the guest demurred repeatedly, but the host would not give up. Finally, the guest laughed and said: 'We call you breeders.'" Other examples:

John Malish hands you the card explaining his muteness, and can virtually predict what happens next. You'll start talking louder, and depending on the day, he'll be exasperated or bemused. (Disability etiquette: What helps and what doesn't help; what is polite and what isn't polite in conversations and teamwork with deaf, visually impaired, mute, wheelchair-using people.)

"I don't care if you're red, yellow, green or purple" or "Gimme five, man!" or "Hey, bro', whaz up?" (Things white people should never say to black people unless they like being identified as possibly prejudiced, or at least nervous.)

"Will you marry me?" (Problems with nonarranged marriages, from the experience and observation of some members of the now established Muslim and Hindu communities in North America.)

Chapter Twenty-One

Mapping Your Daily World

The objective of this simple exercise is to learn the value of finding new and different voices for news stories.[272] Reporters get mired in routine like everyone and need, from time to time, to work on expanding the number of places they go and the variety of people with whom they talk.

Instructions:

1. Use a large sheet of paper to draw a map of your daily world.

2. Begin by drawing your desk or room or building where you have most of your classes, do most of your work, or spend most of your time. Put this location in the center of your page.

3. Then draw your routes to other classrooms or locations that you regularly visit and to your home, dorm room, or apartment.

4. Make notes of the people you normally encounter along your route from work or school to where you live: bus driver, news vendor, worker in a coffee shop or restaurant where you regularly stop, secretary, storekeeper sweeping the sidewalk in front of her store, retired man tending a garden, homeless person on the street corner begging for work or food. Think. Don't leave out anyone.

5. Be detailed in noting locations of stores, restaurants, civic or social centers, and the like along your route. Note the names of as many of the businesses as you can remember.

Now, thinking outside this inner sphere, consider where else you go in a normal day or week. Make a map of your entire city (or community within a larger city), noting adjacent communities, main streets, and so on. Again, be as detailed as possible using street names, businesses, churches, schools, parks.

Indicate areas on the map where you never go or are afraid or uncomfortable to go. Discuss why you've never been to these parts of your community. Have a discussion about being a journalist and how it would be important to be familiar with the entire community.

After completing your maps, analyze what you have created. Google a map of your local community, the one you just described or depicted, and compare the professionally drawn map to the one you just created. How much did you leave out? Write down your observations about the map and the exercise, noting what it says to you about your daily routine. Include in your observations things you might want to change, as a journalist, in order to get to know your community better.

Creating New Maps

Choose a partner or small team and explore your local community before the next class period or meeting or by a specified date if more time is needed. Identify neighborhoods you are not familiar with, go to community stores you've never been in, eat in restaurants in communities where you've never been, wash your clothes in a neighborhood laundry, talk to people you normally would not meet. Take a camera along and take photographs of people, storefronts, streets, businesses, anything that will allow you to build a better picture of the community.

You'll need to put your journalistic skills to use here. Observe, search, investigate, find those communities you didn't know were even there. Print area maps from the Internet, and explore them. Turn off the main thoroughfares, drive through the streets of as many neighborhoods as possible. Find pockets of diversity you never knew existed, and note them for your map. Further, as you explore these new areas, make a list of story ideas that might be developed about these communities. Also list possible sources you might contact for information on other stories. Your source list might include a police officer on a beat, a neighborhood merchant, or the old man tending a garden.

Following your excursion, which could be one day or over several days, prepare a new map of the community in which you identify new neighborhoods, ethnic and racial groups, businesses, churches, and the like that you did not know existed. Use the photographs you have taken to illustrate the map. Post the maps of all the groups on a large bulletin board or wall for the entire class or seminar to study.

As a larger group now, make observations about the communities you have discovered. What did you find of interest? Why didn't you know about these neighborhoods and communities outside your own daily zone? What needs to be communicated to the larger audience? Brainstorm ideas for stories based on your observations and investigations. Combine your lists of possible sources to generate a resource that can be duplicated and shared with the class. List at least a dozen different ideas, and talk about how these ideas might provide improved coverage to the uncovered and undercovered. Trim your list to a few good ideas, and talk more about how these ideas could be developed. Match possible sources from your composite list to use in researching these stories.

This exercise is simply about good journalism, which is being fair, accurate, truthful, and comprehensive. When your reporting, writing, and editing incorporate all those things, you also are being inclusive, and that means reporting on all the communities in your coverage area, including the diverse neighborhoods that might have been overlooked in the past.

Chapter Twenty-Two

Editing for Fairness: Reporting on Disability

The following editing exercise is provided by the National Center on Disability and Journalism.[273] The story should be edited for broadcast style. Edit first; then look at the explanation on the following pages.

A WHEEL-CHAIR BOUND SUSPECT MADE OFF WITH CLOSE TO 10-THOUSAND DOLLARS IN A DOWNTOWN BANK ROBBERY TODAY.

THE THIEF . . . APPARENTLY CONFINED TO A WHEELCHAIR AND AFFLICTED WITH CEREBRAL PALSY . . . PULLED A GUN ON A BANK OF AMERICA TELLER AT THE POST STREET BRANCH.

THE TELLER TOLD POLICE THE GUNMAN WAS SPASTIC . . . WAVING THE GUN AROUND . . . AND MADE EVERYONE NERVOUS. THE SUSPECT WAS GIVEN 10-THOUSAND DOLLARS IN SMALL BILLS

THE HANDICAPPED ROBBER ROARED OUT OF THE BANK AND DISAPPEARED INTO DOWNTOWN TRAFFIC.

THE POLICE LATER CAUGHT HIM WHEN THE WHEELCHAIR GOT STUCK ON A CURB CUT BLOCKED BY A TRUCK.

THE TELLER IDENTIFIED THE SUSPECT . . . 29-YEAR-OLD JASON MILLER OF THE RICHMOND DISTRICT IN A POLICE LINEUP. POLICE SAID HE ALSO SUFFERED FROM CEREBRAL PALSY SINCE BIRTH

After you have finished editing the story, take a look at the comments on the story provided by the NCDJ.

> A WHEEL-CHAIR BOUND SUSPECT MADE OFF WITH CLOSE TO 10-THOUSAND DOLLARS IN A DOWNTOWN BANK ROBBERY TODAY.

A person is not bound to a wheelchair; a wheelchair enables a person to be mobile. Suggestion: "using a wheelchair" or "wheelchair user." Only refer to a person's assistive aids (wheelchair, cane, service animal) when essential to the story. Also, once it has been established that the bank robber uses a wheelchair, it is not necessary to repeat.

> THE THIEF . . . APPARENTLY CONFINED TO A WHEELCHAIR AND AFFLICTED WITH CEREBRAL PALSY . . . PULLED A GUN ON A BANK OF AMERICA TELLER AT THE POST STREET BRANCH.

The word *confined* is similar to "wheelchair bound." Avoid it altogether. Using the wording "afflicted with" makes the assumption that a person with a disability is living a reduced quality of life. Use neutral language. Suggestion: "has cerebral palsy." Only refer to a person's disability when essential to the story.

> THE TELLER TOLD POLICE THE GUNMAN WAS SPASTIC . . . WAVING THE GUN AROUND . . . AND MADE EVERYONE NERVOUS. THE SUSPECT WAS GIVEN 10-THOUSAND DOLLARS IN SMALL BILLS

Muscles, not people, are spastic. Use of this term is considered derogatory when referring to people with cerebral palsy. Also, the sentence beginning, "The suspect was given . . ." is passive voice.

> THE HANDICAPPED ROBBER ROARED OUT OF THE BANK AND DISAPPEARED INTO DOWNTOWN TRAFFIC.

"Handicapped" does not have the same meaning as "disability." It refers to a barrier imposed by society, the environment, or one's own self. Do not use it to refer to a person. Also, consider something less dramatic than "roared."

> THE POLICE LATER CAUGHT HIM WHEN THE WHEELCHAIR GOT STUCK ON A CURB CUT BLOCKED BY A TRUCK.

If you can't define "curb cut," don't use it.

> THE TELLER IDENTIFIED THE SUSPECT . . . 29-YEAR-OLD JASON MILLER OF THE RICHMOND DISTRICT IN A POLICE LINEUP. POLICE SAID HE ALSO SUFFERED FROM CEREBRAL PALSY SINCE BIRTH.

"Suffered from" has the same connotation as "afflicted with" in the second paragraph. Avoid.

Search area newspapers and magazines to find other stories involving people with disabilities. Are the terms used correctly? Read the stories aloud or in groups, and discuss ways as suggested by the NCDJ exercise that these stories could be improved.

If you don't find stories in local papers that cover disability, then that is a question in itself.

Finally, discuss the comments included in the NCDJ analysis of the story. Are references to wheel chair use and the fact that the person has cerebral palsy relevant to this story? Why?

It matters that those who lead the newsroom understand every facet of the community they cover. It is in seeing ourselves whole that we can begin to see ways of working out our differences, of understanding our similarities.

Bob Maynard, 1978

Chapter Twenty-Three

Playing "The Newsroom Diversity Game"

Bob Maynard became editor of the *Oakland Tribune* in 1979 following a distinguished career in journalism that had included a Nieman fellowship to Harvard and service as a correspondent for the *Washington Post* covering civil rights and urban unrest. He also served at ombudsman at the Post and later worked as a member of the editorial page staff. He bought the *Oakland Tribune* in 1983, becoming the first African American to own a major city paper.[274]

Maynard ran the *Tribune* for nearly ten years, building one of the most diverse newsrooms of any major newspaper in America. The newspaper earned a Pulitzer Prize in 1990. He also won the Elijah Parish Lovejoy Award, a national award named for the owner of an abolitionist newspaper in Alton, Ill., who was killed by angry mobs in 1837.

Maynard also was co-founder of the Institute for Journalism Education, a not-for-profit corporation dedicated to creating more opportunities for minority journalists at major national newspapers. It has trained hundreds of journalists of color. Following Maynard's death in 1993, the institute was renamed the Robert C. Maynard Institute for Journalism Education. It offers a number of valuable services, including a media academy that trains first-time newspaper managers, a web-based content auditing service that allows users to easily audit diversity content, a history project that preserves the stories of African American journalists, and other educational programs for journalists of color and those who cover communities of color.

An interesting exercise available only through the Maynard Institute's website is a newsroom diversity game, "Seeing Ourselves Whole,"[275] available by going to the site: http://www.maynardije.org/resources/game/.

Instructions for the game are as follows:

Are You Up for the Challenge?

Welcome to the online interactive game that challenges players to diversify a typical newsroom, while testing their basic knowledge of cultures.

You've just been appointed editor of a mid-size newspaper and the publisher has asked you to move aggressively to diversify newsroom staffing and the paper's content. You must set policy and make strategic decisions that will bring the racial makeup of your newsroom into parity with the surrounding community within four years.

The exercise offers three levels of difficulty. Begin with the first level and work through the exercises individually. In the exercise, you assume the role of a new editor who has been charged with the task of creating a newsroom that matches the diversity of the community, which is 30 percent minority. Your newsroom is only 5 percent.

If you have access to a computer lab, it would be desirable for everyone to be able to work through the exercises at her own pace. After everyone has completed the exercise, work through it again, taking time to discuss the recommended answers. Also look at the comments contained on the wildcards.

An interesting variation on the exercise might be to invite a manager from a local media organization to class on the day of the exercise to get his comments about the decisions recommended by the Maynard Institute's diversity game.

Finally, as a class, using ideas stimulated by the diversity game, create a simple board game that illustrates some of the roadblocks to creating a diverse newsroom, as well as the opportunities for success possible through enhancing both the diversity of the newsroom and the diversity of content.

New Directions in Diversity

Chapter Twenty-Four

A Diversity of Voices

Imagine yourself tuning into television, picking up a newspaper or magazine, or surfing the various news websites and being given a multitude of points of view, from the talking heads on radio and television to the expert sources quoted in print stories.

Imagine tuning into the six o'clock network news to find the evening news being delivered by two females, one black, one Arab American. Imagine the network going live to reporter in a wheelchair doing a story on bans against gay adoption in Florida. Imagine the reporter interviewing a disadvantaged gay couple who want to adopt a biracial child. Imagine the anchor then turning to an in-studio guest, a Native American practicing law in Florida.

Imagine on and on. It's a scenario not likely to unfold anytime soon. Tune into your favorite network news program or continuous news cable channel and you likely will be overwhelmed, with few exceptions, by the knowledge possessed by white males. Whether it's military affairs, squabbling in the Senate, or crime on the street, apparently the white male has a monopoly on wisdom. This exercise is designed to get you thinking about the multitude of sources.

Divide into two or three groups to complete this assignment overnight or within a few days. One group is assigned to do a content analysis of a local newspaper, group two of a network news program, and group three of a local television news program. Each group should analyze a minimum of five stories and list sources used for each. Note the gender of each source and any other information that is discernible. Note observations and conclusions based on the simple analysis.

Next consider what kinds of sources a diversity-aware journalist might consider using. Check the following list to see if any of these seldom approached groups might be appropriate as a source for your story:

_____ Children
_____ Religious group
_____ Rural citizens
_____ Blue-collar workers

_____ Laborers
_____ Homeless people
_____ Students (college or high school)
_____ School teachers
_____ Senior citizens
_____ Gays and lesbians
_____ Merchants
_____ Housewives or househusbands[276]

Consider the five stories selected from newspapers, network news, or local television news. Which of these sources might you have contacted in order to add diversity to each story? What might a college or high school student contribute to a story on troop shortages in Iraq, for example? How about a member of a local United Church of Christ congregation? Or a member of a local gay and lesbian organization? Almost any group listed could add a different angle to a story on the emerging problem of low troop levels.

Finally, with access to a computer lab, use the Society of Professional Journalist's online Rainbow Sourcebook[277] to find additional sources. Find and list both local (in state) and national (all states) sources for each story. List at least three sources for each story and describe the qualifications of each source.

The Rainbow Sourcebook is an excellent resource. A search of sources on gay and lesbian issues, for example, reveals a list of 41 different names of people willing to serve as a resource. Those listed range from a congresswoman to a prisoner advocate to a 78-year-old grandmother who is a charter member of an "older lesbians" organization.

Chapter Twenty-Five

Diversity Resources

The following additional selected resources can be beneficial in providing avenues for further research and study of diversity issues, discovering additional exercises and activities to stimulate discussion of diversity, and ultimately contribute to creating better journalism. Obviously, this is not a complete and comprehensive bibliography; rather, it is culled from the greater body of literature about diversity issues. In choosing materials to include, such criteria as currency, applicability to the goals of this text, and appropriateness for use in classroom or seminar situations have been applied. Happy hunting!

The Best of the Web

Unity: Journalists of Color — http://www.unityjournalists.org
Unity comprises the major journalists of color organizations: National Association of Black Journalists, Asian American Journalists Association, National Association of Hispanic Journalists, and the Native American Journalists Association.

National Association of Black Journalists — http://www.nabj.org
Great site for and about black journalists. Includes information about meetings, jobs, internships, scholarships, and competitions. Contains links to Black College Wire, NABJ publications, and a NABJ census of black newsroom leaders.

National Association of Hispanic Journalists — http://www.nahj.org
Contains latest news and information about Hispanics in journalism, including jobs, annual national, and regional conventions, as well as a link to an excellent stylebook.

Native American Journalists Association — http://www.naja.com
Links to reznet, an informative site of "newz and viewz by Native American students." Also includes news and information and tips about covering Indian Country.

Asian American Journalists Association — http://www.aaja.org
Provides a useful handbook for reporting on Asian Americans and includes information about meetings, scholarships, grants, special programs for high school and college students, and links to other good sites.

South Asian Journalists Association — http://saja.org
SAJA is smaller than AAJA, but the website provides an important emphasis on South Asian culture as well as tips and stylebooks on covering Americans of South Asian descent.

The Asian-Nation - http://www.asian-nation.org/index.shtml
Excellent general source of information about Asians, Asian Americans, and the Asian culture. Describes itself as a one-stop information resource and overview of the historical, demographic, political, and cultural issues that make up today's diverse Asian American community.

National Lesbian and Gay Journalists Association — http://www.nlgja.org
Extremely helpful website includes a guide to lesbian, gay, bisexual, and transgender terminology and the Journalists Toolbox, which offers advice on covering LGBT people. Also news of members, conferences, and competitions.

The Gay and Lesbian Alliance Against Defamation — http://www.glaad.org
Seeks to ensure fair and accurate representation of gays and lesbians in media.
Offers a Media Reference Guide, media awards, conferences, news, and training manuals.

Journalism & Women Symposium (JAWS) — http://www.jaws.org
Jaws' mission is to support "the personal growth and professional empowerment of women in newsrooms and work toward a more accurate portrayal of the whole society." The website provides information on the JAWS Camp, links to jobs, scholarships, listsservs, and more.

The Association for Women in Communications — http://www.womcom.org
Addresses issues relevant to women in all communications disciplines, including print and broadcast journalism, television and radio production, film, advertising, public relations, marketing, graphic design, multimedia design, and photography.

International Women's Media Foundation — http://www.iwmf.org
Sponsors training programs designed to "move women into key position in the news media." Recent workshops in the United States have included the IWMF Leadership Institute of Women Journalists, Women Reaching for the Top: Initiatives for Media Leadership, and Women Journalists of Color in the U.S. Media.

National Federation of Press Women — http://www.nfpw.org
National association of women (and men) working in all areas of communications. Offers professional development, an annual conference, libel insurance competitions, a First Amendment email alert system, and much more.

American Women in Radio and Television, Inc. — http://www.awrt.org
Supports the advancement of women professionals in electronic media and has worked to improve the image of women as depicted in electronic media.

National Center on Disability & Journalism — http://www.ncdj.org
Offers NCDJ newsletter, style guide, tips for reporters covering people with disabilities, and a comprehensive list of links to other sites providing information on a wide range of disabilities.

Religion Newswriters Foundation — http://www.religionwriters.com
Features a resource library, "Religion Online," with an extensive listing of resource material for use in reporting religion in today's world. Links to religionlink.org, which provides story ideas and more resources for reporters, and rna.org, which provides information about religion writer's conferences, contests, and so forth.

American Society of Newspaper Editors — http://www.asne.org
Its diversity page features links to ASNE's annual newsroom employment census, information about Time-out for Diversity, minority fellowship opportunities, and information on awards.

Radio-Television News Directors Association and Foundation — http://www.rtnda.org
Includes information about its annual diversity survey conducted in conjunction with Ball State University, newsletter articles on diversity, and information about the excellent Diversity Toolkit, a DVD training program.

Poynter Online — http://www.poynter.org
The online website for the Poynter Institute, a center for educating journalists and journalism educators. Its diversity page includes numerous articles on diversity; links to resources on diversity; and information about programs, seminars, contests, fellowships, and more. One of the best diversity sites on the Internet.

The Freedom Forum — http://www.freedomforum.org
Information about Freedom Forum's Diversity Institute, Diversity Diaries, Diversity Director, and links to other publications and programs on diversity.

The Society of Professional Journalists — http://www.spj.org
Links to SPJ's Diversity Toolbox, which includes articles and information on reporting on diversity issues, and to its Rainbow Sourcebook, which provides contact information for sources on dozens of diversity issues.

Center for Integration and Improvement of Journalism — http://www.ciij.org
Based at San Francisco University, CiiJ works to make journalism more inclusive both in the newsroom and in journalism education. Offers workshops, publications, and news for students, educators, and professionals. Its Newswatch page includes a Media Guide to Islam, a Diversity Styleguide, and links to other news and information about diversity.

Robert C. Maynard Institute for Journalism Education — http://www.maynardije.org
Features information about Maynard Institute programs, diversity resources, the Knight Foundation sponsored report, "News as American as America," and various columns, including Richard Princes "Journal-isms," news and commentary on issues of diversity.

National Association of Minority Media Executives — http://www.namme.org
Organization of managers and executives of color working in media-related communications fields. Website features news, links to publications and programs, and a jobs listing.

American Civil Liberties Union — http://www.aclu.org
Covers issues relevant to diversity, including immigrants' rights, disability rights, lesbian and gay rights, racial justice, religious liberty, and rights for the poor.

Southern Poverty Law Center — http://www.splcenter.org
Provides educational programs supporting tolerance. Magazines, films, newsletters all provide information that can be used in the classroom and as resources for reporters and editors.

U.S. Census Bureau — http://www.census.gov
Rich site with page after page of detailed information from census surveys. Numbers lovers will have great time surfing the ins and outs of this site. http://www.census.gov/pubinfo/www/hotlinks.html takes you directly to the Census Bureau's minority links.

Association for Education in Journalism & Mass Communications — http://www.aejmc.org
The primary organization for higher education in journalism includes in its mission to "encourage the implementation of a multi-cultural society in the classroom and curriculum." Website includes a Diversity Database, which provides information on educators with research interests and expertise related to diversity issues. Also includes information on the Status of Women and the Status of Minorities.

Newspaper Association of America — http://www.naa.org
Its diversity page features Fusion, an online newsletter offering information on diversity books, reports, articles, websites, a toolbox for better reporting, and a calendar of diversity activities.

The Newsroom Diversity Game — http://www.maynardije.org/resources/game/
Tests your skills at newspaper management when diversity becomes a primary goal. Provided by the Maynard Institute, the educational game includes three levels of difficulty.

How Race Is Lived In America — http://www.nytimes.com/library/national/race
A *New York Times* series on race resulting from a yearlong examination by a team of *Times* reporters. Includes fifteen separate articles on racial issues.

Diversity Syllabi Database — http://newswatch.sfsu.edu/diversity_syllabuses
Provides links to selected syllabi for media diversity courses at ACEJMC accredited colleges and universities. An excellent source for reading lists, films, and documentaries on diversity issues.

DiversityInc — http://www.diversityinc.com
Excellent coverage of diversity news and comment. Also provides information on diversity jobs and careers, diversity-related publications, and a calendar of diversity events.

Offline Resources

All-American: How to Cover Asian America, Asian American Journalists Association, 2000.

The American Indian and The Media, Mark Anthony Rolo, ed. The National Conference for Community and Justice, 2000.

Asian Male Broadcasters on TV: Where Are They? Patricia Riley and Cynthia Kennard, Annenburg School for Communication, University of Southern California, Study conducted for the Asian American Journalists Association, 2002.

Best Practices for Newspaper Journalists, Robert J. Haiman. The Freedom Forum, 2000.

The Children Are Watching: How the Media Teach About Diversity, Carlos E. Cortes. Teachers College Press, 2000.

Coloring the News: How Political Correctness Has Corrupted American Journalism, William McGowan. Encounter Books, 2002.

Controversies in Media Ethics, A. David Gordon and John Michael Kittross. Longman, 1999.

"Covering Communities the Way They Are," Ron Levine. *Fusion* (Supplement to Presstime), Summer 2004.

Covering the Community: A Diversity Handbook for Media, Leigh Stephens Aldrich. Pine Forge Press, 1999.

Cultural Diversity and the U.S. Media, Yahya R. Kamalipour and Theresa Carilli, eds. State University of New York Press, 1998.

Delving into the Divide: A Study of Race Reporting in Forty-five U.S. Newsrooms, Pat Ford, Pew Center for Civic Journalism, October 2001.

Diversity: Best Practices, A Handbook for Journalism and Mass Communications Educators, Accrediting Council on Education in Journalism and Mass Communications, 2003.
Diversity Disconnects: From Class Room to News Room, Mercedes Lynn de Uriarte with Christina Bodinger-de Uriarte and Jose Luis Benavides, funded by the Ford Foundation, 2003.

Diversity in the Washington Newspaper Press Corps, a joint project of UNITY: Journalists of Color, Inc., and the Phillip Merrill College of Journalism, University of Maryland, 2005.

Diversity: The Invention of a Concept, Peter Wood. Encounter Books, 2003.

Diversity Toolkit: Instructional Guide for Diversity Training (including a DVD Companion). Radio and Television News Directors Foundation, 2004.

Does Your Newspaper's Staff Reflect the Racial Diversity of the Community It Serves? Bill Dedman and Stephen K. Doig, Knight Foundation, http://powerreporting.com/knight/california.html, 2004.

Doing Ethics in Journalism: A Handbook with Case Studies, Jay Black, Bob Steele, and Ralph Barney. Allyn and Bacon, 1999.

The Elements of Journalism: What Newspeople Should Know and the Public Should Expect, Bill Kovach and Tom Rosenstiel. Three Rivers Press, 2001.

The Essence of Excellence: Covering Race and Ethnicity (and doing it better), Keith Woods. Columbia University Graduate School of Journalism, 2001.

Facing Difference: Race, Gender, and Mass Media, Shirley Biagi and Marilyn Kern-Foxworth, eds. Pine Forge Press, 1997.

"50 Years Later: Brown v. Board of Education," *Teaching Tolerance*, Spring 2004.

Freedom of the Press: A Framework of Principle, William Ernest Hocking. The University of Chicago Press, 1947.

Gender, Race and Class in Media: A Text-Reader, Gail Dines and Jean M. Humez, eds. Sage Publications, 1995.

Good Ideas In Newspaper Diversity, tips from winners and nominees for the Robert G. McGruder awards for diversity leadership, compiled by the Freedom Forum, 2003.

Grutter v. Bollinger et al., United States Supreme Court, 539 U.S., June 23, 2003.

Guide to Research on Race and News, the Missouri School of Journalism, University of Missouri-Columbia, 2000.

"Handling Race/ethnicity in Descriptions: A Teaching Module," Keith Woods, Poynter Institute, Poynteronline, http://www.poynter.org, 2002.

How Long Must We Wait? The Fight for Racial and Ethnic Equality in the American News Media, Juan Gonzalez and Joseph Torres, independently published and released during UNITY 2004, http://images.democracynow.org/howlong.pdf

I Have Chosen to Stay and Fight, Margaret Cho. Riverhead Books, 2005.

Intercultural Encounters: The Fundamentals of Intercultural Communication, Donald W. Klopf. Morton Publishing Company, 2001.

Journalism Across Cultures, Fritz Cropp, Cynthia M. Frisby and Dean Mills, eds. Iowa State Press, 2003.

A Journalist's ToolBox: Techniques for Building Better Journalism, four tapes on interviewing, framing, other voices, and tapping your community. The Pew Center for Civic Journalism, http://www.pewcenter.org.

Latinos in the United States: A Resource Guide for Journalists, National Association of Hispanic Journalists, 2002.

"Redefining Our Sense of Place: Strong Connection to Changing Communities Produces Richer, Smarter Stories," Carol Weber Thomas, Knight Ridder News, Spring 2003.

Lesbians and Gays in the Newsroom: 10 Years Later, Leroy Aarons and Sheila Murphy, principal investigators, Annenberg School of Communication, University of Southern California, 2000.

Media Ethics: Cases and Moral Reasoning, Clifford G. Christians, Kim B. Rotzoll, Mark Fackler, Kathy Brittain McKee, and Robert H. Woods, Jr. Pearson, Inc. 2005.

Media Ethics: Issues and Cases, Phillip Patterson and Lee Wilkins. McGraw Hill, 2005.

Mass Communication Ethics: Decision Making In Postmodern Culture, Larry Z. Leslie. Houghton Mifflin Company, 2004.

"News As American As America," Sally Lehrman, Robert C. Maynard Institute for Journalism Education, 2005, http://www.maynardije.org.

Nickel and Dimed: On (Not) Getting By in America, Babara Ehrenreich, Owl Books, 2002.
The Newspaper Credibility Handbook: Practical Ways to Build Trust, Michele McLellan, American Society of Newspaper Editors' Journalism Credibility Project, April 2001.

Newsroom Diversity: Meeting the Challenge, Lawrence T. McGill. The Freedom Forum, 2000.

Pictures of Our Nobler Selves: A History of Native American Contributions to News Media, by Mark Trahant, The Freedom Forum First Amendment Center, 1995.

"The Push for Connections: Covering the Untold Stories," *Poynter Report: Special Issue,* Spring 2004.

Race: How Blacks and Whites Think and Feel about the American Obsession, Studs Terkel, Anchor, 1993.

Race Matters, Cornel West. Vintage Books, 2001.

Race, Multiculturalism, and the Media: From Mass to Class Communication, Clint C. Wilson II and Felix Gutiérrez. Sage Publications, 1995.

The Reading Red Report, the Native American Journalists Association and News Watch, http://www.naja.com, 2003.

Regents of the University of California v. Bakke, United States Supreme Court, 438 U.S., June 28, 1978.

Report of The National Advisory Commission on Civil Disorders, Otto Kerner, chair, U.S. Government Printing Office, 1968.

The State of the News Media 2004: An Annual Report on American Journalism, Tom Rosenstiel, the Project for Excellence in Journalism, 2004.

The Source Book of Multicultural Experts, 2004/05, Lisa Skriloff, ed. Multicultural Marketing Resources, Inc., 2004.

Thinking Clearly: Cases in Journalistic Decision-Making, Tom Rosenstiel and Amy S. Mitchell, eds. Columbia University Press, 2003.

We Are All Multiculturalists Now, Nathan Glazer. Harvard University Press, 1997.

"What Works?" Lori Robertson. *American Journalism Review,* August/September 2004.

White Lies: Race and the Myths of Whiteness, Maurice Berger. Farrar, Strauss and Giroux, New York, 1999.

White News: Why Local News Programs Don't Cover People of Color, Don Heider. Lawrence Erlbaum Associates, Publishers, 2000.

"White Privilege: Unpacking the Invisible Knapsack," Peggy McIntosh, *Working Paper 189, White Privilege and Male Privilege: A Personal Account of Coming To See Correspondences through Work in Women's Studies,* 1988. Wellesley College Center for Research on Women, Wellesley, Mass. 20181.

Why Are All the Black Kids Sitting Together in the Cafeteria? And Other Conversations About Race, Beverly Daniel Tatum. Basic Books, 1997.

Within the Veil: Black Journalists, White Media, Pamela Newkirk. New York University Press, 2000.

The Working Poor : Invisible in America, David K. Shipler, Knopf, 2004.

Film and Video

A Class Divided, about an Iowa schoolteacher who, the day after Martin Luther King Jr. was murdered in 1968, gave her third-grade students a first-hand experience in the meaning of discrimination, 1985, PBS. Features students involved in the experiment and their reactions fourteen years later. The story of Jane Elliot's blue-eyes, brown-eyes exercise was originally told in ABC News' *Eye of the Storm.* Other films focusing on the exercise and subsequent workshops include *The Angry Eye, Blue Eyed, The Essential Blue Eyed* and *The Complete Blue Eyed, The Thirty Minute Blue Eyed,* and *The Stolen Eye.*

The Color of Fear, a film about the state of race relations in America as seen through the eyes of eight North American men of Asian, European, Latino, and African descent, who engage in an open and candid dialogue on race and ethnicity, Lee Mun Wah, 1994.

Images of Indians, a five-part PBS series exploring Native American stereotypes: *The Great Movie Massacre, How Hollywood Wins the West, Warpaint and Wigs, Heathen Injuns and Hollywood Gospel,* and *The Movie Reel Indian,* 1982.

Matters of Race, a four-hour production of KQED and PBS, examining the relationship between race and power, http://www.kqed.org/tv/community/mattersofrace, 2003.

Laramie Project, a 2002 HBO film that tells the story of Matthew Shepard's murder through interviews conducted by a group of young actors and writers from a New York City theater company who seek out Laramie residents to discover how their lives were changed on October 6, 1998.

Mickey Mouse Monopoly: Disney, Childhood and Corporate Power, a documentary produced and written by Chyng Sun, directed, filmed, and edited by Miguel Picker. Takes a close and critical look at the world created by Disney films and the stories they tell about race, gender, and class, 2001.

Normal, an HBO film that tells the story of a seemingly "normal" Midwestern factory worker who stuns his family and community by revealing he wants a sex change operation, Sundance selection, 2003.

Not in Our Town, a documentary about the people of Billings, Montana, who took a stand against hate violence in their community. Spawned efforts by other communities to speak out and take actions against racial and ethnic violence, 1995.

Smoke Signals, feature-length movie by and about Native Americans, directed by Chris Eyre, tells the story of a cross-country trek by an unlikely pair whose differences lead to friendship and discovery, Sundance selection, 1998.

Skins, feature-length movie filmed on location at the Pine Ridge Oglala Lakota reservation in South Dakota, a shocking look at life on the modern reservation, directed by Chris Eyre, 2002.

Time of Fear, traces the lives of the 16,000 Japanese-Americans during WWII who were sent to two camps relocation camps in southeast Arkansas, a PBS video.

Two Towns of Jasper, tells the story of a 1998 incident in which three white men in the small town of Jasper, Texas, chained a black man to the back of their pickup truck and dragged him to his death. The film relates how it affected all the residents of the town, both black and white.

When Billy Broke His Head . . . and Other Tales of Wonder, documentary about disability, civil rights, and the search for intelligent life after brain damage, directed by Billy Golfus and David E. Simpson, 1994.

Getting the Right Words

Following are some of the most used terms relating to diversity. Consult the NABJ, NAHJ, AAJA, NAJA, SAJA, and NLGJA websites and individual guides listed in the resource appendix for additional terms.

Abayah — long robe-like clothing worn by some Arab women; also called jilbab or chador.

Aboriginal — those who have inhabited an area from the earliest known times; indigenous people.

Afflicted with, suffers from, victim of — avoid the assumption that every person with a disability "suffers" or is a "victim."

African American — an individual living in the United States who has African ancestry; although often used interchangeably with black, all black people living in the United States are not of African decent. Hyphenate only when using as an adjective.

Afro-American — archaic term; avoid.

Ageism — discrimination or prejudice against people based on age.

Agnostic — a person who believes that, at our present level of knowledge, we cannot know whether or not a God exists.

AIDS — Acquired Immune Deficiency Syndrome, medical condition in which the body's immune system does not adequately combat certain diseases; caused by HIV destruction of white blood cells.

AIM — American Indian Movement; activist organization founded in 1968 to promote civil rights for Native Americans.

Alaskan Native — refers to indigenous people of Alaska.

Alien — being from another planet; a citizen of another country; someone who does not belong; increasingly associated with a negative connotation and should be avoided.

Allah — God.

All American — can be offensive when used in a narrow sense meaning "white, blond," and the like.

AME — African Methodist Episcopal Church; independent Methodist church founded in Philadelphia in 1794.

Amerasian — a person who has both American and Asian parentage; not a synonym with Asian American, which is a term applying to an individual whose parents are both Asian but who is an American citizen by either birth or naturalization.

America — the entire Western Hemisphere, including North, South, and Central America; not solely the United States.

American Indian — interchangeable with Native American; use tribal affiliation (Cherokee, Navajo) depending on preference of the source in question.

Anti-Semitism — hatred toward Jews; discrimination or prejudice against people because of their belief in Judaism.

Arab — a person from an Arabic-speaking country.

Arab American — an individual who descends from an Arabic-speaking country and who is an American citizen by either birth or naturalization; not all Arab Americans are Muslims.

Asian American — applies to someone with Asian parents who is a U.S. citizen by either birth or naturalization; some argue that the continued use of the Asian identifier perpetuates the sense of being outsiders regardless of how long their families have lived in the United States.

Asian Indian — avoid as a means of distinguishing from American Indians; instead say "people from India" or "Indian Americans" when referring to U.S. citizens and permanent residents with Indian ancestry.

Atheist — someone who does not believe in the existence of God or other deities.

Barrio — section of a town or city dominated by Latino residents; like the word *ghetto*, it has a negative connotation and should be avoided.

BIA — Bureau of Indian Affairs; largely made up of tribal members, BIA is the federal agency charged with overseeing (enhancing the quality of life, promoting economic opportunity, and so on) the affairs of tribal nations.

Biracial — an individual who traces his or her heritage to two races; "mixed" is not an acceptable synonym; use only when relevant.

Birth defect — avoid; when appropriate use "born with a disability" or "person who has had a disability since birth."

Bisexual — an individual, male or female, who may be attracted to either sex.

Black — generally the preferred term, unless subject prefers otherwise, when referring to race; use lowercase and only as an adjective: black journalist, black people; however, use only when race is relevant.

Black diaspora — referring to black people of African descent dispersed by way of slavery and colonization throughout the world.

Black Muslim — archaic reference to sect of black Muslims; members prefer to be called Muslims.

Blind — adjective; describes a person with complete vision loss; a person may be legally blind but still have some vision. When appropriate to refer to the disability of those who are not totally blind, use "visually impaired" or "partially sighted."

Blue collar — refers to a manual laborer, usually one who works for wages as opposed to a set salary or commission.

Born Again Christian — a person who has repented of his sins and accepted Jesus as Lord and Savior. Conservative Protestants believe that this is the only way one can get to heaven. Some of these denominations do not require that a person repent first.

Brave — offensive; do not use as a term to describe American Indian males.

Buck — avoid; racial slur historically used to refer to young black and Native American males.

Burka — loose garment with veiled eyeholes worn by some Muslim women, particularly in India and Pakistan.

191

Central America — the land mass between North and South America; between Mexico and Columbia.

Chador — face scarf or robe worn by some Arab women as a sign of modesty or hijab.

Chicano — a popular 1960s term for Mexican Americans, particularly on the West Coast; not universally accepted and should not be used as an identifier without asking first.

Chinaman — racial slur typically used in a broad sweep to describe anyone of Asian descent; should be avoided.

Chink — negative racial term applied largely to Chinese and Chinese Americans; should be avoided.

Cinco de Mayo — May 5, a popular celebration having significance for Mexican communities in Mexico and the United States; relates to the 1862 Battle of Puebla in which Mexican forces defeated a much larger French army; sometimes mislabeled Mexican Independence Day, which actually is September 16.

Civil Rights Act — culmination of civil rights movement in the mid-twentieth century; Congress passed the Civil Rights Act in 1964 and the Voting Rights Act in 1965 guaranteeing basic civil rights to all people regardless of race.

Civil union — refers to a legal arrangement between two people of the same sex that provides rights similar to those enjoyed by married couples.

Classism — discrimination or prejudice against people based on economic or social class.

Closeted — a person who is "in the closet" does not wish to share his or her sexual orientation.

Colored — archaic; use only in historic quotes or referring to organizations, names, or events that still use the term as a part of an official designation.

Coming out — the process of coming out of the closet or making one's sexual orientation known.

Confined to a wheelchair — avoid; people with disabilities who "use wheelchairs" don't think of themselves as being confined; in fact, a wheelchair provides mobility.

Cripple, crippled — avoid; if necessary to describe a person's disability use an accurate description: "walks with assistance" or "uses a wheelchair."

Cross-dresser — one who wears clothing usually associated with the opposite sex; not necessarily an indication of sexual orientation.

Cuban American — a citizen of the United States with Cuban ancestors; one who came to the United States and became naturalized or who is of Cuban descent born in the United States.

Dark continent — offensive; avoid as a term referring to Africa.

Deaf — adjective; refers to a person with total or near complete hearing loss. Those whose hearing loss is not as advanced may, when appropriate, be referred to as "hearing impaired" or "hard of hearing" or having a "hearing loss."

Deaf-dumb, deaf-mute — avoid; these terms have a negative connotation.

Deformed — avoid; has negative connotation; if necessary, describe the specific disability.

Diaspora — refers to the dispersion of people of one race who once were concentrated in a single place; the Black Diaspora, for example, refers to black people of African descent throughout the world.

Differently abled, handi-capable — avoid trendy terms such as these and others like "physically challenged" and "inconvenienced." "Person with a disability" is preferred.

Disabled, disability — preferred terms; when possible use "person with a disability" rather than "disabled person."

Disadvantaged — social class of people who are historically oppressed due to a lack of economic, social, and political power.

Domestic partners — an unmarried couple of the same or opposite sex who live together as partners; may or may not have legal implications depending on state law.

Down low — usually refers to men of color who have sex with other men without the knowledge of their female partners; MSM or "men who have sex with men" is used to convey an equivalent meaning.

Drag — dressing in the clothes of the opposite sex.

Drag queen — usually a male performer who dresses in female clothing for entertainment.

Dyke — avoid; derogatory term for a lesbian.

Eid Al-Fitr — celebration at the end of the Muslim holy month, Ramadan.

Eskimo — people who inhabit Arctic coastal areas of North American, parts of Greenland, and northeast Siberia; sometimes considered offensive; Inuit can be substituted in most instances, depending on the native language.

ESL — English as a Second Language.

Ethnicity — group identity based on language and social-cultural background.

Eurocentric — focusing on Europe or European concerns, often in an arrogant, "Europe is the center of the world" sort of way.

Evangelical — strong believer; one who is zealous in their support of the Christian religion and extremely eager to have other people share his or her beliefs.

Executive Order 9066 — 1942 order by F.D.R., which led to the internment of more than 100,000 Japanese Americans, two-thirds of whom were U.S. citizens, during WWII.

Fag, faggot — avoid; derogatory term for a gay male.

Faithism — discrimination or prejudice against someone based on faith or religious belief or nonbelief.

First Nations — refers to the indigenous people of Canada.

Fit — seizure is preferred.

Five Pillars of Islam — refers to the sacred expectation of followers of Islam: faith in shehada (there is no god but God, and Muhammad is his prophet); salat (prayer five times daily); sharing of alms with the poor; fasting during Ramadan; and completing hajj (pilgrimage to Makkah).

Fundamentalist — one who believes in strict adherence to the basic beliefs of a faith; often associated with the Evangelical Christian movement.

Gay — preferred umbrella term when referring to homosexual men; refer to homosexual women as lesbian; use gay men and lesbian when referring to both men and women; use only when it is appropriate to refer to individuals by their sexual orientation.

Gay lifestyle — should be avoided; being lesbian, gay, bisexual, or transgender is not just a lifestyle that one chooses; it is life.

Ghetto — avoid due to negative connotation; refers to poor inner city.

Guide dogs — also called assistance animals, service animals, and Seeing Eye (registered trademark) dogs.

Gullah — refers to descendants of African slaves living on the barrier islands along the coast of South Carolina, Georgia, and Florida; the Gullah language can still be heard on some of the islands where Gullah culture continues to flourish.

Hajj — pilgrimage to Makkah; all Muslims are expected to make the pilgrimage at least once during their lifetime.

Half-blood or half-breed — avoid; derogatory term, used in the past to refer to an American Indian with mixed heritage.

Handicap, handicapped — avoid due to the negative connotation ; "disability" or "person with a disability" is preferred; replace even terms like "handicap parking" or "handicap seating" with "parking" or "seating for people with disabilities."

Heterosexual — refers to people who are attracted to members of the opposite sex.

Hijab — modesty, the trait that leads some Arab women to wear robes and face scarves; also refers to a type of veil or face scarf.

Hispanic — term created and used in the 1980 census by U.S. government to describe people from or descended from a Spanish-speaking country; often used interchangeably with Latino; determine an individual's preferred identification when relevant.

HIV — human immunodeficiency virus, the virus that causes AIDS.

Hmong — ethnic groups inhabiting parts of China, Laos, Thailand, and Vietnam; several thousand Hmong refugees relocated to the United States following Vietnam-era fighting in Laos.

Homo — pejorative term and is never acceptable.

Homophobia — irrational dislike, fear, or even hatred of people who are gay or lesbian.

Homosexual — refers to people who are attracted to members of the same sex; use lesbian and gay men instead.

Hyphenated Americans — when referring to groups of people by their race or national origin, use the nonhyphenated form: Korean American, Asian American, African American; as an adjective, use the hyphen: Korean-American family, African-American culture. President Teddy Roosevelt, in 1915, criticized "hyphenated Americans" for not contributing to the mainstream of America. Consider if it's ever necessary to identify people by race or country of origin, particularly those who may have been in America for generations.

Illegal alien — an individual who has entered the country without legal documentation; preferred term is "undocumented immigrant."

Illegal immigrant — "undocumented worker" or "undocumented immigrant" is preferred.

Imam — one who leads prayer at a mosque; leader in an Islamic community; also called a sheik.

Infantile paralysis — polio.

Inner city — avoid this and other stereotypical references to poor communities of color.

Internment — confinement of someone regarded as a security threat; often refers to the confinement of Japanese Americans, many of them American citizens, in concentration camps during WWII.

Invalid — avoid; pejorative term that refers to someone with a disability.

Islam — with over one billion followers, the Islam religion is the second largest in the world; followers of the Islam belief are Muslims.

Jack and Jill of America — an African-American cultural, social, and civic organization for black children; founded in 1938, currently has over 8,000 members.

Jihad — Arabic term referring to the Islamic concept of the struggle to do good; is not synonymous with Holy War, which is a term used by Muslim extremists.

Jim Crow laws — refers to laws and practices, largely in the South, that imposed racial segregation through the mid-sixties.

Juneteenth — June 19, black Emancipation Day, celebration of the end of slavery.

Kafiyyeh — traditional, nonreligious, checkered head covering worn by some Arab men to exhibit pride in their culture.

Kwanzaa — African-American cultural holiday, Dec. 26 through Jan. 1; derived from traditional African harvest festivals.

Lame — avoid when referring to a person.

La migra — slang for Immigration and Naturalization Service (INS).

Latin America — in its broadest sense applies to all those countries in the New World whose national language is Spanish, as well as Brazil, Haiti, and other Caribbean islands.

Latino — ethnic description; people who are from or who are descended from a Spanish-speaking country; sometimes used interchangeably with Hispanic; when appropriate to use the ethnic identification, use that preferred by the source or subject; note that while Latino refers to men, boys, and mixed gender groups, the correct term for girls and women is Latina.

Lesbian — the currently preferred term for a female homosexual when it is appropriate to identify an individual by sexual orientation.

LGBT — lesbian, gay, bisexual, and transgender.

Little person — refers to a person of short stature; avoid dwarf or midget; avoid the trendy "vertically challenged"; if necessary to refer to the height of a person of short stature, ask for his preference.

Makkah (preferred) or **Mecca** — birthplace of Muhammad and Islam holy site located in western Saudi Arabia near the Red Sea; millions of Muslims make a pilgrimage there each year.

Mexican — a citizen of Mexico; incorrect when used as a label for Hispanic or Latino people, all of whom are not from Mexico.

Mexican American — a citizen of the United States with Mexican ancestors.

Minimum wage — the minimum amount required by the federal Fair Labor Standards Act for qualifying employees; currently $5.15 per hour. A person earning minimum wage and working forty hours per week with no time off would make $10,712 in a year.

Minority, minorities — increasingly viewed as a somewhat negative term because of the unempowered status of most things that are minor or seen in a minority perspective; people of color can be used as an alternative in most instances.

Mosque — Muslim place of worship.

Muhammad — preferred over Mohammad; the Muslim prophet and founder of Islam.

Mulatto — archaic term once used to refer to an individual with one white and one black parent; should be avoided.

Muslim — a follower of the Islam belief, the second largest religion in the world; all Muslims are not Arabs, and not all Arabs or Arab Americans are Muslim.

Negro — while still a part of some organizational names such as the United Negro College Fund and is acceptable in such references, it should not be used in references to individuals; use black or African American.

New World — avoid; implies that there was no one in the Americas prior to the arrival of the Europeans.

Niggardly — tight or stingy; often viewed with a derogatory connotation due to its similarity to the word *nigger*; best to avoid.

Nigger — a highly inflammatory racial slur; should not be used.

Nondisabled — reference, if necessary, to a person who does not have a disability; avoid the trendy "temporarily abled."

Nuyorican — someone who is of Puerto Rican descent but who was born and grew up in New York City.

Oreo — black on the outside, white inside; refers to a black person who acts white; similar to the use of Uncle Tom; should not be used.

Oriental — avoid; no longer used when referring to people of Asian descent; use Asian or Asian American.

People of color — increasingly popular term for describing people of diverse races and ethnicities; also use journalists of color, students of color, and the like.

Permanent resident — person with a green card; has legal status to live and work in the United States on a permanent basis.

Pink triangle — symbol of gay pride; gay men were required to wear the label in Nazi concentration camps during WWII.

Poverty — according to the U.S. Department of Health and Human Services, a person who earns less than $9,310 or a family of four earning less than $18,850 would fall below the poverty threshold.

Powwow — a traditional Native American celebration and social gathering honoring sacred traditions through dancing, singing, and drumming.

Queer — has had its ups and downs as a term for gay; once considered pejorative, it currently is being used as an umbrella term by some LGBT people; still best to avoid.

Quran — the preferred spelling of the Muslim holy book; do not use Koran.

Race — a classification of humans by skin color and physical characteristics; has little real significance and is generally inappropriate as a means of identifying people.

Rainbow flag — symbol of the diversity of the LGBT community.

Ramadan — ninth month of the Muslim calendar, a month of fasting ending in celebration.

Refugee — a person from one country admitted to another because of a fear of persecution; Montgnards, for example, sought refuge in the United States because of their fear of persecution in Vietnam.

Religion — an organized system of beliefs by which someone lives; usually associated with a belief in the existence of a divine power.

Reservations — areas of land reserved by the U.S. government as permanent tribal homelands; only about 40 percent of Native Americans live on reservations today.

Sexual preference — use "sexual orientation" instead; preference implies that one chooses his or her sexual orientation.

Sovereign — self-governing or independent; free from external control.

Spanglish — combination of Spanish and English to create new words or sentences that combine words from both languages.

Spic — offensive term sometimes used to refer to people of Spanish or Mexican descent; do not use.

Squaw — avoid; not acceptable as a term applying to Native American women.

Straight — acceptable common term for heterosexual.

Synagogue — Jewish house of prayer; place of worship and communal center for followers of Judaism.

Tejano, Tejana — one of Mexican descent living in Texas.

Third World — viewed as a Eurocentric label; "developing world" is preferred.

Transgender — applies to all stages of becoming or being transsexual (preoperative, postoperative, or nonoperative), as well as to cross-dressers and drag queens or kings.

Transsexual — a person who identifies as a member of the opposite sex; acquires the physical characteristics of the opposite sex; not an indication of sexual orientation.

Transvestite — avoid; the correct term is cross-dresser.

Tribe — historically, people united by family, language, religion, and political systems; some dislike the term, preferring instead Indian nations, legally recognized as self-governing sovereign entities; others use the two (tribes or nations) interchangeably.

Twinkie — avoid; derogatory term referring to someone who is Asian but acts white, similar.

Undocumented immigrant — preferred over illegal alien; a person living in the United States who does not have the federal documents needed to legally live and work here.

Vegetable, vegetative state — do not use to refer to people; comatose or nonresponsive is preferred.

Warpath — avoid this and similar terms (wampum, for example), which tend to evoke stereotypical images.

Wheelchair — when necessary to the story, refer to a person as one who "uses a wheelchair" rather than as being "wheelchair bound" or "confined to a wheelchair."

Wigger — negative term, avoid; white person who takes on the dress, language, and so on of black people; white person who wants to be black.

End Notes

Introduction to Part One

[1] Ernest Sotomayor, "Letter to the Industry," *UNITY Online*, December 5, 2004
http://www.unityjournalists.org/przmsg_120504.html

[2] Sotomayor.

[3] "U.S. Interim Projections by Age, Sex, Race, and Hispanic Origin," U.S. Census Bureau, August 26, 2004
http://www.census.gov/ipc/www/usinterimproj

Chapter One

[4] Kay Mills, "JAWS Herstory," Journalism & Women Symposium, March 30, 2002
http://www.jaws.org/members/herstory/index.html

[5] "ASNE Sets New Vision for Newsroom Diversity Beyond 2000," American Society of Newspaper Editors, October 20, 1998 http://www.asne.org/index.cfm?id=1400

[6] Keith Woods, "The Essence of Excellence: Covering Race and Ethnicity (and doing it better)" (Columbia University Graduate School of Journalism, 2001) 5.

[7] Keith Woods, "The Woods Theorem: A New Formula for Diversity in American News Organizations," *The Values and Craft of American Journalism: Essays from the Poynter Institute*, Roy Peter Clark and Cole C. Campbell, eds. (Gainesville: University Press of Florida, 2000), 106.

[8] "Diversity at Appalachian State University," *AppState*, 2005
http://www.diversity.appstate.edu/diversityDefined.html

[9] "Defining Diversity: ISU's Definition of Diversity," Iowa State University, 2005 http://www.public.iastate.edu/~aao/eod/definitions.html

[10] "Defining Diversity: Other Definitions of Diversity," Iowa State University, 2005
http://www.public.iastate.edu/~aao/eod/definitions.html

[11] Beverly Daniel Tatum, *Why Are All the Black Kids Sitting Together in the Cafeteria?* (New York: Basic Books, 2003), 22.

[12] "Diversity Mission," American Society of Newspaper Editors, April 29, 2002
http://www.asne.org/index.cfm?id=3468

[13] Beverly Kees, "The Diversity Standard," *Diversity: Best Practices* (The Accrediting Council on Education in Journalism and Mass Communications, 2003), 6.

[14] Kees, 5.

[15] Peter Wood, *Diversity: The Invention of a Concept* (San Francisco: Encounter Books, 2003), 88.

[16] Potter Stewart, concurring opinion, *Jacobellis v. Ohio*, 378 U.S. 184, June 22, 1964.

[17] "AAJA All-American Stylebook: Glossary Updates," *All-American: How to Cover Asian America* (Asian American Journalism Association, 2000), a1–a2.

[18] Roberto R. Ramirez and G. Patricia de la Cruz, "The Hispanic Population in the United States," *Current Population Reports* (U.S. Census Bureau, June 2003), 1.

[19] Bureau of Indian Affairs, Department of Interior, *Federal Register*, Vol. 67, No. 134, July 12, 2002.

[20] "Indian Country Resource Guide," *The American Indian and the Media*, Mark Anthony Rolo, ed. (The National Conference for Community and Justice, 2000), 82.

[21] "100 Questions and Answers About Arab Americans: A Journalist's Guide," *Detroit Free Press*, 2001
http://www.freep.com/jobspage/arabs

22 Don Heider, *White News: Why Local News Programs Don't Cover People of Color* (Mahwah, New Jersey: Lawrence Erlbaum Associates, Publishers, 2000), 5.

23 "Diversity Dictionary," *Diversity Database: Moving Towards Community,* University of Maryland, 2001 http://www.inform.umd.edu/EdRes/Topic/Diversity/ Reference/divdic.html

24 "Culture," *Encarta World English Dictionary,* Microsoft Corporation, 2005 http://encarta.msn.com/dictionary /culture.html

25 Jesse McKinnon, "The Black Population in the United States," *Current Population Reports* (U.S. Census Bureau, April 2003), 1.

26 "NABJ Style," National Association of Black Journalists, 2004 http://www.nabj. org/newsroom/style-book/index.html

26 "Indian Country Resource Guide," 80.

28 "The Diversity Style Guide," News Watch, 2004 http://www.ciij.org/ newswatch/?news_section_id=16

29 National Association of Hispanic Journalists, 2005 http://www.nahj.org/home/ home.shtml

30 "How Not to Cover Asian America," *All-American: How to Cover Asian America* (Asian American Journalism Association, 2000), 33.

31 "How Not to Cover," 34.

32 Tatum, 15.

33 B. Lee Artz, "Hegemony in Black and White: Interracial Buddy Films and the New Racism," *Cultural Diversity and the U.S. Media,* Yahya R. Kamalipour and Theresa Carilli, eds. (New York: State University of New York Press, 1998), 67.

34 Heider, 8.

35 William McGowan, *Coloring the News: How Political Correctness Has Corrupted American Journalism* (San Francisco: Encounter Books, 2002), 9.

36 "The Face and Mind of the American Journalist," *American Journalist Survey* (Indiana University School of Journalism, 2003), Poynteronline http://www.poynter.org/ content/content_view.asp?id=28235

37 "Newsroom Employment Census," *American Society of Newspaper Editors/Diversity*, April 20, 2004 http://www.asne.org/index.cfm?id=1138

38 Mae Cheng, "Increasing Newsroom Diversity: It's Time to Make It Personal," UNITY Online, April 12, 2005 http://www.unityjournalists.org/news25.html

39 Bob Papper, "Running in Place," *Communicator*, July/August 2005: 26–32 http://www.rtnda.org/research/research.shtml

40 Papper, 26.

41 "Diversity in the Washington Newspaper Press Corps," *UNITY: Journalists of Color and the University of Maryland Philip Merrill College of Journalism*, August 2005 http://www.unityjournalists.org/index.html

42 "Diversity in the Washington Newspaper Press Corps," 6.

43 "Diversity in the Washington Newspaper Press Corps," 7.

44 Leroy Aarons and Sheila Murphy (principal investigators), *Lesbians and Gays in the Newsroom 10 Years Later* (Annenberg School of Communications, University of Southern California, 2000), 60.

45 Aarons, 11.

46 Aarons, 64.

47 Aarons, 63.

48 Robert Dodge, "Messages," *Lesbians and Gays in the Newsroom 10 Years Later*, Leroy Aarons and Sheila Murphy, principal investigators (Annenberg School of Communications, University of Southern California, 2000), 6.

Chapter Two

[49] Justice Lewis Powell, *Regents of the University of California v. Bakke*, 438 U.S. 265, June 28, 1978, 16.

[50] Justice Sandra Day O'Connor, *Grutter v. Bollinger* et al, 539 U.S. __, June 23, 2003.

[51] John C. Merrill, "Overview: Foundations for Media Ethics," *Controversies in Media Ethics*, by A. David Gordon and John Michael Kittross (New York: Longman, 1999), 1.

[52] Bob Steele, "Doing Ethics: Ask Good Questions to Make Good Ethical Decisions," handout at Diversity Across the Curriculum Seminar, Poynter Institute, 2003.

[53] Commission on Freedom of the Press, *A Free and Responsible Press*, Robert D. Leigh, ed. (Chicago: The University of Chicago Press, 1947), 21.

[54] "The News Media and the Disorders," *Report of the National Advisory Commission on Civil Disorders* (Washington, D.C.: U.S. Government Printing Office, 1968), 212.

[55] "The Face and Mind of the American Journalist."

[56] Cornel West, *Race Matters* (New York: Vintage Books, 2001), 93.

[57] Powell, 310.

[58] John Robinson, "The Editor's Log: My Sunday Newspaper Column," New-Record.com, November 27, 2004 http://www.blog.news-record.com/jrblog/ archives/2004/11/my_Sunday_newsp.html

[59] Powell, 310.

[60] Powell, 316.

[61] Ruth Bader Ginsburg, dissenting, *Gratz v. Bollinger* et al., 539 U.S. __ 2003.

[62] West, 95.

[63] Peter Wood, 145.

[64] McGowan, 7–8.

[65] West, 96–97.

[66] Ramirez, 1.

[67] Alfredo Garza, "Ignoring the Latino Consumer Is a Risky Business," *Viva: The Latino Culture Magazine* 2004: Vol. 1, Edition 1.

[68] Howard Buford, "Getting Serious About Winning the African American Market," *The Source Book of Multicultural Experts* (New York: Multicultural Marketing Resources, 2004), 9.

[69] Saul Gitlin, "The Rise of the Multicultural Consumer," *The Source Book of Multicultural Experts* (New York: Multicultural Marketing Resources, 2004), 15.

[70] Howard Buford, "Understanding Today's Gay Consumer Market," *The Source Book of Multicultural Experts* (New York: Multicultural Marketing Resources, 2004), 48.

[71] Gitlin.

[72] Don Williamson, "Finding Gold in Diversity," *People & Product: Supplement to Presstime*, March 2000 http://www.naa.org/diversity/people-and-product/index.html

[73] Williamson, 1–2.

[74] "ASNE Diversity Mission," American Society of Newspaper Editors, April 29, 2002 http://www.asne.org/index.cfm?id=3468

[75] "Time-Out for Diversity and Accuracy," American Society of Newspaper Editors, 1999 http://www.asne.org/kiosk/diversity/1999timeout/premise.htm

[76] "Time-Out."

[77] Clint C. Wilson II and Felix Gutiérrez, *Race, Multiculturalism, and the Media: From Mass to Class*

Communication (Thousand Oaks, California: Sage Publications, 1995), 24.

[78] David Yarnold, "Diversity Toolbox: Why Diversity?" Society of Professional Journalists, 2002 http://www.spj.org/diveristy_toolbox_why.asp

[79] "A Complete Picture," handout at Diversity Across the Curriculum Seminar, Poynter Institute, 2003.

[80] Keith Woods, *The Essence of Excellence*, 3.

[81] "Time-Out."

[82] "Time-Out."

[83] "Code of Ethics," Society of Professional Journalists, 2005 http://www.spj.org /ethics_code.asp

[84] Jesse Jackson, address, Democratic Convention, July 17, 1984.

[85] Martin Luther King, "Letter from a Birmingham Jail," April 16, 1963.

Chapter Three

[86] "Newsroom Employment Census," ASNE http://www.asne.org/ index.cfm?id=1138

[87] Commission on Freedom of the Press, 21.

[88] National Advisory Commission on Civil Disorders, 210–211.

[89] National Advisory Commission on Civil Disorders, 212.

[90] "Newsroom Census," ASNE.

[91] Sotomayor, "Letter to the Industry."

[92] "Newsroom Census," ASNE.

[93] Lawrence T. McGill, *Newsroom Diversity: Meeting the Challenge* (Arlington, Virginia: The Freedom Forum, 2000), 3 http://www.freedomforum.org/publications/ diversity/meetingthechallenge/meetingthechallenge.pdf

[94] McGill, 6.

[95] Bill Kovach and Tom Rosenstiel, *The Elements of Journalism: What Newspeople Should Know and the Public Should Expect* (New York: Three Rivers Press, 2001), 188.

[96] Bryan Monroe, "Newsroom Diversity: Truth vs. Fiction," *Nieman Reports*, Fall 2003, 29.

[97] Monroe, 31.

[98] Mary Sanchez, "Anytown, Anytime," Poynteronline, August 11, 2003 http://www.poynter.org/content/content_print.asp?id=42848&customs=

[99] Carol Weber Thomas, "Redefining Our Sense of Place," Knight Ridder News, Spring 2003, 26.

[100] Sue Ellen Christian, "Different Takes on What Makes a Newsroom Diverse," *Society of Professional Journalists Quill*, January 2005.

[101] Christian.

[102] Lori Robertson, "What Works?" *American Journalism Review*, August/ September 2004, 39–41.

[103] Carmen L. Manning-Miller and Karen Brown Dunlap, "The Move Toward Pluralism in Journalism and Mass Communication Education," *Journalism and Mass Communication Educator*, Spring 2002, 45.

[104] "Diversity: Best Practices," 14.

[105] "Diversity: Best Practices," 15.

[106] "Diversity: Best Practices," 21.

Chapter Four

[107] Keith Woods, "Talking Across Difference," handout at Diversity Across the Curriculum Seminar, Poynter Institute, 2003.

[108] Teresa Cosby, participant, "A Beginning Conversation on Diversity and State Planning," ed. Lillian Moy, *Management Information Exchange*, Winter 2001, 38.

[109] "Conversation Guidelines," Michigan Great Start Project, 2004
http://www.michigan.gov/greatstart/0,1607,7-197-27385-82434—,00.html

[110] Keith Woods, "Talking Across Difference."

[111] Aly Colon, "At Ease With Diversity," Poynteronline, August 19, 2003 http://www.poynter.org/content/content_print.asp?id=444882&custom=

[112] Colon, "At Ease With Diversity."

[113] Dori J. Maynard, "Why Journalists Can't Talk Across Race," Maynard Institute, 2004 http://maynardije.org/columns/dorimaynard/040514_assessment

[114] Ruth Seymour, "Bias Survey: A Teaching Module," Poynteronline, August 6, 2002 http://poynteronline.org/content/content_view.asp?id=9521&sid=5

[115] Peggy McIntosh, "White Privilege: Unpacking the Invisible Knapsack," *Working Paper 189 White Privilege and Male Privilege: A Personal Account of Coming To See Correspondences through Work in Women's Studies* (Wellesley, Mass.: Wellesley College Center for Research on Women, 1988).

[116] McIntosh, "White Privilege."

[117] Maynard, "Why Journalists Can't Talk Across Race."

Chapter Five

[118] Based on conversations with Turner Catledge in 1981 and 1982 when Catledge would return to his alma mater, Mississippi State University where the author was a member of the journalism faculty, to spend time with students and faculty.

[119] Matt Thompson, "The Invisible Reporter: Q&A with Anne Hull," Poynteronline, October 8, 2003 http://www.poynter.org/content/content_print.asp?id=50594&custom=

[120] Pankaj Paul, "Tips for Reporting on Race and Ethnicity," handout distributed during a reporting and diversity seminar at the 2004 UNITY: Journalists of Color conference in Washington, D.C., August 6, 2004.

[121] Wanda Lloyd, "Tips for Reporting on Race and Ethnicity," UNITY 2004.

[122] Elizabeth Llorente, "The 'Beat' Generation: Ten Tips for Reporting on the Diverse Community," People & Product: Tenfold, NAA, March 2000 http://www.naa.org/diversity/people-and-product/tenfold.html

[123] Matt Thompson, "The Invisible Reporter: Q&A with Anne Hull."

[124] General email to "all users," forwarded following the incident to the students on the campus where this occurred in February 2005.

[125] Keith Woods, "Covering Race Relations: Guidelines and Tips," handout distributed at the 2004 UNITY: Journalists of Color conference, Washington, D.C., August 2004.

[126] Keith Woods, "The Language of Race," Poynteronline, July 1999 http://www.poynter.org/content/content_view.asp?id=5468&sid=5

[127] Aly Colon, "The Color Connection," Poynteronline, July 2003 http://www.poynter.org/content/content_print.asp?id=40631&custom=

[128] "Jogger Is Raped in Predawn Darkness," *The St. Petersburg Times*, October 7, 1999.

129 "Racial Identification: Some Guidelines," Poynter Institute, handout at Diversity Across the Curriculum Seminar, Poynter Institute, 2003.

130 Abe Rosenberg, "Trade Secrets: Don't Let Racism Creep into Your Writing," *RTNDA Communicator*, July/August 2002 http://www.rtnda.org/trades/racism.shtml

131 Llorente, "The 'Beat' Generation."

132 Rosenberg, "Trade Secrets: Don't Let Racism Creep into Your Writing."

Chapter Six

133 Courtland Milloy, "Out From Under the Thumb of White Bias," washingtonpost.com, January 26, 2005 http://www.washingtonpost.com/wp-dyn/articles/A36395-2005Jan25.html

134 "NABJ@30: Telling Our Story," National Association of Black Journalists, December 12, 2004 http://nabj.org/front/nabj/v-print/story/921p-1446c.html

135 "NABJ@30: Telling Our Story."

136 National Advisory Commission on Civil Disorders, 201–212.

137 "Newsroom Census," ASNE.

138 "Newsroom Census," ASNE; Papper, "Recovering Lost Ground"; and U.S. Census Bureau.

139 Rosenberg, "Trade Secrets: Don't Let Racism Creep into Your Writing."

140 Encarta.

141 Keith Woods, "Taking Race Over a Slice of Watermelon," Poynteronline, July 2003 http://poynteronline.org/column.asp?id=58&aid=42722

142 Buford, "Getting Serious About Winning the African American Market."

143 Republicans Are Running for Office in the South," Associated Press, June 15, 2004 http://e.thetimes-news.com/Default/Client.asp?Enter=true&skin=_FreeBur&Daily=FreeBur

Chapter Seven

144 "Hispanic Population Passes 40 Million, Census Bureau Reports," *U.S. Census Bureau News*, June 9, 2005 http://www.census.gov/prod/2001pubs/c2kbr01-3.pdf

145 Ramirez, "The Hispanic Population in the United States."

146 Marie Arana, "The Elusive Hispanic/Latino Identity: Variations on a Theme," *Latinos in the United States: A Resource Guide for Journalists* (Washington, D.C.: National Association of Hispanic Journalists, 2002), 7–8.

147 "U.S. Born Hispanics Increasingly Drive Population Developments," *Pew Hispanic Center Fact Sheet*, January 2002 http://pewhispanic.org/files/factsheets/2.pdf

148 "U.S. Born Hispanics Increasingly Drive Population Developments."

149 "Spanish in the United States," Wikipedia, January 2006 http://en.wikipedia.org/wiki/Spanish_in_the_United_States

150 Alex López Negrete, "For Hispanics, Main Street Becomes the Boulevard of Dreams," *The Source Book of Multicultural Experts*, 21–22.

151 Juan Antonio Lizama, "Latino Liaison for Kaine Set for Statewide Outreach," *Richmond Times Dispatch*, TimesDispatch.com, January 21, 2006 http://www.timesdispatch.com

152 Ramirez, "The Hispanic Population in the United States."

153 Mary Sanchez, ed., "Periodismo," *Latinos in the United States: A Resource Guide for Journalists*, 24.

154 Sanchez, ed., 24.

155 *Latinos in the United States: A Resource Guide for Journalists*, 18.

156 Michelle Crouch, "Driver in Fatal Wreck Charged with DWI," *The Charlotte Observer*, charlotteobserver.com, January 23, 2006 http://www.charlotte.com/mld/ observer/news/local/13689071.htm

157 Javier J. Aldape, ed., "How do You Write It?" *Latinos in the United States: A Resource Guide for Journalists*, 64.

Chapter Eight

158 Saul Gitlin, "The Rise of the Multicultural Consumer," 16.

159 Gitlin.

160 Genaro C. Armas, "Black, Asian Women With Degrees Earn More," *Associated Press News*, March 28, 2005 http://groups.yahoo.com/group/asianamericanartistry/ message/5918

161 "How Not to Cover Asian Americans," *All-American: How to Cover Asian America*, 36.

162 "How Not to Cover Asian Americans," 37.

163 C. N. Le, "Population Statistics and Demographics," *Asian-Nation: The Landscape of Asian America*, 2006 http://www.asian-nation.org/population.shtml

164 Terrence Reeves and Claudett Bennett, "The Asian and Pacific Islander Population in the United States," U.S. Census Bureau, May 2003 www.census.gov/prod/ 2003pubs/p20-540.pdf

165 Tony Ramirez, ed., "All-American Stylebook: Glossary Updates," *All-American: How to Cover Asian America*, a1.

166 "Asia and America: A Field Guide," *All-American: How to Cover Asian America*, 53.

167 U.S. Asian Population, Census 2000, Infoplease http://www.infoplease. com/ipa/A0778584.html

168 Txong Pao Lee and Mark E. Pfeifer, "Building Bridges: Teaching about the Hmong in our Communities," Hmong Cultural and Resource Center, 2005 http://www.learnabouthmong.org/presentation/index_files/frame.htm

169 "Montagnards: Their History and Culture," Culturalrientation.net, 2005 http://www.culturalorientation.net/montagnards/vintro.html

170 "SAJA Stylebook for Covering South Asia & the South Asian Diaspora," South Asian Journalists Association, 2005 http://www.saja.org/stylebook.html#S

171 Tony Ramirez, ed., "All-American Stylebook: Glossary Updates," a1.

172 "A Guide to Asian Names," *All-American: How to Cover Asian America*, 28.

173 "Glossary," *All-American: How to Cover Asian America*, 20.

174 "Glossary," *All-American: How to Cover Asian America*, 23.

175 Stephanie Ebbert, "Asian-Americans Step Up to the Ballot Box," *The Boston Globe*, April 25, 2005.

176 Katie Hong, "John McCain's Racist Remark Very Troubling," seattlepi.com, March 2, 2002 http://seattlepi.nwsource.com/opinion/hongop.shtml

177 Amy Leang, "Newsrooms Must Walk the 'Diversity' Walk, Not Just Talk the Talk," *ASNE Reporter 2001*, April 6, 2001 http://asne.org/2001reporter/friday/amy6.html

178 Margaret Cho, *I Have Chosen to Stay and Fight* (New York: Riverhead Books, 2005), 42.

179 Cho, 5.

Chapter Nine

180 Barbara Munson, "Not for Sport," *Teaching Tolerance*, Spring 1999 http://www.tolerance.org/teach/magazine/features.jsp?p=0&is=18&ar=183

181 "American Indian and Alaska Native Heritage Month: November 2004," U.S. Census Bureau, October 25, 2004 http://www.census.gov/Press-Release/www/2004/cb04ff20-2.pdf

182 "American Indian and Alaska Native Heritage Month: November 2004."

183 "Indian Entities Recognized and Eligible to Receive Services from the U.S. Bureau of Indian Affairs," *Federal Register*, Vol. 67, No. 134, July 12, 2002.

184 "Indian Country Resource Guide," *The American Indian and the Media*, 82–83.

185 "Indian Country Resource Guide," *The American Indian and the Media*, 85.

186 "Indian Country Resource Guide," *The American Indian and the Media*, 89.

187 "American Indian and Alaska Native Heritage Month: November 2004."

188 "American Indian Census Facts: American Indians by the Numbers," U.S. Census Bureau, 2003 http://www.aigc.com/articles/ai-census-facts.html

189 "The American Indian and Alaska Native Population: 2000," U.S. Census Bureau, 2002 http://www.census.gov/prod/2002pubs/c2kbr01-15.pdf

190 Mark Anthony Rolo, "Introduction," *The American Indian and the Media*, 8.

191 Wesley Pulkka, "Reconnecting Artists, Cultures," *Albuquerque Journal*, August 16, 2005.

192 David Melmer, "School Mascot Logos Still Hot-buttone Issue with Tribes," *Indian Country Today*, September 28, 2005.

193 Jeff Tuttle, "A Tribe by Any Other Name," *Covering Indian Country Blog*, Western Knight Center for Specialized Journalism: Covering Indian Country, March 11, 2005 http://wkconline.org/index.php/blogs/na_category /C17

194 "Cherokee Tribe's Voters Oust Council Chairman," *The Asheville (N.C.) Citizen*," September 2, 2005.

195 Deborah Locke, "The Non-Indian Reporter," *The American Indian and the Media*, 43.

196 William Claiborne, "Some Ideas for New Reporters," as presented by Denny McAuliffe at the Western Knight Center "Covering Indian Country" Seminar, 2005.

197 "Indian Country Resource Guide," *The American Indian and the Media*, 93.

198 Claiborne.

199 John F. Kennedy, "Introduction," *The American Indian*, Native Voices Foundation http://www.nativevoices.org/articles/Kennedy.html

Chapter Ten

200 "Her Syndicate Runs Edited Version of Ann Coulter Column," *Editor & Publisher*, February 27, 2005 http://www.editorandpublisher.com/ eandp/ news/ article_display.jsp?vnu_content_id=1000818305

201 "Stop Hate Crimes Now," *Human Rights World Report*, Human Rights Watch, 2001 http://www.hrw.org/press/2001/09/usreprisal0921.htm

202 Joyce Davis, "Covering Muslims in America," *Poynter Report*, Winter 2003, 18.

203 Angela Brittingham and G. Patricia de la Cruz, "We the People of Arab Ancestry in the United States," U.S. Census Bureau, March 2005 http://www.census.gov/ prod/2005pubs/censr-21.pdf

204 "100 Questions and Answers about Arab Americans: A Journalist's Guide," *Detroit Free Press*, 2001 http://www.freep.com/jobspage/arabs

205 "100 Questions and Answers about Arab Americans."

206 "100 Questions and Answers about Arab Americans."

207 "100 Questions and Answers about Arab Americans."

208 "Religions of the World," Religious Tolerance.org, 2003 http://www.religioustolerance.org/worldrel.htm

209 "100 Questions and Answers about Arab Americans."

210 "100 Questions and Answers about Arab Americans."

211 "100 Questions and Answers about Arab Americans."

212 "100 Questions and Answers about Arab Americans."

213 Joyce Davis, "Covering Muslims in America," 17–18.

214 "100 Questions and Answers about Arab Americans."

215 "Guidelines for Countering Racial, Ethnic and Religious Profiling," Society of Professional Journalists, 2005 http://www.spj.org/diversity_profiling.asp

216 Donna Abu-Nasr, "Muslim and Arab Voices Urge Calm Over Cartoon Issue," The Associated Press, February 9, 2006.

217 Hassan M. Fattah, "Stampede During Annual Pilgrimage to Mecca Kills 345," *The New York Times*, January 13, 2006.

218 "100 Questions and Answers about Arab Americans."

Chapter Eleven

219 "New NBC Show Called Anti-Christian Bigotry," NewsMax.com, 2006 http://www.newsmax.com/archives/ic/2005/12/28/114017.shtml

220 Randy Dotinga, "How to Cover LGBT People: Education and Resources for Journalists," Journalists' Toolbox, National Lesbian and Gay Journalists Association, September 3, 2003 http://www.nlgja.org/pubs/toolbox_intro.htm

221 Congressman Barney Frank, address to a session during the Association for Education in Journalism and Communications conference, August 2001, in Washington, D.C. The author attended the session and notes that there was considerable resistance from media representatives to Frank's criticism of news coverage of LGBT issues.

222 David Hawpe, "Don't Forget the Context," *NewsWatch*, Spring 2001, 6.

223 Hawpe, 7.

224 Barney Frank, "Favorite Quotes," the Gay and Lesbian Information Bureau, December 1999 http://www.glib.org/discus/messages/83/84.html?1100125951

225 Alberta Lindsey, "Cleics Sign Ad Accepting Gays: 44 Methodist Ministers in Area Say They'll Let Homosexuals Join Church," *Richmond Times-Dispatch*, December 24, 2005.

226 "Stylebook Supplement: Gay, Lesbian, Bisexual and Transgender Term-inology," National Lesbian & Gay Journalists Association, March 2004 http://www.nlgja.org/pubs/style.html

Chapter Twelve

227 Vickie Beck, address to a session during the Association for Education in Journalism and Communications conference, August 2001, in Washington, D.C.

228 "Style Guide," National Center on Disability and Journalism, 2002 http://www.ncdj.org/styleguide.php

229 Beck.

230 "Beyond the AP Stylebook: Language and Usage Guide for Reporters and Editors," The Advocado Press, Inc., 1992 http://www.raggededgemagazine.com?mediacircus/styleguide.htm

231 Lindsay Kastner, "School Board Settles Lawsuit: It Has a Plan to Address Disabled Access," *Richmond Times-Dispatch*, January 18, 2006.

232 Jack McNeil, "Americans with Disabilities: Household Economic Studies," U.S. Census Bureau,

February 2001 http://www.census.gov/prod/2001pubs/p70-73.pdf

[233] "Beyond the AP Stylebook."

[234] "Tips for Journalists: Interviewing People with Disabilities," National Center on Disability and Journalism, 2002 http://www.ncdj.org/interviewing.html

[235] "Tips for Journalists: Interviewing People with Disabilities."

[236] "Tips for Journalists: Interviewing People with Disabilities."

[237] Kathryn Coffin, "How It's Said Matters," from a two-page printout from Spinal Network (date unknown) distributed at UNITY, Washington, D.C., 2005.

[238] Jeff South, "Disability as Diversity," *The Quill*, August 2003, 20.

[239] Jack McNeil, "Americans with Disabilities."

Chapter Thirteen

[240] "Religions of the World."

[241] Diane Connolly, "The Faith Connection: Tips for Telling Smarter Stories," *Poynter Report*, Winter 2003, 12.

[242] Terry Mattingly, "Religion Coverage: Past as Prologue?" *Poynter Report*, Winter 2003, 15.

[243] Mattingly, 16.

[244] David Crumm, "Covering Religion on Any Beat," Journalism.org, 2005 http://www.journalism.org/resources/tools/reporting/beats/religion.asp

[245] Connolly, 12–14.

[246] Julie Meyer, "Age: Census 2000 Brief," U.S. Census Bureau, October 2001 http://www.census.gov/prod/2001pubs/c2kbr01-12.pdf

[247] "Poverty Guidelines," United States Department of Health and Human Services, 2005 http://aspe.hhs.gov/poverty/05poverty.shtml

[248] Carmen DeNavas-Walt, Bernadett D. Proctor, and Robert J. Mills, "Income, Poverty, and Health Insurance Coverage in the United States:2003," U.S. Census Bureau, August 2004 http://www.census.gov/prod/2004pubs/p60-226.pdf

[249] "Introduction," *For an Economy that Works for All*, Ford Foundation Project coordinated by Douglas Gould Co., Inc., http://www.douglasgould.com

[250] "Executive Summary," For an Economy that Works for All," 3.

[251] "Executive Summary," 4.

[252] "Setting the Frame," For an Economy that Works for All," 5.

Chapter Fourteen

[253] "Name that Group," from an exercise used with freshmen orientation groups at Elon University, Elon, North Carolina, 2005.

[254] McIntosh, "White Privilege: Unpacking the Invisible Knapsack."

Chapter Fifteen

[255] Keith Woods, "The Listening Post."

[256] Ruth Seymour, "Pushing Forward in New Ways," *Poynter Report*, Spring 2000.

[257] Victor Merina, "Using Listening Posts, Finding Community Guides," Poynter.org— Diversity Update,

February 1, 2000 http://www.poynter.org/ diversity/diversity/0131-00.htm

258 Elizabeth Llorente, "Penetrating an Immigrant/Ethnic Community," Poynter.org— Diversity Update.

259 Carol Weber Thomas, "Redefining Our Sense of Place," Knight Ridder News, Spring 2003, 25–27.

Chapter Sixteen

260 Ruth Seymour, "Perspective Shift: Disability," handout used at a Poynter Institute Diversity Across the Curriculum seminar attended by the author in 2001.

Chapter Seventeen

261 The idea for the assignment and the actual bias survey are based on an assignment used by Ruth Seymour at a Poynter Institute Diversity Across the Curriculum seminar attended by the author in 2001.

Chapter Eighteen

262 Keith Woods, "The Power of a Word," a handout used at a Poynter Institute Diversity Across the Curriculum seminar attended by the author in 2001.

263 "Dead Man Had Gasoline Stashed throughout His Home," *The St. Petersburg Times*

264 "3 Teens Charged with Man's Murder," The St. Petersburg Times, March 19, 1998.
"Woman Loses 3 of 8 Fetuses," The St. Petersburg Times, October 2, 1996.

265 "Woman Loses 3 of 8 Fetuses," The St. Petersburg Times, October 2, 1996.

266 "Cross-dressing Man Sentenced for Battering Woman at Bar," The St. Petersburg Times, September 25, 1999.

267 "Gay Man Barred from Adopting," Fort Lauderdale Sun Sentinel, November 1996.

Chapter Nineteen

268 "Code of Ethics and Professional Conduct," Radio-Television News Directors Association, 2005 http://www.rtnda.org/ethics/coe.shtml

269 "Code of Ethics," Society of Professional Journalists, 2005 http://www.spj.org/ethics_code.asp
Chapter Twenty

Chapter Twenty

271 Ruth Seymour, "Story Stances," a handout used at a Poynter Institute Diversity Across the Curriculum seminar attended by the author in 2001.

Chapter Twenty-One

272 Lillian Dunlap, "Mapping Our 'Daily World' Exercise," based on a handout used at a Poynter Institute Diversity Across the Curriculum seminar attended by the author in 2001.

Chapter Twenty-Two

273 Editing exercise and analysis, National Center Disability and Journalism, 2005 http://www.ncdj.org

Chapter Twenty-Three

[274] "Robert C. Maynard: Life and Legacy," Maynard Institute for Journalism Education, 2005 http://www.maynardije.org/about/history

[275] "Seeing Ourselves Whole: The Newsroom Diversity Game," Maynard Institute for Journalism Education, 2005 http://www.maynardije.org/resources/game/

Chapter Twenty-Four

[276] "Giving Voices to Other Voices," based on a handout used at a Poynter Institute Diversity Across the Curriculum seminar attended by the author in 2001.

[277] "Rainbow Sourcebook," Society of Professional Journalists, 2005 http://www.spj.org/diversity_search.asp

Index

Other books for writers from Marion Street Press, Inc.

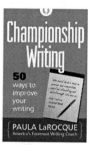